The Grace of Incorruption

DONALD SHEEHAN

The Selected Essays of Donald Sheehan
on Orthodox Faith and Poetics

Edited by Xenia Sheehan
Foreword by Christopher Merrill

PARACLETE PRESS
BREWSTER, MASSACHUSETTS

2015   First Printing

The Grace of Incorruption: The Selected Essays of Donald Sheehan on Orthodox Faith and Poetics

Copyright © 2015 Carol W. Sheehan

ISBN 978-1-61261-601-8

The author's preferred Scripture translation was the King James Version; however, as he often corrected the English to the Septuagint Greek (generally Rahlfs' *Septuaginta*), most translations herein are in some measure the author's own.

The Paraclete Press name and logo (dove on cross) is a trademark of Paraclete Press, Inc.

Library of Congress Cataloging-in-Publication Data
Sheehan, Donald, –2010.
  [Essays. Selections]
  The grace of incorruption : the selected essays of Donald Sheehan on Orthodox faith and poetics / Donald Sheehan ; edited by Xenia Sheehan ; foreword by Christopher Merrill.
      pages cm
  Includes bibliographical references and index.
  ISBN 978-1-61261-601-8
  1. Orthodox Eastern Church—Doctrines. 2. Bible. Psalms. I. Sheehan, Xenia, editor. II. Title.
  BX323.S524 2015
  230'.19—dc23   2014044627

10 9 8 7 6 5 4 3 2 1

Published by Paraclete Press
Brewster, Massachusetts
www.paracletepress.com

Printed in the United States of America

CONTENTS

PART TWO

Orthodox Poetics and the Great Psalm

"To die, to be buried, to depart . . . And yet to have lived and died in such a way that your presence, discretely and from a distance as if a fragrance from someone absent, can give others the possibility to breathe divine fragrance!"
—Archimandrite Vasileios (*Beauty and Hesychia in Athonite Life*)

FOREWORD

Donald Sheehan's conversion to Eastern Orthodox Christianity, detailed in the opening essay of *The Grace of Incorruption*, had not only personal but professional implications for the literature professor and longtime director of The Frost Place. Scripture, patristic writings, and the liturgy—these profoundly shaped the last third of his life, during which he translated the Septuagint Greek Psalter and wrote this book, which unites his literary training, his poetic imagination, and the fruits of his prayer life. *The Grace of Incorruption* explores the mystery, music, and connections between faith and poetry, with uncommon wisdom.

The first half of this book, "Reflections on Life, Literature, and Holiness," examines works by Shakespeare, Dostoevsky, Saints Ephraim and Isaac, Frost, and Salinger, as well as contemporary poets like Jane Kenyon, Sydney Lea, and Nicholas Samaras, raising questions about the nature of penitence, prayer, personhood, freedom, depression, and the right relationship to the earth. Sheehan weaves in elements of his autobiography, travels, and writings by Church Fathers such as Dionysius the Aeropagite and John Climacus, discovering that "to achieve genuine sight of one's sinfulness without blaming others is to be with God." Humility is the cornerstone of his faith; the quality of attention on display in these pages, a form of prayer dedicated to revealing the sacred aspects of literature, is rooted in his belief that knowledge is limited; his observations, drawn in part from his experience of working with a range of poets at The Frost Place in Franconia, New Hampshire, shed light not only on the creative process but on the religious imagination. In this book the subdeacon and the professor work hand in glove.

Take the famously dark vision of Frost's "An Old Man's Winter Night," which Sheehan reinterprets from an Orthodox perspective, likening its movement to the thought of Dionysius the Aeropagite, discerning in its negations the sort of reverse affirmation dear to the author of *The Mystical Theology*. For Dionysius "the denial of all denials of course asserts that something *is*," which offers a gloss on Frost's assertion: "A light he was to no one but himself, / Where now he sat, concerned with he knew what, / A quiet light, and then not even that." Sheehan argues that the poem "goes the way of negation so as to achieve affirmation; it goes the way of deliberately turning out the lights so as to find the way of keeping a whole countryside. As Dionysius tells us to do, the poem goes into darkness to encounter that which illumines beyond all the false lights. And the central fact of this darkness is—as I have said—that it is fully alive, fully aware, fully creative." It is the heart of the mystery of Orthodoxy that Sheehan celebrates.

For example, he suggests that one key to understanding Salinger's *Franny and Zooey* lies in *The Way of a Pilgrim*, an anonymous nineteenth-century Russian spiritual work about the Jesus Prayer: "Lord Jesus Christ, Son of God, have mercy on me, a sinner." Which is to say: the fictional world of a seminal twentieth-century American writer was informed by a Russian believer's question: how to pray without ceasing, as St. Paul counseled? What the Jesus Prayer offers Salinger Sheehan finds in "the bright darkness of the Psalms," the daily reading of which profoundly shaped his thinking: "that darkness wherein all the false lights are extinguished, and where we can thereby behold the light 'concealed from all the light among beings.'"

The second half of the book thus addresses the Psalms, focusing on the Great Psalm (118 in Orthodoxy, 119 in Western Christianity), an alphabetic acrostic that spells out God's plan for Creation. This is the longest psalm and chapter in the Bible, and in twenty-two eight-line stanzas, each beginning with a Hebrew letter and containing a variety of rhetorical strategies and musical motifs, the universe is figured anew, which is why the psalm remains the source of so much inspiration and interpretation. Sheehan devotes considerable energy to explicating its secrets, literary and spiritual. He makes three important points at the outset: "First, psalmic poetics are aural and oral—in the ear and mouth—sung (chanted), not silently read. Second, psalmic poetics are communal, holding the meaning of the entire Israelite community. Third, psalmic poetics are actions of blessedness, actions that secure whole communities from demonic violence: 'God is . . . working salvation in the midst of the earth' (Ps 73:12)." Among the many virtues of *The Grace of Incorruption* is its determination to serve as an instruction manual in the proper way to hear and chant the Psalms so that they heal, bless, and save individuals and communities alike.

Sheehan believes that the Orthodox practice of reciting the Great Psalm in its entirety at Matins on both Holy and Lazarus Saturday, coupled with the decision by its Greek translators to retain the letters of the Hebrew alphabet as titles for its stanzas, reveals its resurrectional meaning and movement: "The artistic technique of Psalm 118 can therefore be best understood as the poetics of resurrection"—the poetics, that is, that came to govern the lifework of a singular man, blessed with faith and learning, who brings us the good news of life everlasting.

Christopher Merrill
Iowa City, Iowa

EDITOR'S INTRODUCTION

"Truly, truly I say to you, unless the seed of wheat fall into the ground and die,
it abides alone; but if it die, it brings forth much fruit."
(*John* 12:24)

Donald Sheehan spoke often of "downward mobility," usually with some amusement, as a goal to be sought. Because he knew this, he was able to follow St. John's great teaching with more courage (which he thought he lacked) and richer fruit (visible to others around him, though seldom to himself) than anyone I've known. Now that his body has been committed by others to the ground to which he committed himself in so many other ways, I pray that, with this publication of more of his work, his fruit may increase in abundance and truth.

It has been a moving and challenging process for me to gather and edit these essays, filled with my husband's long-familiar voice. The essays in Part One are like old friends. I was there when they were born, I talked with him about them, and I attended most of the lectures for which they were written—at Dartmouth College; Middlebury College; Hellenic College/Holy Cross Seminary; Marlboro College; The Frost Place in Franconia, New Hampshire; The Frost Farm in Derry; The Orthodox Monastery of the Transfiguration in Ellwood City, Pennsylvania; Holy Resurrection Orthodox Church in Claremont, New Hampshire; and St. Jacob of Alaska Orthodox Church in Northfield, Vermont. They span just over two decades, roughly 1984 to 2006, though I have not arranged them chronologically.

Writing each lecture, Don would respond with care to whatever need or request had called it into being; at the same time he would take the occasion to weave together and bring into focus significant events in his life, books he'd been reading, topics he was teaching, things he was thinking about, and above all, his daily psalmic prayer and growing understanding of the Eastern Orthodox Church and her teachings. Increasingly, over his years teaching as an Orthodox believer, it was this latter understanding that he sought to integrate into his academic life and even to make the measure of that life. One might read the essays, therefore, with the thought that in them he is working his way toward maturity as an *Orthodox* teacher of literature, finding the connections, testing the ground to see what's solid and firm, panning for gold, as it were. And he had an excellent eye for gold.

The essays in Part Two were written during the last five or six years of Don's life. He intended one day to make them into a book, and to this end I typed them at his bedside from his handwritten pages during the final weeks of his life, assisted by our son David. He had been unable to write the final chapter, having discarded several drafts, one of them only days before his repose. The book remains unfinished.

These poetics essays, on a subject that was nearly always on his mind and in his journals, are the ones that most deeply integrate his faith into his scholarly calling. Adapted to no particular audience, they come straight from his profoundly insightful mind and heart, working in unison; and because Don never did really understand that his own mind/heart could move more quickly and lightly than many, they can be hard to penetrate. He was humbly willing to provide steppingstones for others, but he would often not think to do so unless the person (often myself) were there before him asking questions.

In one of the later essays in Part Two, Chapter VI on "The Drama of Intimacy," Don quotes St. Isaac the Syrian speaking of "a noetic ray running between the written lines." He follows with this comment of his own: "The noetic ray acts so as to become the roots that enter into the soil. And once they take root in that soil, the words can become for us the various flowers of incorruption: and thereby can scatter in us that inner discourse our arrogant hearts otherwise sustain." As I read and reread Don's words in the poetics essays, without his presence to trigger my understanding (as it always did), hoping—praying—for points of entry, my persistence is from time to time rewarded with fleeting glimpses of the great realities that move between the lines and behind the words of Psalms. Don cautions, though: "You cannot *will* the gift of stillness. But you must choose actively to await its giving." Better readers will surely come to this more easily than I; others may struggle. But I urge you to keep choosing and waiting. For Don has now passed on to us the task of panning for gold, and there is much here to be found.

Whatever understanding he came to as he followed the psalmic call to "endure patiently His way" (Ps 36:34) to its earthly end, I am sure that it continued further along the ways he indicates here. He became silent and much simpler and did not—could not—share what he was thinking, if he was "thinking" at all in the ordinary sense. Mostly, I think he was praying, from long practice, beneath the pains and mundane discomforts of his final illness. It culminated, in his last hours, in the deep and patient simplicity of his labored, sometimes joyous, one-word notes to his young goddaughter (Good!!—in response to her offering him a blessing) or his children (SING!), and the profound peace in which he finally passed on, described in the Epilogue by our friend Lydia Carr.

▪   ▪   ▪

Between the bookends of Don's opening account of his painful beginnings and Lydia's account of his death, we are privileged to be witnesses to a process of conversion by which his father's ungoverned brilliance, alcoholic violence, and Irish blarney are wholly transformed *within the author* to a unique and sober sort of brilliance that shows us the path to stillness—and, yes, still retains a touch of blarney. It is a sort of blarney, however, that, transfigured in this way, opens doors into worlds of faith and understanding that can only be reached by this road less traveled that he chose to take. That is, he sometimes simply found shortcuts to truth, jumping over a few things that seemed to present themselves as facts, just as he jumped—or was carried or thrust by the angel who guided and guarded his life—through the hoops of his afflicted upbringing. I can't really explain why this is okay. But people who have traveled those shortcuts with him will understand it, as you will too when you read this book.[1]

It took an army sergeant to turn Don in his seventeenth year from a trou- bled street gang hooligan—forged in the image of James Dean (*Rebel Without a Cause*), who burst into his life in 1955—into a lover of poetry who could learn and follow the ways by which, in his words, "the ruining oppositions of actual experience are held within the musical disciplines of lyric art" and thereby changed into beauty and truth. And it took seven years after his father's death for him to learn the forgiveness that would open the doors of heaven to him. Thus, this book is above all a story of beauty, truth, and the forgiveness that knows how to seek and find them. If there are at times errors in his facts, I urge you not to judge too quickly or close your ears to what he is saying. He did not, after all, seek out this publication of his work or have a chance to revise it. Rather, ask yourself: Am I able to forge this kind of truth and beauty out of the facts—or even the blarney—of my own life? Can I love and lift up toward incorruption even half so gracefully the people in my life who may have harmed me? And can I do this, as he did, by heading straight into the wind of it all "until God Himself can be seen in the very ruins themselves: seen, and felt, and overwhelmingly and gratefully loved"? For myself, I do not think that I can answer "yes" to these questions.

▪ ▪ ▪

Now, about my editing: As an editor (by inclination and profession), I have changed very little of what Don wrote, and when I felt the urge to say something I generally just added an endnote. The truth is, much as I enjoy wordcraft, I don't *like* to change even Don's phrasings or punctuations, because the *person* I have loved and trusted and grown with for over fifty years (still ongoing) is so much in them. But I have made two significant exceptions. First, I have integrated Don's notes or writings from several sources to construct an introduction to Part Two and slightly clarify (based on his journal notes) the opening of Chapter 1 of that part. Second, for a variety of reasons, I came to the difficult and painful decision to delete material drawn from, or dependent on, the work of Fr. Pavel Florensky, a writer Don had loved. Spiritual counselors and theology student friends to whom I expressed my concerns concurred with this decision: Fr. Florensky, though a brilliant scientist and philosopher who braved the Soviet authorities by wearing his priest's cassock to work in their labs and died a martyr's death in their gulags, was and is a problematic figure in the realm of Orthodox theology, and, for those following the Orthodox way, not a reliable guide either theologically or pastorally.

One of the issues that arose in Don's work was Florensky's borderline Sophiology or Sophianism: an equation or confusion of God's Holy Wisdom (Gk. *sophia*) with the person of the Mother of God; or an understanding of Sophia as a sort of fourth person of the Trinity. This has vast and devastating implications for our understanding of both the divine and the human and hence for our salvation. The accepted Orthodox understanding is that God's Holy Wisdom is the Person of Christ Himself (cf. 1 Cor 1:24). Florensky was also closely associated with a movement called Imiaslavie, a dogmatic line of thought asserting that the Name of God is actually God Himself. This latter understanding appears to have carried over into a quasi-magical understanding of—what affects us here—icons. Both movements were judged heretical by the Russian Orthodox Church during the twentieth century, though Fr. Florensky was not personally condemned.

Don, who always saw people in their best light—and Florensky's was indeed a bright one—was fascinated by his work and had not, at the time he wrote some of these essays, picked up on the problems inherent in Florensky's thought. Don was a teacher of literature, not a theologian. But I can say with assurance as his closest confidante over many years that he would not have wanted to propagate a theology that led to spiritual confusion. Nor was Fr. Florensky one of the sources he drew sustenance from in his final years. As I did this editing, I also consulted Don's and my spiritual father and counselor, who supported entirely my decision to excise the Florensky material. He would, I am confident, have counseled Don to do the same had the matter come up between them, and Don would have obeyed such counsel unhesitatingly, even with joy.

In doing this editing, and even in publishing his work at all, I have thus taken, we could say, Don's final step in this world—or, better (to use his words), at this boundary between worlds—a final step toward the Church and the faith that he chose to give his life to (and led me to). In all of Don's steps in his journey to, and through, Orthodoxy, his conscious and deliberate focus was ever one of obedience. It seems fitting to me, then, that bringing his literary work to light should involve a final act of obedience to Orthodox dogmatic teaching, and that this obedience should be carried out on his behalf by another. As he says of his pilgrimage to Alaska in his essay on Orthodox holiness, "I had traveled six thousand miles in order to be carried by someone for the final three yards. It is always so: in every ascetic action we must let go of all our own control." But if I have introduced errors or infelicities or given offense to anyone by doing this, I ask your forgiveness, and his.

■　　■　　■

Finally, I wish to express my profound gratitude to those people who have especially helped to bring the book to completion: First, my son

Benedict (Rowan), with his wife, Maria (Talia), for their loving support for me and Don over so many years—even in those moments when Benedict feared that his Dad might not be making any sense. But then he came to see that they just used different languages: Don, in his own medium, poetry, did something very like what he and Maria do so gracefully and insightfully in theirs, music. Hierodeacon Herman (Majkrzak), Don's godson, who continues to pray for us and has always been there with sensible advice and help when I needed it. Father Nektarios, whose prayers have—I'm sure more often than I know—mysteriously untangled many knotty problems. Mother Michaila, who set me on a good path. John Taylor Carr, whose help with the Greek and its transliteration (not always consistent in essays spanning twenty years) has greatly improved the book's usefulness to scholars; Lydia Carr for her moving and insightful account of Don's passing; and both of them, with Lucia as well, for their love for Don. Christopher Merrill for his honesty and loyal support of my efforts to publish Don's work, despite his reservations about the cuts I made. Miriam Warren for her skillful photo editing and help in tracking down sources for some images. Fr. Deacon Theophan Warren and Dr. Harry Boosalis for their kind theological assistance and support. My longtime friend Ann Brash, a fine editor, who helped and supported me in the final stages. Fr. Moses Hibbard for his conscientious labors in constructing the foundations of the glossary in the midst of a full seminary and family life. Mark Montague, who contributed a number of valuable refinements to the glossary. A founding member of the Dostoevsky study group described in "Seed and Fruit" and companion and guide to Don and our sons on their 2003 pilgrimage to Mt. Athos, Mark was enlisted at the eleventh hour to finish checking the Greek and to guide me in getting some last linguistic and theological points as right as we could without harming Don's work. His final assessment: "Don doesn't have to be right about all the details to give us incredibly rich food for thought and deep insight. For every questionable detail there are a hundred gems. He's poured his heart out onto the page here, and what a treasure for us it is!"

I am grateful, more than I can ever say, to all who have prayed or labored that these essays might find their way into the light and bear good fruit. Thank you.

■   ■   ■

My goal in compiling *The Grace of Incorruption* has been to offer in it the best of Don Sheehan's work as an Orthodox Christian teacher and scholar, to allow him to tell you in his own gentle, fervent, and intelligent voice, all at one time and place, some of the fine literary and spiritual understandings he spent over a quarter century weaving together, the events and encounters that touched him deeply and changed his life and the lives of those around him, the things that remained closest to his heart until the very end—the saving things he would have wanted you to know.

Xenia (Carol) Sheehan

South Canaan, Pennsylvania

PART ONE

Reflections on Life, Literature, and Holiness

1
Coming Home

I was raised in a violent home, where, until I was nine years old, my father's alcohol addiction fueled his open or just barely contained violence, a home where my mother was beaten over and over (I remember her face covered with blood). Alcohol broke apart my home in a violent paroxysm the night of July 4, 1949, the summer I was nine. The police were in our living room in the small hours of July 5. I remember all of this very clearly.

Some three weeks earlier, in June, I was shot in the chest with a pistol, the bullet entering two inches below my heart. The gunman was my best friend, also age nine, and we had found his big brother's target pistol while we were playing at his house.

What I remember most vividly about the shooting—I remember viscerally, without having to make any conscious effort at all to remember—is lying on the operating table and seeing the doctor over me, his hands at the wound very skillfully and tenderly probing for the bullet—his great arms and torso coming down to me, his face silent in concentrated stillness bending over me, his hands intimate and strong and exact and delicate.

And I remember, too, my father and mother coming into the operating room, my father hastily dressed as he fought through a thick hangover to put clothes on, both their faces made into vivid masks of desperate panic. But I remember feeling absolutely serene in the hands of this doctor; my parents' terror did not touch me as I attended peacefully to these hands that were giving my life back to me, hands that were undoing the death my hapless friend had almost dealt me. Some three weeks later my home would break apart, and my mother would take the three of us children (my sister, brother, and me) to her brother's home. But the terror of the July 4th catastrophe would not grip me the way it would have a month before; it would not shake me the way a dog shakes a tiny animal it has seized, to break its neck. By the time of the breaking, I had had other hands at my heart, I had had my life given back to me.

That summer of 1949, my family's home slowly but surely moved to the July 4th catastrophe. By the last week of June, I had almost fully recuperated from my gunshot wound, but my father's drinking had grown worse. He would come home every afternoon those days fairly drunk, and then throughout the evening he would get very drunk. And as he got drunker, he would begin a pattern of outbursts of rage and smashing of things, followed by periods of eerie calm. After each outburst, the four of us—my mother, sister, brother, and I—would tiptoe around, speaking only in soft whispers, so as not to trigger the next round of rage.

But on this particular evening in late June, the bouts of raging had grown longer, and the calm spells meant only that he was regathering his will for the next round of violence. The second round that evening had been about twenty minutes of raging at all of us in the kitchen—and breaking some dishes—and then he stormed out of the kitchen and through the dining room and into the living room: and all was suddenly quiet. Making my way on tiptoe across the dining room, I peeked around the living room door. He was sitting on the couch, staring at his hands.

Then I did something that still takes my breath away. I walked across the living room and sat down on the couch right next to him. I picked up a magazine from the coffee table and opened to the first pictures I came to, and I pointed to one. "Look, Dad, isn't that interesting?" I didn't dare look at him.

No answer. After a moment, I looked up at him, and I found that he was looking down at me. Over fifty years later I can still see my father's eyes. They were sad eyes, yet peaceful, warm, and profoundly *young*, with all the wildness gone out and, in place of it, something like *stillness*. And I felt all at once peaceful, the way I'd felt on the operating table at the hospital three weeks before.

He looked at me for a long, long minute, and then he spoke. "You're the only one not afraid of me."

I was just old enough to know what gratitude sounded like in my father's voice. And so to this day and hour, I know what *the person my father is* sounds like when he speaks.

The moment was quickly swept away, for that summer of our family's life was wholly in the violent hands of Satan. But that moment was—beyond every logic I know—a seed.

In late March of 1983, I was moved to visit my father's grave. He had died seven years before, and I had not yet fully taken in the irrevocable fact. It was for me, I think, as if his death had happened so often and so deeply and for so many years that, when he actually died in 1976, I somehow couldn't face the fact of such a long, steady, and deep loss. But now, that March, I knew I had to go to his grave.

Carol, my wife, gladly and lovingly joined me on the 1,300-mile journey from the New Hampshire mountains to Memphis, Tennessee, and our two sons, David (age 14) and Rowan (age 3), came along with us.

The night before we went to the cemetery, we stayed in a Memphis motel, and I spent two or more hours writing my father a long letter. Here, in part, is what I wrote that night to my father:

> Where were you? In the years—long, long lost years—of my little-boyhood, when I was frightened, or mean, or crazy, or tired: Did you hold me? Did you tell me I was all right, that everything was all right? Or were you always too frightened or crazy or mean or exhausted yourself? When Mom was cold or contemptuous, were you there to get her through it? Or did her contempt frighten you too much?
>
> And can I give up—freely and fully—my attachment to the pain of our past: not give up our past—just being attached, needing so much, to the pain of our past? The wounds to our bodies heal quickest: just flesh wounds. But I can still see bright as day, and ghastly, the cut on Mom's temple, the blood down her face, you pulling us downstairs, Mom against a white wall, her face a mask of terror: you are saying, "There's your Mother, look at her."
>
> Today I see all this—and I surrender my clinging to the pain of it. It indeed hurts—but I open my hands, see: it slides away. The pain is a thing, a substance—green, viscous, malleable, semi-solid—and IT IS NOT ME.
>
> Are we ever (any of us) through accusing our fathers? Are we ever through loving them? Will we ever love without mercilessness? Is ruthlessness our first response?

I say now: you are free now of love-ruthlessness. For the heavenly untwisting continues for you, in me because for you; it must so act, that what you do now, after death, changes what I am now, in life . . .

Thus I've come, Dad, to bury forever my needing to be in pain through you. And to let begin to grow from this seed of today a deeper, fuller loving between us.

I love you. You love me. Do not forget this.

Your son in loving,

Donald

After I finished writing this letter, I found a Bible in the motel room. It took me a while but I finally found the passage in Genesis I was looking for—when Abraham raises the knife over his son Isaac, but the angel stays his hand.

The next morning was Friday, and the warm Tennessee spring sunlight was shining everywhere as we came to my father's grave. While Rowan scampered away to look at the exotic southern flowers, the three of us knelt down at the grave. I then read my letter aloud to him, my voice sometimes quavering but carrying forward to the end where I asked for forgiveness.

Then I read to him from Genesis, and when I came to the verse—"Abraham stretched forth his hand, and took up the knife to slay his son" (22:10)—I could not go on, for I was too shaken by sobbing. But then I did go on and after I finished reading I waited a long minute, and then I found myself saying the thing I'd come all this long way to say: "I didn't die, Dad, you didn't kill me, we're fine now, we're really fine."

The long journey back to New Hampshire was peaceful. But because Carol and I needed to be at work Monday morning—and David at school—we drove as straight through as we could manage. So it was near midnight of Easter Sunday, April 3rd, when we arrived home. We got our sleepy sons out of the car and into their beds, and then we unloaded the car and, too exhausted even to talk, we sank into our bed like stones dropped into water. It was around 1:00 AM.

At dawn on April 4, I was all of a sudden awakened, fully and completely. What awoke me were these words sounding in my mind: *Lord Jesus Christ, Son of God, have mercy on me, a sinner.* For an instant I thought someone had spoken aloud, but then I realized the words were in me. I sat up, fresh and alert. The words repeated themselves. And then repeated again. I looked over at the window, and the first light of dawn was coming in. The words kept on being repeated.

So I got out of bed. The words in me were calm, neither slow nor fast, level in emphasis, each word distinct yet flowing into the next, with a tiny pause after the last words and then the whole beginning again.

I got dressed and went downstairs, faintly wondering why I felt so fine after such a long journey and so brief a rest. Only *faintly* wondering, because the prayer now occupied every tiny fraction of mental attention I had—for, perfectly and gently, without the slightest air of even the least compulsion, *the prayer simply filled all of me.*

I had no idea what was happening. But I was not even slightly disturbed. And as I sat in our tiny kitchen, I knew that I could completely stop the experience at any instant I chose. But I did not want to end it, so peaceful and fresh I felt as the prayer kept flowing on in me, clear, substantial, and real.

About an hour of this beauty in silence went by, and then I had to awaken the family. To my surprise, I found I could talk with them and do things without the prayer at all diminishing. After breakfast I got myself out to the car and down the highway to the school where I was then teaching. The prayer kept on, steadily unceasing yet wholly uninsistent.

I negotiated the whole day, teaching classes and speaking with people, with the prayer never once skipping a beat. By late afternoon, heading home, I couldn't remember a single thing I'd said all day, but apparently no one had noticed anything odd about me, so probably, like most days, I'd said nothing in particular (what teacher does?).

The prayer continued all evening and awakened me the next morning. And all the next day, it kept on as before. I spoke of it to no one, not even to Carol, to whom I told everything important and most of what wasn't. For I had no idea what was happening.

So the days followed one another that April of 1983, and three weeks went by in this way. Then one afternoon, I was striding through the College library, and all at once I stopped and took a book off the shelf. It was *The Way of a Pilgrim*, an anonymous nineteenth-century Russian book.[2]

Then I suddenly remembered. Years before I had read J. D. Salinger's beautiful story *Franny and Zooey*,[3] where Franny has a great desire to say this prayer, called the Jesus Prayer, and she carries around with her a little book with this title. I was stunned. Among other wonders, I never knew until this moment that it was a *real book* Franny was carrying. I'd thought Salinger had invented it for his story.

I found a chair, and I read the opening twenty or so pages of *The Way of a Pilgrim*. Here was this very prayer, and it was long known (so a footnote told me) in the Eastern Orthodox Church in Russia. I had never even heard the name of such a church. But the book told me the essential fact I most needed. My prayer had a home.

That night I spoke with Carol—but only very tentatively. I didn't speak at all of my continuing experience in this prayer, because I didn't know any words that seemed even remotely true. So I spoke about the book and the Pilgrim's beautiful love for Christ. She was surprised, a bit baffled, but kind and loving.

During the next months, I began something different, something more deliberate. The prayer was beginning to ebb now, so when I got up just after dawn (when I now always awoke, regardless of when I went to bed), I read psalms aloud from an old copy of *The Book of Common Prayer*, slowly and softly. When I said the prayer now, I seemed to be saying it deliberately, saying it the way I was now saying the psalms. During the day, the prayer would come and go, but it was still active in me.

And I still wondered now and then what an Orthodox Church was. Were there any in this country?

Then, late in January 1984, I acted on a whim. I went to visit a tiny Benedictine monastery in Connecticut. This was a place that a poet I knew and liked had often visited and deeply loved. I found that the abbot, Fr. John Giuliani, was a warm and perceptive and reassuringly uncomplicated man. On the second of my three days at the monastery, I asked him after morning Mass if I could talk to him alone, my heart all at once in my mouth.

And so I told Fr. John the whole story of my now ten months of experience with the prayer. He listened to it all with a great depth of stillness, a depth that buoyed me up in this my first time of telling. I sat with my head bowed, looking down at my hands, talking for a very long time. When I finished, I looked up at him—and was startled. His eyes were bright with tears.

"You know, my dear, that your father has given you a very great gift. When you went to his grave, you found that it was open—the way Christ's tomb always stands open—and that loving does not die but binds together all the worlds. He has given you this prayer, my dear, because such loving as this between you never ceases but keeps working on and on."

He lifted his hand in a graceful gesture.

"You must keep on going the way God is calling you. This gift of your father's is a very precious seed." I felt awed and grateful for what he had told me.

As we went to the door, he turned back to me. "Oh, you know, dear one, the Orthodox Church is everywhere. Just look around."

This was January 28, 1984. I returned home with something like the seed of a great understanding. And all that winter and spring, when I prayed the psalms and the prayer each morning and evening, I somehow felt the memory of my father's presence as clear, light, and essential. And I wondered what Fr. John meant by the Orthodox Church being everywhere. New York? Boston?

Then, in the middle of May 1984, I opened the phone book to look up a number I knew perfectly well, and my eyes saw a listing for the Holy Resurrection Orthodox Church in a nearby town just to the north. It literally took my breath away.

I waited three days so I could call calmly. The phone was answered by the wonderful priest who was to become my first father in Orthodoxy, Fr. Vladimir Sovyrda. I knew I was coming home.

By the time of my baptism as an Orthodox Christian on September 8, 1984, the prayer in me had entirely ceased. My little spiritual drama was over and the seed had vanished. But before me now stood open the immense and unending fruitfulness of the Orthodox way. And I knew at that moment what I know to this day: my father goes before me on this way.

POSTSRIPT: Don died peacefully at home a little after 1 AM on May 26, 2010. It was one of his last wishes to rectify what he considered to be a serious omission in this account—something he had simply dropped out of his mind when he wrote it. Only twenty-six years after the event did it rise to the surface, to become the substance of his final confession, after hearing read to him a spiritual counsel concerning the importance of paying all of one's debts before one departs this life. He had no voice at this point but wrote down the name "Fr. O'Brien." Then his voice began to return—unexpectedly and for a brief time—and he said he remembered having read a book, some time before his visit to his father's grave, by Fr. O'Brien and that the book spoke of the Jesus Prayer.[4] He wished now, at the end of his life, to pay this spiritual debt to Fr. O'Brien and to acknowledge that somewhere in his heart the Prayer had already been planted by this good man, bearing fruit only in the soil of his own experience of forgiveness and repentance, and leading to his subsequent entry into the Orthodox Church. I hope that this telling of the story will help to pay that debt.

—Xenia (Carol) Sheehan

2
The Syrian Penitential Spirit
The Witness of Saints Ephraim and Isaac[5]

Anyone newly Orthodox in this country is often enough shocked to discover the deeply *countercultural* meaning of Great Lent. Everything that Orthodox are given to do in Lent acts to separate them from the great tidal power of a vast consumerist culture: the extent and depth of the fasting; the length and variety of the liturgical services; above all, the quality and mode of the Lenten prayers. This shock is real and profound, and even in the monasteries, it is deeply felt. This shock is (if you will) spiritually *seismic,* for it is meant to reconfigure the whole of one's life in the oceans of actual existence. The shock of Lent accomplishes this seismic configuration in two steps. First, it opens up an immediate gap: we turn off TVs and radios in our homes in order to stop the world's ceaseless *ongoingness.* Then, in the silence that follows, we can in stillness begin to remember who and what we foundationally are in God: children of the light He has created—and *not* children of the darkness we create for ourselves.

Central to the Orthodox experience of Lent is the brief prayer called "The Prayer of St. Ephraim the Syrian." In every Lenten weekday service for almost seven weeks this prayer is chanted or spoken by the priest as the entire congregation follows him in the prescribed pattern of prostrations. In this way, the prayer may be said to knit together all the Lenten services and to focus each person on the central meaning of Lent. To comprehend this brief prayer is thus to understand the very heart and whole mind of Orthodox Lent. Here is the Greek text of the prayer, along with the translation commonly used today in the Orthodox Church in America:

Κύριε καὶ Δέσποτα τῆς ζωῆς μου, πνεῦμα ἀργίας, περιεργίας, φιλαρχίας, καὶ ἀργολογίας μή μοι δῷς.

Πνεῦμα δὲ σωφροσύνης, ταπεινοφροσύνης, ὑπομονῆς, καὶ ἀγάπης χάρισαί μοι τῷ σῷ δούλῳ.

Ναί, Κύριε Βασιλεῦ, δώρησαι μοι τοῦ ὁρᾶν τὰ ἐμὰ πταίσματα, καὶ μὴ κατακρίνειν τὸν ἀδελφόν μου, ὅτι εὐλογητὸς εἶ, εἰς τοὺς αἰῶνας τῶν αἰώνων. Ἀμήν.

O Lord and Master of my life! Take from me the spirit of sloth, despair, lust of power and idle talk. (Prostration)

But give rather the spirit of chastity, humility, patience and love to Thy servant. (Prostration)

Yea, O Lord and King! Grant me to see my own transgressions and not to judge my brother, for blessed art Thou, unto ages of ages. Amen. (Prostration)

But before we begin to reflect on this prayer, let me say a few words about St. Ephraim himself. He was born early in the fourth century AD in the ancient city of Nisibis (modern Nuseybin, in southeast Turkey), a city of some considerable significance for well over a thousand years prior to his birth. His parents were Orthodox Christians (he speaks of them very beautifully in his poems), and his Christian community had—a century earlier—suffered severe Roman persecution under the Emperor Diocletian (one of the Syriac martyrs of this period is the woman Saint Febronia). But now, in the early fourth century, the Orthodox community of Nisibis was free, prosperous, and thriving. The language spoken was Syriac, an east Aramaean dialect, and the ecclesiastical Syriac language that has come down is strong, assured, and very beautiful. Thus, fourth-century Syrian Christians of Nisibis had created a culture and a church that richly harmonized Semitic and Greek elements. And amidst this great and flourishing culture, Ephraim became one of the greatest of Christian poets the world has yet seen, leaving as his legacy some twenty-five volumes of extraordinarily accomplished poetry, a body of work only now beginning to find its modern English translators. From the wealth of St. Ephraim's life and work, I shall here highlight only two facts so as to approach his Lenten prayer.

First, despite how he is usually depicted on Orthodox icons, St. Ephraim was never a monk. He was an ordained deacon who remained celibate all his life. Partly, his not being a monk can be explained by noting that Egyptian monastic practice—the model for all Orthodox monasticism—had not, in Ephraim's lifetime, yet reached southeast Turkey. But this only partly explains it, for evidence does exist that accurate *knowledge* of monasticism had reached Nisibis in the first quarter of the fourth century; and travel to established monasteries, while difficult by our standards, was assuredly possible to do then. In other words, Ephraim can be understood as having *chosen* to become a deacon rather than becoming a monk.

Second, Syriac Orthodoxy of the fourth century was in active dialogue with Greek Orthodox culture. There is compelling evidence that some of Ephraim's poetry and homilies were translated into Greek during his lifetime;

St. Ephraim the Syrian. Icon by Stefan Nedetu.

and we know that within thirty years of his death a good deal of it was already in Greek. Ute Possekel, a scholar of St. Ephraim, puts it this way: "Hellenism was an integral part of fourth-century Syriac culture."[6] Thus, while retaining strong—indeed, definitive—ties to Semitic Christianity, Syriac Orthodoxy used with great skill the full range of Greek poetry and philosophy in its theological and artistic expressions.

Now, these two facts—St. Ephraim's life as a deacon in a large urban parish and his Christian culture's widespread use of Greek—can help greatly in understanding something of his Lenten Prayer. I shall here use the ecclesiastical Greek translation of the Syriac as my text (for I have no Syriac), fairly confident that in doing so I shall be able to achieve some secure accuracy. Also, I shall assume throughout that St. Ephraim intended the prayer to speak with equal power to *all* Orthodox, lay and monastic as well as clerical: for his mind is shaped by parish and not monastic life.

Let us, then, consider this prayer in Greek. The prayer is three sentences long. The first sentence deals with an undesirable spirit that possesses four qualities, while the second deals with a wholly desirable spirit also possessing four qualities. Note well at the outset: the prayer speaks of two distinct spirits, each with four qualities—and *not* of eight spirits.

The first sentence asks "the Lord and Master of my life" *not* to give me this first spirit. (An aside: the usual English translation asks God to "take from me"—a mistranslation of the Greek, one with interesting implications, as we shall later see.) The first quality of this spirit is, in Greek, *argia*, a word meaning sloth, most literally "a-working," with the same meaning in the prefix as "a-moral."[7] That is, *argia* does not mean simply "not-working"; it means the *total absence of any capacity to act*. The second quality uses the same root as the first to form the word *peri-ergia*, which literally means: running all around in crazed busyness. These first two qualities are therefore opposite sides of the same devastating coin: the total absence of the capacity to work; the hyper-presence of extreme working. The sequence here seems to me crucial: the sloth creates the psychic condition for crazed busyness *as response.*

And this response of crazed busyness creates, in turn, the condition for the third quality of this terrible spirit: *philarchia*, a word best translated here as "the hunger to control things." That is, every experience of crazed busyness produces in us this terrifying hunger to manage and dominate and rule over all things. But—and here is one of St. Ephraim's great insights in this prayer—this hunger leads, in turn, to the fourth quality: *argologia*, a word we can most literally construe as speech that has no capacity to achieve work (*ergia*). In other words, the more we hunger to dominate, the less our speech has any power to effect genuine consequences. The Greek beautifully signals this point by having the first part of *argologia* repeat the first of the four qualities, *argia*.

In this way, then, the first sentence gives us the total state of our soul when held by this dread spirit. Our sloth produces our crazed busyness, which in turn creates in us the hunger to dominate—and this hunger leads to speech that achieves nothing: and so we return to sloth: and then the devastating cycle begins again.

Now, the Greek verb that steers this first sentence is: "Do not give me"—and *not* "Take from me." The Greek could not be plainer and more straightforward—nor, for that matter, could the Slavonic, which fully agrees with the Greek on this point. We may therefore rightly ask, how can the Lord and Master of our life be understood as *giving* this dreadful spirit to us?

The best response is to consider this passage from Homily 42 of St. Isaac the Syrian's great book, *The Ascetical Homilies*. St. Isaac is St. Ephraim's monastic counterpart, from the same Syriac Orthodox culture some three centuries later. Here is the passage from Homily 42:

> But the trials that God allows to fall upon men who are shameless, whose thinking is exalted in the face of God's goodness, and who abuse His goodness in their pride, are the following: manifest temptations of the demons which also exceed the limit of the strength of men's souls; the withdrawal of the forces of wisdom which men possess; the piercing sensation of the thought of fornication which is allowed to assault them to humble their arrogance; quick temper; the desire to have one's own way; disputatiousness; vituperation; a scornful heart; an intellect completely gone astray; blasphemy against the name of God; absurd notions that are entirely ridiculous, or rather, lamentable; to be despised by all men and to lose their respect; to be made

by the demons both openly and secretly by every kind of means a disgrace and a reproach among men; the desire to mingle and have intercourse with the world; always to speak and behave foolishly; endlessly to seek out some new thing for oneself through false prophecy; to promise many things that are beyond one's strength.[8]

This dreadful list can be seen as an *elucidation* of St. Ephraim's four qualities, the seventeen magnifying the four, yet presenting the same understanding. And Isaac's point in the Homily is everywhere clear: God bestows such terrible afflictions upon us in order that (and here I am quoting Isaac) "you may comprehend the subtle pathways of your mind by the kinds of trials that beset you" (*Homilies*, 42:210). That is, when we see that—for example—we have fallen into "the desire to have one's own way," we are thereby *being shown by God* that which is hidden in the depths of our minds. Syriac ascetical tradition everywhere asserts that such unveiling is directly from God—and, equally, the remedy for such spiritual sickness is also from God.

For, a page later, Isaac says this: "The remedy for them all is one . . . And what is it? Humility of heart" (211). In other words, God sends us the dreadful spirit precisely so that we may see hidden within us that spiritual sickness called arrogance. And once we so see it, we may then begin to seek what alone will cure that sickness, namely humility. But—and this is crucially important—such sickness begins when (says Isaac) "a man . . . begins to appear wise in his own eyes" (211), and such sickness can easily become next to incurable. Isaac puts it this way: "Do not be angry with me that I tell you the truth. You have never sought out humility with your whole soul" (212). And therefore St. Ephraim prays in his prayer: Do not give me—do not lay upon me; do not weigh me down with—this dread spirit, for I may well not possess the humility and wisdom I need to be cured of such affliction. "Take from me" as a translation thus misses important aspects of God's action in our penitential awareness—though, clearly, it is God who grants us the humility that heals us. In this way, the action of repentance in us reflects the great line from Psalm 99: "Know that the Lord, he is God, that he has made us, and not we ourselves" (l. 3).[9]

In this context, then, St. Ephraim's second sentence possesses sharp significance. In this sentence, the four qualities of the penitential spirit— better: the four pathways of this spirit in us—are beautifully given. The first of the four is, in Greek, *sophrosyne*, a word of high antiquity in classical Greek culture, going back through Plato and Aristotle all the way to Hesiod and Homer. The word is translated variously as discretion, moderation, sanity, self-control, prudence, temperance, and chastity. All the word's meanings, both classical and Christian, include two key aspects: integrated wholeness and unified singleness.

Now these two aspects are best understood in the light of Syriac Orthodoxy's teachings on celibacy and virginity, teachings that everywhere held that celibacy—including the celibacy voluntarily chosen by a husband and wife—was the condition in which a person achieved self-integration. The Syriac translation of the Gospels rendered the Greek word *monogenes* (only begotten) with the Syriac word meaning "singleness," using the same word for both the Son of God and the human person. In one of his poems, St. Ephraim says: "let such a man who is divided / collect himself together and become one before You."[10]

Self-collection and becoming one before God: here is *sophrosyne*. It is the state of self-integration in which each person achieves oneness in order to be in God's presence. The Syriac Church reads this oneness as the fulfillment of Christ's commandment in the Gospel: "when your eye is single, your whole body is then full of light" (Matt 6:22). Such singleness of sight results when one's eye sees every other person *not* as the receiver of one's hungers and desires—not, that is, in the thousand disintegrations of one's craziness—but, instead, sees everyone in the world as a child of God, completely integrated and entirely beautiful and wholly illumined. *Sophrosyne* is thus both the means and the end of such illumined seeing. As Psalm 35 says: "For with thee is the fountain of life, in thy light we shall see light" (l. 9).

The second of the four spiritual qualities St. Ephraim asks for is, in Greek, *tapeinophrosyne*, or humility of mind. This compound word is, again, one possessing a high and long history before it reaches this Syriac prayer. The first part of the compound, *tapeino-*, means humility, while the second part signifies the mind in its conscious intentionalities, its deliberately chosen focus. Taken together, the two parts signify the mind's voluntary obedience to the way of humility. And—here is yet another of St. Ephraim's insights in this prayer—this humility of mind incarnates and makes actual the way of *sophrosyne*. That is, our freely chosen humility of mind heals our intellectual arrogance in such a way that *sophrosyne* can be made real in us.

Thus, an interesting verbal pattern now can be seen. In the first sentence about the dreadful spirit, the initial pair of words used the same root in a *contrastive* manner: sloth became its opposite, crazed busyness, yet stayed the same spirit. In this second sentence, the initial pair also shares the same root, but the use is not contrastive but *actualizing*: chastity, or *sophrosyne*, becomes actualized by humility. In the first sentence, the movement is a whipsaw motion; in the second, the movement is one of grounding and making real.

Similarly, the third quality—in Greek, *hypomone*, meaning "patience"— is best understood as arising from humility. St. Isaac perfectly states this connection in the same Homily 42: "in proportion to your humility you are given patience in your woes" (212). In other words, just as humility incarnates *sophrosyne*, so it gives rise to patience. In the same way that— in the first sentence—sloth and crazed busyness produced the condition for the hunger to control things (*philarchia*), so, too, *sophrosyne* and humility together yield patience as their fruit. But note again the difference in *movement* between the two sentences. In sentence 1, the sequence may rightly be characterized as *vicious*: whipsawing from sloth to busyness, then to domination and submission. Here, in sentence 2, the sequence is *incarnative*, with each quality—or pathway—giving itself wholly to the actualization of the next. *Sophrosyne* gives itself into humility, and together they become incarnated in and as patience. This incarnative movement thus perfectly expresses the action of *kenotic*, or self-emptying, love.

Thus, the fourth and final quality of this beautiful spirit is stated: *agape*, or love. A later homily of St. Isaac's possesses this sentence: "Love is the offspring of knowledge, and knowledge is the offspring of the health of soul; health of soul is a strength which comes from prolonged patience" (62:298). Isaac's sequence here thus interestingly matches Ephraim's sequence in the prayer, for in both, the endpoint of love fulfills the whole sequence. Even the differences between Isaac's and Ephraim's formulations can be understood as harmonic and not divergent. For St. Ephraim's *sophrosyne* is a superb reading of St. Isaac's "health of soul," while St. Isaac's "knowledge" perfectly fits St. Ephraim's "humility of mind." And again, the sequence of the second sentence is the movement of incarnation and kenotic love, the divine becoming always more fully realized in our flesh as we become always more divinized in God.

Then the prayer's third and final sentence emerges. Here St. Ephraim prays that God give him the sight to see fully his own transgressions. We may understand this sight as completing the prayer's movement into incarnation. That is, St. Ephraim prays that he may see himself fully in the way that God sees him: in all his sinfulness. St. Ephraim also prays that he be given *not* to judge his brother in this awareness of his own sinfulness, not to blame another even slightly for his own sin.

And in so praying, St. Ephraim makes the second great sentence of the prayer become fully incarnate. To be able to withstand—for even an instant—fully knowing one's own sinfulness without even remotely blaming another for any of that sinfulness: here is the heart and mind of the Orthodox Lent. For such knowledge would be akin to seeing ourselves in the way God beholds us: seeing our transgressions and never judging another. To Syriac Orthodoxy, such seeing is the supreme end of all ascetic labors.

For such knowledge, Saints Isaac and Ephraim are saying, would yield in us the immense fruitfulness of actual loving: of God and of one's brother or sister in God. In Homily 62, St. Isaac asks, "What is knowledge?" and then answers: "The perception of life immortal." "And what is life immortal? Consciousness in God" (298). In this way, then, the third sentence of St. Ephraim's prayer moves the penitent's mind into the mind of God, and we achieve what St. Paul calls the mind of Christ (1 Cor 2:16). And from within the mind of Christ, St. Ephraim beholds Christ's eternality: "for blessed art Thou, unto ages of ages."

From this perspective, St. Ephraim's prayer—"Grant me to see my own transgressions"—can be understood to incarnate, in and as repentance, what Our Lord prays in John 17: "I am no longer in this world . . . and I come to You, Holy Father" (John 17:11). To achieve genuine sight of one's sinfulness without blaming others is to be with God. "Now I come to You," Our Lord continues, "and these things I speak in the world, that they may have My joy fulfilled in themselves" (John 17:13). Note very carefully: as Christ says this great priestly prayer, He is "no longer in this world" at the very moment

He is speaking "these things . . . in the world." In other words, this prayer of Christ's is spoken at the boundary between worlds, where heaven and earth touch, combining within Himself the life here and the life there. And at this boundary, Christ gives all His joy to be incarnated and made full in us. Just so, in its final phrase the Prayer of St. Ephraim achieves the blessedness of heaven—and the penitent gives all this blessedness to his brother in the action of surrendering all his judgment of him. Here is the fullest incarnation of humility and patience; here is the deepest heart of Orthodox Lent.

■　■　■

My first Lent as an Orthodox was the spring of 1985. I can still recall how moved I was by this extraordinary prayer. It was as if my eyes and heart had truly opened for the first time. When Pascha came, with its shock of genuine joy, I felt strongly that I needed still to keep this Lenten prayer before me. So, in the days following Easter, during Bright Week, I went to my priest, Fr. Vladimir Sovyrda, who had received me into the Church the previous September 8, 1984, at Holy Resurrection Church in Berlin, New Hampshire. I asked Father: Could I continue to say this prayer at my morning and evening prayer at home? He gave a warm and quick smile. "Oh, sure, after Pascha season is over, keep on praying this prayer as long as you like." And he gave me a blessing. I kissed his hand.

Since that day in mid-April 1985, I have—except during the Pascha season—said this prayer every morning and evening of my life.

I didn't know—who of us could have known?—that April day in 1985 that Fr. Vladimir would, two years later, sicken with cancer and die, on April 5, 1987, the week before Holy Week began. During that week I traveled to the hospital each day to be with my first father in Orthodoxy. I would sit by his bed, sometimes chanting psalms to him, trying to help in tiny ways Matushka Ann and their three adult children to comfort him. And I tried not to get in their way.

The final hour came swiftly. During the afternoon of Sunday, April 5, 1987, I had sat by his bedside as his breathing grew always hoarser and more labored and more dreadful. Matushka Ann, softly at first and then more strongly, began to sing the Liturgy of the Presanctified Gifts, celebrated Wednesday evenings (and sometimes on Fridays, too) during Orthodox

Lent. The two daughters and son joined their mother, and their strong and beautiful Orthodox voices rose wonderfully above—yet beautifully holding—Father's terrible breathing.

A few times in that last hour I tried to sing with them, but I could not because of my unceasing tears, which choked me. So I sat by his bed, my eyes closed as his now were, and all at once and sharply there arose in my mind's eye a powerful image: Father was traveling a dry and harsh road into death, a road where no water was and no rest from fearsome labor. And every long and shuddering and frightful breath was carrying him closer to death. I wept for this torment.

Then I heard Matushka Ann and her daughter Marina begin to sing antiphonally: "Let my prayer arise in Thy sight as incense, and let the lifting up of my hands be an evening sacrifice." Then, when they ended the song, his son Mark began: "Lord and Master of my life, give me not the spirit of sloth, despair, lust of power and idle talk . . ." chanting the whole prayer straight through. They made a single prostration at the end of the bed—or cross—where Father was. And suddenly Father's breathing grew quieter and shallower, and Marina touched her father's feet under the covers, whispering to us: "They're cold." Matushka Ann then alone began to sing the Hymn of the Entrance: "Now the powers of heaven do serve invisibly with us . . ." And then Father shuddered once all over, and his breathing stopped completely. He was dead.

I raised my head in the sudden silence—I had put my forehead down on his bed by his hand—and I saw Matushka Ann and her children, heads bowed now in immense grief. The silence of death weighed heavily on us. Then Marina opened the prayer book and began chanting the prayers for the parting of the soul from the body. We stood around the bed, and Marina kept chanting in a clear and good Orthodox voice that was now beginning to be free from tears: "Look down on me from on high, O Mother of God, in mercy hear my plea, that beholding You I may go forth from the body rejoicing."[11]

Then all at once and suddenly, a great and immense *peacefulness* descended into the hospital room, a peacefulness that seemed to fill all of us and everything in the room, a peacefulness that seemed to me—I cannot explain this—to change the very air in the room we were in, the air now a very faint and very beautiful blue-green color. All the weight lifted at this peacefulness of color we could *breathe* in and rejoice. We saw in each other's eyes the reality of a great joy. It was the air of the Mother of God, the very blue-green color she carries in every Orthodox icon.

When I left the hospital that night I knew in my heart what I now say aloud for the first time: Fr. Vladimir had been praying the Prayer of St. Ephraim in his final hour. And I know, too, that in blessing me to pray the prayer he had placed in my heart a very clear and very good light.

St. Ephraim begins one of his poems with a beautiful line: "Blessed is the Messenger who came bearing / a great peace."[12] This messenger is of course Christ Himself, who was—I am certain—the author of the peacefulness that had descended into the hospital room that night in 1987. He ends this poem by describing the "wise women" around the cross who "with their soft words / changed dirges into prophecy" (*Hymns*, 123). Matushka Ann and her family had accomplished this same wondrous change, their grief becoming prophetic.[13]

■   ■   ■

On June 9, in the year 373, St. Ephraim died of the plague. He had contracted the sickness from those in the city to whom, as Father Deacon Ephraim, he had been ministering since the disease had begun ravaging the city all that spring. Nothing more is known of his final hours. But it is not unfitting to imagine this prayer on his dying lips, this prayer of all our lives.

3

"A New Man Has Arisen in Me!"
Memory Eternal in Dostoevsky's *Brothers Karamazov*[14]

Central to Eastern Orthodox Christendom is the singing, at the end of every Orthodox funeral, of the song known as "Memory Eternal" (in Church Slavonic: *Vechnaya Pamyat*). This song also concludes Dostoevsky's great, final novel, *The Brothers Karamazov*, when, following the funeral of the boy whom Alyosha Karamazov (and the circle of schoolboys around him) had deeply loved, Alyosha speaks to the boys about the funeral and about the meaning of the resurrection, with this brief song as their steady focus. My thesis is simply this: to know something of this song's meaning is to comprehend both the Eastern Orthodox faith and Dostoevsky's greatest novel.

In the fourth century AD the Orthodox Fathers known as the Cappadocians articulated the relational reality of personhood. It is summed up in this way by J. D. Zizioulas in his wonderful essay called "The Contribution of Cappadocia to Christian Thought":

1 We are persons because we know ourselves as foundationally free, under not even the tiniest bondage to, or limitation of, either earthly history or the material world—a freedom even prior to and greater than the Church herself because (as Zizioulas says) such freedom "constitutes the 'way of being' of God Himself."

2 We are persons because we can give ourself freely and entirely to another in self-emptying love; that is, we can voluntarily surrender all our selfhood entirely into the hands of another in the action of loving that other. Zizioulas puts it beautifully: "Love is a relationship, it is the free coming out of one's self, the breaking of one's will, a free submission to the will of another."

3 We are persons when we understand ourself as wholly unique, as entirely unrepeatable and forever irreplaceable. As members of a species we are merely replaceable and countable individuals in a

set, biological, historical, or sociopolitical. As members of a set (or sets), we can be compelled to serve extrinsic, even hostile, purposes; we can, that is, be treated as things. But as persons, we are unique and unrepeatable; hence, we cannot (as Zizioulas says) "be composed or decomposed, combined or used for any objective whatsoever."[15]

These three conditions of personhood—foundational freedom, self-emptying love, and absolute uniqueness—shed great light on what the Orthodox Church—and Dostoevsky—mean by the phrase "Memory Eternal." It means this: in the same way that the wise thief of Luke 23:42 ("Lord, remember me when Thou comest in Thy kingdom") achieves personhood by entering into loving Christ freely (and this freedom is emphasized in the crucifixion scene by everyone else mocking Christ while the thief freely and deliberately chooses to love); just so we become persons in freely surrendering our own will, in an action of love, into the hands of another.

Dostoevsky gives beautiful expression to this Orthodox understanding of personhood early in *The Brothers Karamazov* when he describes the relation between Alyosha Karamazov and his spiritual father, the Elder Zosima. "What, then," asks the narrator, "is an elder?" He answers:

> An elder is one who takes your soul, your will into his soul and into his will. Having chosen an elder, you renounce your will and give it under total obedience and with total self-renunciation. A man who dooms himself to this trial, this terrible school of life, does so voluntarily, in the hope that after the long trial he will achieve self-conquest, self-mastery to such a degree that he will, finally, through a whole life's obedience, attain to perfect freedom—that is, freedom from himself—and avoid the lot of those who live their whole lives without finding themselves in themselves. (27–28)

This perfectly expresses the Orthodox understanding of the relational reality of personhood. And the whole of *The Brothers Karamazov* can usefully be read as a vast commentary on this single passage. At age 19, Alyosha Karamazov struggles to achieve the "perfect freedom" found only in loving obedience to his spiritual father, the Elder Zosima. At age 28, Dmitri at first rejects the Orthodox way of personhood by plunging into a life of entirely autonomous desires and their endlessly self-willed fulfillment. But then, in the course of the novel, he discovers a profounder and more directly Orthodox experience when he discovers the relational reality of personhood through his love of Grushenka. The middle brother, Ivan, age 24, rejects the ways of both his brothers in the name of a still more terrifying autonomy: not the passional autonomy his older brother Dmitri attempts but a spiritual autonomy, one wherein he asserts his own will as more perfective than God's will in creating the world. Ivan's spiritual and psychic agony in the novel's final hundred pages stands as Dostoevsky's revelation of what inevitably happens to those who attempt to deny or unmake the Orthodox reality of relational personhood. It is the attempt to unmake Memory Eternal through self-willed oblivion.

In this light, then, I want to consider that astonishing moment in the novel when Dmitri, having been falsely arrested and imprisoned for two months for the murder of his father (and about to be wrongly convicted of it), says this to his brother Alyosha, who visits him in prison:

> "Rakitin wouldn't understand this," he began, all in a sort of rapture, as it were, "but you, you will understand everything. That's why I've been thirsting for you . . . Brother, in these past two months I've sensed a new man in me, a new man has arisen in me! He was shut up inside me, but if it weren't for this thunderbolt, he never would have appeared. Frightening! What do I care if I spend twenty years pounding out iron ore in the mines, I'm not afraid of that at all, but I'm afraid of something else now: that this risen man not depart from me! Even there, in the mines, underground, you can find a human heart in the convict and murderer standing next to you, and you can be close to him, because there, too, it's possible to live, and love, and suffer! You can revive and resurrect the frozen heart in this convict, you can look after him for years, and finally bring up from the cave into the light a soul that is lofty now, a suffering consciousness. You can revive an angel, resurrect a hero! And there are many of them, there are hundreds, and we're all guilty for them! Why did I have a dream about a 'wee one' at such a moment? 'Why is the wee one poor?' It was a prophecy to me at that moment! It's for the 'wee one'

that I will go. Because everyone is guilty for everyone else. For all the 'wee ones,' because there are little children and big children. All people are 'wee ones.' And I'll go for all of them, because there must be someone who will go for all of them. I didn't kill father, but I must go. I accept! All of this came to me here . . . Within these peeling walls. And there are many, there are hundreds of them, underground, with hammers in their hands. Oh, yes, we'll be in chains, and there will be no freedom, but then, in our great grief, we will arise once more into joy, without which it's not possible for man to live, or for God to be, for God gives joy, it's his prerogative, a great one . . ." (591–92)

I want to pull three strands from this complex and revelatory speech. The first strand occurs when Dmitri says: "A new man has arisen in me! He was shut up inside me, but if it weren't for this thunderbolt, he would never have appeared." This newly risen (or resurrected) self is, above all, a remembered self; that is, it is a self that was always "shut up inside" him but that could only be made manifest—that is, be remembered—by the "thunderbolt" of relationality let loose by his father's death. Hence, the second strand: "I didn't kill father, but I must go. I accept!" The walls of autonomy are here fully breached as Dmitri voluntarily accepts the Orthodox reality wherein "everyone is guilty for everyone else" because each person possesses personhood only relationally. The result in Dmitri is the rush of understanding that, as the false freedom of self-willed autonomy vanishes, genuine joy arrives. Here is the third strand: "Oh, yes, we'll be in chains, and there will be no freedom, but then, in our great grief, we will arise once more into joy, without which it's not possible for man to live, or for God to be . . ." This third strand explicitly links the arrival of real joy to the ending of false freedom, a joy that is essential, Dmitri says, to both human life and divine being. Together, these three strands—the resurrected self, the relational self, and the joyful self—are the three defining aspects of personhood in *The Brothers Karamazov*. And all three aspects can be best understood—in Dostoevsky and in Orthodox Christendom—as aspects of the meaning of Memory Eternal.

Everywhere operative in Eastern Christendom is the spiritual activity called *theosis*, wherein the human person is understood to become like

God. Theosis is considered to be the normative goal of every person on earth—and not the rare experience of a spiritual elite. What propels the person toward achieving theosis is, very simply, obeying what Christ, in the gospels, calls "the first and great commandment" (Matt 22:38): "Thou shalt love the Lord thy God with all thy heart, and with all thy soul, and with all thy mind" (Matt 22:37).

In this scene we are examining, Dmitri perfectly illustrates this love when he ends his speech to Alyosha by saying: "And then from the depth of the earth, we, the men underground, will start singing a tragic hymn to God, in whom there is joy! Hail to God and his joy! I love him!" (592). Here, then, is the engine that moves the process of theosis: the power of loving God. Furthermore, this is also the engine that moves what Christ (in the same passage in St. Matthew) calls the second of the two great commandments: "Thou shalt love thy neighbor as thyself" (Matt 22:39). In loving the neighbor—that is, loving the one who is always right now before you, "nigh" or near you—in the same way in which you love God, you are directly experiencing the way wherein the Other is always oneself. These two great commandments are, to the Orthodox heart, Christ's direct injunctions to each of us to enter into the way of theosis.

Then Dostoevsky gives us the fullness of theosis when Dmitri says to Alyosha, on the eve of his trial, what Christ Himself says to His disciples on the eve of His arrest and crucifixion: "I am." Dmitri says: "And it seems to me there's so much strength in me now that I can overcome everything, all sufferings, only in order to say and tell myself every moment: I am! In a thousand torments—I am; writhing under torture—but I am. Locked up in a tower, but still I exist, I see the sun, and if I don't see the sun, still I know it is. And the whole of life is there—in knowing that the sun is . . ." (592).

This speech is, if you will, pure ontological song wherein the singer's affirmation of being ("I am!") communicates ontological ecstasy to every living thing in such a way that each created thing remains entirely and perfectly itself at the very same moment each thing becomes a single note in the singer's vast song. In other words, the singer's love for God converges fully with the love flowing from God to the singer. Thus, the result of entering into ontological song is what can be termed the unceasing aliveness of the state of theosis. For this is an aliveness in which the human person comes to participate through love directly in God's eternal aliveness.

In the "Talks and Homilies of the Elder Zosima," assembled by Alyosha Karamazov after his beloved Elder's death, there occurs this extraordinary passage:

> Much on earth is concealed from us, but in place of it we have been granted a secret, mysterious sense of our living bond with the other world, with the higher heavenly world, and the roots of our thoughts and feelings are not here but in other worlds. That is why philosophers say it is impossible on earth to conceive the essence of things. God took seeds from other worlds and saved them on this earth, and raised up his garden; and everything that could sprout sprouted, but it lives and grows only through its sense of being in touch with other mysterious worlds; if this sense is weakened or destroyed in you, that which has grown up in you dies. Then you become indifferent to life, and even come to hate it. So I think. (320)

This passage is, as Victor Terras rightly says, "the master key to the philosophic interpretation, as well as to the structure," of the entire *Brothers Karamazov*.[16] For it elucidates two powerful and connected ideas: (1) that we can strongly (albeit obscurely) intuit the way wherein this empirical world of our actual lives is, in fact, rooted in the higher heavenly world of God; and (2) that what bears fruit in this world does so only when we nurture in our lives those three seeds Dmitri discovers, which God has directly sowed in us: the capacities to remember our real self, to breach the walls of our autonomy, and to seek and embrace the real joy that follows the ending of false freedom. Such nurturing occurs when we fall to the ground and die so that these seeds may begin first to bud and then to bear fruit. These two ideas, then, help us to understand why Dostoevsky chose as the epigraph to his novel this saying of Christ's: "Truly, truly I say to you, Unless the seed of wheat fall into the ground and die, it abides alone; but if it die, it brings forth much fruit" (John 12:24). This way of fruitfulness is the way of Memory Eternal.

Thus, we can see how both the artistic structure and the philosophic significance of the novel are held in these two ideas. We can see the three brothers, throughout the novel, drawing near to enacting these two ideas—or else missing them altogether or (with Ivan) deliberately turning away from them. And what connects these two ideas is, again, Memory Eternal, here understood as the way the seed genetically "remembers" the fruit it springs from and will, if conditions are right, soon become. True remembering is therefore directly connected to—indeed, hardwired into—the process wherein we die so as to enter into fruitfulness. And this process is the one of remembering God and of being remembered by Him.

We are now able to see something of the lovely shapeliness of the final scene in the novel. In this scene, Alyosha talks to the dozen boys with whom he has just attended the funeral of Ilyusha, the boy they all had come to love in his final days of life. Toward the end of his speech to the boys, Alyosha says this: "Let us first of all and before all be kind, then honest, and then—let us never forget one another. I say it again. I give you my word, gentlemen, that for my part I will never forget any one of you; each face that is looking at me now, I will remember, be it even after thirty years" (775). This shape is, of course, the Orthodox shape of Memory Eternal: the present seed of actual love is already becoming the unceasing fruitfulness of memory. And this fruitfulness of memory is a triumph over death—made possible, in the words of the triumphal song that fills the Orthodox Paschal Liturgy, by Christ's "trampling down death by death." This can occur for us, not at all because we erase the dead in our mind's oblivion (what secular culture calls "getting over it"), but precisely because we keep them so strongly, indeed so brightly present in our love. And Dostoevsky is luminously clear in his Orthodox understanding of Alyosha's speech. By holding another in our love, we are becoming like God in that we are remembering the seed of God in ourself at the very instant we are seeing the fully ripened fruitfulness of the other in God. In this way, the other begins to become our very self. Alyosha concludes this way: "You are all dear to me, gentlemen, from now on I shall keep you all in my heart, and I ask you to keep me in your hearts, too! Well, and who has united us in this good, kind feeling, which we will remember and intend to remember always, if not Ilyushechka, that good boy, that kind boy, that boy dear to us unto ages and ages! Let us never forget him, and may his memory be eternal and good in our hearts now and unto ages of ages!" (775).

The point is magnificently clear. The fruitfulness of Memory Eternal arises always and solely from an actual person—here, Ilyusha—who unites in love all the Orthodox believers who sing his passing and have taken him into their hearts. Thus, what begins in isolative grief concludes in relational joy. Such is the shape of Memory Eternal in Orthodoxy and in Dostoevsky.

And thus emerges still another significance: through the action of Memory Eternal, the person who has died continues to act back into the lives of those who continue to love him or her. In the middle of the novel, in the chapter called "Cana of Galilee," Alyosha kneels by the coffin of his spiritual father, the Elder Zosima, while the episode in St. John's Gospel telling of Jesus' changing water into wine is being read aloud. As the episode is read, Alyosha prays silently, and then he dozes slightly—and then he instantly enters into a vision wherein he sees Father Zosima sitting at the wedding table in Cana where Jesus Himself is sitting. As the Elder catches sight of Alyosha and rises and walks toward him, smiling in beautiful welcome, Alyosha registers perfectly the Orthodox comprehension of what is now occurring: "Why, he is in the coffin . . . But here, too" (361). That is, Alyosha fully sees how his spiritual father lies dead in the coffin and yet—simultaneously—is standing alive before him. In the actions of Memory Eternal, death on earth is defeated by unceasing aliveness in God.

The scene continues with Alyosha listening to his beloved teacher speaking words of wisdom to him. And then Alyosha, the vision ended, goes out under the immense night sky where, the narrator tells us, "the silence of the earth seemed to merge with the silence of the heavens, the majesty of the earth touched the majesty of the stars" (362). Then Alyosha suddenly falls to earth, weeping in joy and kissing the earth; and the Elder's voice rings again in Alyosha's soul: "Water the earth with the tears of your joy, and love those tears . . ." (362). The narrator then says: "It was as if threads from all those innumerable worlds of God came together in his soul, and it was trembling all over, 'touching other worlds'" (362). This last phrase is, of course, the Elder Zosima's phrase, here remembered by Alyosha, yes, but above all directly given by the Elder to Alyosha in this moment, directly shaping and indeed directly creating this moment. "Never, never in all his life," the narrator says, "would Alyosha forget that moment" (363).

This moment is, for Alyosha, a moment of *theosis*, one in which he participates fully in divine aliveness, a moment, that is, of Memory Eternal. And this moment, Dostoevsky makes abundantly clear in the chapter, is a moment that is entirely given by the dead to the living in an action of love. The chapter ends this way: "'Someone visited my soul in that hour,' Alyosha would say afterward, with firm belief in his words" (363). In Memory Eternal, the beloved dead act in love directly in the lives of the living.

▪ ▪ ▪

After Fr. Zosima dies, Alyosha composes a biography of the Elder from (in the title Alyosha gives it) "His Own Words." In the early pages of this biography, Fr. Zosima says this: "From my parental home I brought only precious memories, for no memories are more precious to a man than those of his earliest childhood in his parental home, and that is almost always so, as long as there is even a little bit of love and unity in the family. But from a very bad family, too, one can keep precious memories, if only one's soul knows how to seek out what is precious" (290).

Here, then, is perhaps is the most beautiful understanding of Memory Eternal both in Eastern Orthodoxy and in Dostoevsky. It is the soul's seeking out what is precious—that is, what is unceasingly alive—even in the darkest, most afflicted of circumstances. And the crucial point, in the novels and in the Church, is that such seeking can succeed most fully and directly through what Dostoevsky calls "a whole life's obedience" to the historical Orthodox Church and her long traditions of fasting and prayer. For in this obedience, we avoid the terrible fate of those who (like Ivan Karamazov) seek to find themselves in themselves. Instead, like Alyosha and (in the end) Dmitri, we come to understand that we are precious not in our self-assertion but only in our self-emptying.

4
Seed and Fruit
St. Isaac the Syrian's *Ascetical Homilies* and
René Girard's Writings on Violence

I

begin this essay on violence with an autobiographical note. To use
novelist Carolyn Chute's wonderful remark about her autobiographical novel: the subject has been involuntarily researched by the author.[17] I
was raised in a violent home, where, until I was nine years old, my father's
alcohol addiction fueled his open or just barely contained violence, a home
where my mother was beaten over and over (I remember her face covered
with blood). Alcohol broke apart my home in a violent paroxysm the night
of July 4, 1949, the summer I was nine. The police were in our living room
in the small hours of July 5. I remember all of this experience very clearly.

Some three weeks earlier, in June, I was shot in the chest with a pistol,
the bullet entering two inches below my heart. The gunman was my best
friend, also age nine, and we had found his big brother's target pistol while
we were playing at his house.

What I remember most vividly about the shooting—I remember
viscerally, without having to make any conscious effort at all to remember—
is lying on the operating table and seeing the doctor over me, his hands at
the wound very skillfully and tenderly probing for the bullet—his great
arms and torso coming down to me, his face silent in concentrated stillness
bending over me, his hands intimate and strong and exact and delicate.

I offer this piece of autobiography as a tiny verbal icon of the way I
want to approach my subject of St. Isaac the Syrian's *Ascetical Homilies* and
René Girard's writings on violence.[18] The Girardian discourse is, I want to
suggest, a revelation of our violent home life: only here our home is our
shared historical, cultural, and anthropological life. Thus, in reading and
studying the Girardian discourse, we soon come to see just how terrifyingly
evil our shared home life has for so long been and just how desperately we

have been trying all this time to keep its violence veiled from everyone's eyes and, above all, from our own.

But—to continue my analogy—with St. Isaac's *Ascetical Homilies*, we have other hands at our heart. In reading and studying St. Isaac, we find that his *Homilies* come close to our woundedness, that they bend down over us and remove affliction from our heart, giving our life back to us.

And so my suggestion is this. In the same way that I could bear the breaking of my home only because I had known those healing hands at my heart, we can only genuinely comprehend what Girard is saying about violence in the Orthodox light of St. Isaac's *Ascetical Homilies*. Now, as we shall see, St. Isaac does not in any way *soften* the Girardian revelation; indeed, if anything, he deepens it by making even our most ordinary circumstances and relationships become far worse to us. But—and this is my main point— my gunshot wound sharply worsened my childhood home for me by all at once ending every method of coping I had devised in nine years to deal with the violence—and immediately brought me to an operating table where something like grace could touch me. So, too, St. Isaac's ferocity worsens our case by revealing the violence within even our apparently most harmless ordinariness—and carries a grace that enacts our healing.

II

In a 1996 interview, René Girard gives a telling answer when asked why he thinks so many people have misunderstood his analysis of mimetic desire:

> There are many people who prefer to say that the real problem is the wish to kill one's own father or mother, and they ignore or resist the possibility that the most common problem—our predicament—is that of trying to beat a rival at his own game. So there is a resistance to shedding light on the role of rivalry in our lives.[19]

In a single phrase—"trying to beat a rival at his own game"—Girard here discloses his essential insight into the *mimetic* nature of human desire. This insight says that, in the presence of another's desire for something, one's own instantly flares up—just as the flare-up of one's own desiring instantly intensifies the other's. Desire is therefore mimetic in the sense that we "catch" it from others. And one of Girard's crucial points is that such contagion does not in any way *lessen* the intensity of the desiring. If anything, the intensity actually *increases* as the desire passes from one person to another. I give a simple example that I draw from Gil Bailie's book *Violence Unveiled*.[20] A toddler in a day care idly picks up a toy, and instantly another child wants precisely that toy and reaches to take it—at which point the first child's desire instantly escalates to exceed the second one's desire, and so on, reciprocally. Desire increases as it moves from one to the next.

Now, modern psychology, as it comes down to us from Freud, can shed very little light on this mimetic phenomenon of desire. The reason why this is so, Girard holds, is that Freud abandoned the specifically mimetic nature of desire. And in the place of mimesis, Freud set classical Greek myths (Oedipus, Electra, etc.) to explain desire: "the wish to kill one's own father or mother," as Girard says in the interview. These psychological myths do two things at once. First, they veil the mimetic nature of desire by isolating the individual into a separate "bundle" of complexes and compulsions. And second, the myths feed the individual's desires by cloaking them with the dark grandeur of vivid narrative, a grandeur that makes every desire it touches into an inexorable need that must be fulfilled—an inexorability perfectly expressed in the Oedipus narratives wherein blindness also occurs. (In a recent essay, Girard says that "the Oedipus myth . . . may well be the myth par excellence of our post-Christian and neo-pagan confusion"; see *Reader*, 206.) These two primary actions of psychological myths—the simultaneous veiling and feeding of desires—can shed very little, if any, light upon "our predicament" as Girard describes it: "trying to beat a rival at his own game." Psychology can only tacitly *affirm* the predicament by glorifying the desire.

Why do we resist knowing this? We resist it for the same reason that the two toddlers loudly resist any solution to their quarrel that overrides either one's claim to *originary* desire:

"I had it *first*! I wanted it *first*!"
"You were just *holding* it! I wanted to *play* with it!"

As anyone who has tried well knows, no adequate response can be made to such assertions of originary desire. Indeed, as Girard astutely points out, "the lie of spontaneous desire" rejects any challenge to its foundational "illusion of autonomy" (*Reader*, 43) because all of us—from earliest childhood—are passionately committed to this primary delusion that our desires are our "own."[21] The strength of our resistance to seeing the mimetic basis of our desiring therefore perfectly measures the depth of our commitment to this lie of autonomy. Thus, the "lie of spontaneous [i.e., non-mimetic] desire" follows the curve of our mimetic contagion, running always slightly ahead of it so as to provide the "wiring" for our mimetic desiring to move through. The speed of our desiring therefore outstrips even the possibility of our resisting, for the lie of passional autonomy entirely hides from us the mimetic basis of our desiring. In this sense, then, the roots of our psychological resistance may be said to be in that moment when Eve in the Garden of Eden "catches" desire from the serpent and spins the lie of autonomous (hence, envious) human desire: "And when the woman saw that the tree was good for food, and that it was pleasant to the eyes, and a tree to be desired to make one wise, she took of the fruit . . ." (Gen 3:6).

What happens in this decisive moment is that the lie of autonomous desire takes hold in human self-consciousness. So complete is the grip of this lie that, in fact, this moment in Genesis comes to seem to us not a catastrophe but a *liberation into genuine consciousness, an awakening of selfhood and the possibility of individuation.* Indeed, for Girard, most of what we know and accept and revere as modern thinking expresses precisely this lie. And, again, our resistance even to seeing it—let alone abandoning it—measures the strength and depth of its hold on us.

In this light, we may best understand one of Girard's most compelling essays. Published in 1993, and revised slightly for the 1996 *Reader*, the essay was first entitled "How Can Satan Cast out Satan?" Now, this is the question, of course, that Jesus asks in the Gospels (Mark 3:23), but for an answer, we must turn, says Girard, to the Passion narratives as the very "center of all significance" in the Gospels (*Reader*, 195). Why, asks Girard, does Jesus call the Passion "the hour of Satan"? He answers this way: "Because it is Satan's attempt to cast out Jesus, to expel him as if he were another Satan, a worse Satan than Satan himself" (ibid.). Here is the central premise of Girard's essay: Satan is paradoxically "both the exorcized demon and the exorcist" (*Reader*, 202).

Girard explains the paradox in this way. On the one hand, Satan sees Jesus as a demon to be exorcized, as a force that immediately and deeply challenges all his realm and all his rule, wreaking havoc everywhere. On the other hand, all the forces that conspire to crucify Christ—that is, the Temple rulers; the Roman authorities; the disciples whose panicked flight constitutes silent collaboration (but especially Peter, who actively collaborates while warming himself at the night fires of violence); and, steering all the forces, the crowd in the city streets whose relentless homicidal purpose and ruthless voice directly shape the event—taken collectively (for so they act), *all these forces are Satan*. Thus, Satan is simultaneously the exorcist and the exorcized.

In the essay, Girard strikes an important analogy. This paradox of Satan resembles what contemporary physics calls "self-organizing systems" (*Reader*, 202). These are "complex entities," Girard says, "in which the principle of order and the principle of disorder are one and the same" (202). In such systems, he goes on, "as soon as disorder reaches a certain threshold . . . the forces of disruption turn into a force for reintegration and reordering," and he says, "The Satan of the Gospels is a self-organizing system" (202). My point here is this: both the disorder and the order that Satan engineers are premised upon the same lie of autonomous desire. That is, both these phenomena directly reject God's presence and sovereignty.

Let me give an example to illustrate the point, an example drawn from contemporary psychotherapy. Now, it is nearly axiomatic in marriage counseling that each partner in a marriage must have his or her unique needs met. The scenarios of marital affliction are therefore very familiar indeed, nearly all of them driven by this single axiom of fulfilling one's needs.[22] The resulting disorder is also equally familiar, for the resentments and bitternesses and disappointments and blindnesses are plain to see. In Girard's terms, such disorder is Satanic. It arises straight from the resentment born of the lie and it leads directly—and this is Girard's crucial point—to the overwhelming desire to victimize the other person as the source of one's own discontent: "If only I could get rid of her [or him], I'd be fine." This is sacrificial violence, and as such it is Satanic disorder.

But equally Satanic is that order which results, says Girard, when "the forces of disruption turn into a force for reintegration and reordering" (*Reader*, 202). Our poor couple seeks counseling. Inexorably, they are guided toward a premise which says that, just as the sources of their unhappiness lie *within each of them*, so, too, the sources of a new happiness lie also *within*. Almost inevitably, then, the counseling process will lead to finding a culprit whom the couple can *agree* is the common cause of their shared discontent: her abusive father, his manipulative mother, and so on. Such a culprit—now become the couple's sacrificial victim—is *safe;* that is, the new sacrifice acts to strengthen the bond between them. The disruptive forces in their marriage thus turn into the force for a new reintegration. Of course, says Girard, such a self-organizing system leaves Satan undisturbed.

But will it work? In other words, can Satan really cast out Satan? A few verses after Jesus asks this question in St. Mark's Gospel, He says, "If Satan rises up against himself, and is divided, he cannot stand, but has an end" (Mark 3:26). Our couple may well achieve a time of apparent peace. But since the system remains unchanged, the disorder will inevitably return—often enough, in entirely new ways not foreseen in the counseling. Jesus is therefore very clear on the point. Once Satan self-divides, he cannot stand, in the precise sense that he can give nothing whatever of what St. John calls the light of life (1:4). That is, Satan can only shed what the poet John Milton magnificently calls "darkness visible,"[23] which we may here take to be the self-generative and self-sustaining system of violence, a darkness that keeps the reality of the violence's "systemness"—that is, in our example, the capacity of the violence to be both the manifest disorder of the afflicted marriage and the apparent order of the marriage counseling—entirely veiled. It is this reality that the light of Christ unveils. And in and by that light, Satan's foundational lie of autonomous desire is utterly unmade.

In this way, then, Girard's description of the mimetic basis of our desire achieves two great ends. First, in providing a trenchant critique of psychology and culture, it discloses the nature and depth of our resistance to seeing this basis. Second, in focusing upon the Gospels as its source of illumination, it helps restore to us a way of recomprehending Scripture in all its explanatory power, a way of regrasping Scripture in the very terms of that extraordinary verse from LXX Psalm 118 (119): "Thy word is a lamp to my feet / And a light to my paths" (l. 105).

III

What also opens for us is a way to reascend that extraordinary height of spiritual wisdom about Scripture known as the Eastern Orthodox patristic tradition. In the unbroken tradition of Orthodox Christendom, the seventh-century presence of St. Isaac the Syrian is so essential that, as one contemporary Orthodox monastic wrote, "If all the writings of the desert fathers . . . were lost and the writings of Abba Isaac the Syrian alone survived, they would suffice to teach one from beginning to end concerning the life of stillness and prayer."[24] For, in his *Ascetical Homilies*, St. Isaac offers to us the one entirely certain antidote to all our mimetic poisoning: stillness. In Greek *hesychia*, stillness is the term that helps cohere the entire tradition, for every important Orthodox teacher of prayer has, for sixteen centuries, employed this term in a fundamental way. St. Isaac defines stillness as a voluntary "silence to all things" (21:112), a silence undertaken so that one can come to hear the voice of the Creator of all things, a voice now almost entirely drowned out by the willful noise that all things—especially humans—are constantly making. This is the silence, St. Isaac says, that Christ Himself sought in the desert at night, withdrawn "from all the clamour and tumult," so that He "could pray in stillness" (75:371). Thus, in choosing stillness as the ground of our prayer, we follow Christ Himself in His prayer to the Father.

Now, the fullness of this redemptive stillness can be achieved only by that practitioner of stillness (called in Greek a *hesychast*) who, St. Isaac says, "esteems . . . withdrawal above association with men" (44:218). St. Isaac recounts a story from the life of St. Arsenios, in which the saint twice receives this injunction from God: "Arsenios, flee, be silent, be still. Though the sight and intercourse of the brethren be very profitable, yet association with them will not profit you so much as to flee them" (44:219).

St. Arsenios obeys this injunction in both letter and spirit, and he becomes so inaccessible to all other persons that, St. Isaac tells us, when once the Archbishop of Alexandria visited him so as to fulfill a "desire to see him and to enjoy that honor" (44:218), Arsenios sat with his head bowed and did not speak a single word to him. St. Isaac exclaims, "Do you see how marvellous the elder was? Do you see his shunning of association with men? This is the man who harvests the fruit of stillness!" (44:219).

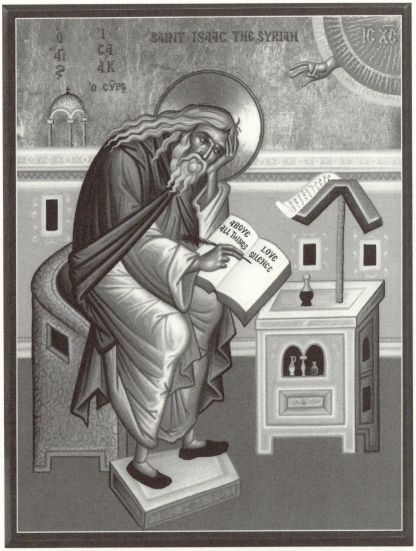

St. Isaac the Syrian. Holy Transfiguration Monastery, Brookline, MA.

But then St. Isaac tells us an even more riveting story, this time about a saint he does not name:

> We know of another saint whose brother after the flesh, a recluse
> in another cell, fell ill. During the whole period of his brother's
> sickness he restrained his compassion and did not go forth to visit

him. Now at the time of his departing from this life, his brother sent word to him, saying, "Though you have not yet come to me, come even now, though it be during the night, and I shall see you before my departure from the world and embrace you and I shall be at peace." But that blessed man was not persuaded, not even at that hour when nature is wont to be compassionate to other men and to overstep the limit set by the will. He said, "If I go out, my heart will not be pure before God, because I have neglected to visit my spiritual brothers, whereas I would have honored nature above Christ." And his brother died and did not see him. (44:220)

In the nearly four hundred pages of *The Ascetical Homilies*, no other single passage more sharply—even alarmingly—confronts certain of our basic assumptions about human relationships than does this one. In the account of the Archbishop's visit to St. Arsenios, we can catch the unmistakable odor of mimetic contagion in the bishop's "desire to see" Arsenios and "to enjoy that honor"—and that one whiff is enough to make plain to us that, if we catch and transmit mimetic desire through the networks of our associations, then we can begin to gain immunity to the contagion by stepping out of those networks. Like the Gospels, the *Homilies* are persuasively clear that the sins arising from our envy and driven by our hunger for safety, comfort, and prestige are sins that run wide and deep in us. All this, I think, is fairly plain sailing.

But in reading this account of the saint who refuses to see his dying brother, we raise a swarm of increasingly hostile questions. Why, in this instance, is reclusive stillness not just another form of the lie of autonomy—even a spiritually worse form? Is not exclusive stillness here a cover-story for an icily contemptuous pride? It may, admittedly, be a good thing for you to walk away from (say) bawdy songs in a crowded barroom, or even from a bishop hungering for the prestige of your company; but is it not an entirely different (and plainly bad) thing to refuse a dying brother's death-bed plea for your compassion? What does this awful hiding away really mean? Who does this Isaac think he is? God? (And please note: our questions become more like assertions as they grow more hostile.)

Let me begin with the final question—but let me first rephrase it. The real question this story raises is, I suggest, not simply about St. Isaac, nor about the unnamed saint, nor about you or me. The real question is about the nature of personhood, and it is simply: *What is a person?*

As the entire Orthodox patristic tradition everywhere assumes and often articulates, human personhood has two primary dimensions. First, the human person is foundationally *relational*. That is, because the person is formed in the image and likeness of God, and because God is trinitarian in His essence (i.e., He is Father, Son, and Holy Spirit), so, too, the human person as such is known only in his/her *relation* to other persons. Now, the relations within the Trinity are relations characterized by a love that is both wholly *self-emptying* (*kenotic* in Greek, from *kenosis*) and wholly reciprocal: each Person of the Trinity is ceaselessly giving Himself in love to the other two Persons. Let me dare to say this: each Person of the Trinity gives Himself as, simultaneously, *seed* that the Others may bear fruit and *ground* that the Others may take root and grow in Him. Just so, our human personhood exists—has "living-beingness" or (in Greek) *ontos*—wholly in this divinely grounded kenotic love for others; for as God is three Persons in one nature, so we, all humanity, are many persons in one nature, held in that same relation of seed to fruit, fruit to seed. For St. Isaac, this foundation of our personhood means that *who we are* is ontologically distinct—to the point of opposition—from the associational networks of mimetic desiring in precisely the same way that self-emptying love is ontologically distinct from, opposite to, violent envy. And, again for St. Isaac, so distinct are these two realms of being that we must *separate ourselves entirely* from the state of envious violence in order to enter the kingdom of self-emptying love, for no *détente* is spiritually possible. We must leave Egypt, cross over the sea, and enter into the desert. Only so, St. Isaac holds, will the lie of autonomy that drives all our violent envy finally fall away in the presence of the real relation to another: the relation of kenotic love. Imagine, then, this. At the very moment when we feel the pull into envying the good that has come to another, we instead offer ourselves as ground in which that person's goodness might grow into greater fruitfulness.[25] And imagine this, too. At the very moment when another unjustly offends us, we offer the offender not our advice or correction but our very *person* as seed to that other's ground—never knowing when, where, or even *if* such offering will ever bear fruit—and we do so without even the secret reward of self-congratulation. In such actions lies the way of kenotic love, wherein the whole of human nature is potentially cohered.

Thus, this first dimension of human personhood may be characterized as *horizontal*: it connects us to all other human persons on the plane of earthly life.

The second dimension of personhood is vertical and connects us to God, who is the seed and ground and fullness and substance of all our loving: the One, that is, with whom we are *in love*. The vertical dimension may be understood this way: because the human person is made in the image and likeness of God, the human person has a divine core. This divine core or (to use the Orthodox term) *heart* of the human person is most clearly revealed in what St. Isaac terms *theoria*. *Theoria* is perhaps the most difficult word in all of St. Isaac to understand because it presupposes a certain spiritual experience; indeed, the English translators call it the most puzzling of his terms "because," they say, "experience of this is the only unerring guide to understanding it" (cx). The simple explanation of *theoria* is "divine vision" or "the perception of divine mysteries." In Homily 37, St. Isaac describes the action of *theoria* as he defines what he calls "spiritual prayer," a form of prayer that, he says, "only one man in ten thousand is accounted worthy of":

> [S]piritual prayer . . . is the mystery of the future state and life, for herein a man is raised on high and his nature remains inoperative and unmoved by any motion or memory of things present. The soul does not pray a prayer, but in awareness she perceives the spiritual things of that other age which transcend human conception; and the understanding of these is by the power of the Holy Spirit . . . He brings them [i.e., those who have reached the perfection of purity] forth from prayer into *theoria*, which means "vision of the spirit." (182–83)

Now, this experience of *theoria* begins in the withdrawal from mimetic associations so as to achieve the silence of inward and outward stillness, and then it plunges the hesychast into what St. Isaac calls the "awestruck wonder at God" (43:214), an ecstatic state of deepest stillness in which the person comes to see—with immediate spiritual sight—first the divinely created state of earthly humanity *before the Fall* and then, in a final movement of sight, when "the veil of the passions is lifted from the eyes of his mind" (ibid.), he directly beholds the supreme glory of God—and falls passionately in love. This entire spiritual sequence—from withdrawal to stillness to wonder to the direct vision of the created earth and the heavenly Creator—is, for St. Isaac, both the revelation and the fulfillment of the heart of our personhood, a heart that wholly belongs not to us (for we would not then be in love) but to God. A beautiful line in LXX Psalm 21 catches St. Isaac's meaning: "those who seek Him will praise the Lord, their hearts will live forever" (l. 26).

Thus, this vertical dimension of our personhood crosses the horizontal dimension at the point of the human heart, where our love of God becomes one with love of our neighbor.

And it is to this juncture that St. Isaac takes us in Homily 44; for there, some two sentences after he concludes his account of the saint who refused to see his dying brother, St. Isaac writes this:

> The commandment that says, "Thou shalt love the Lord thy God with all thy heart, and with all thy soul, and with all thy mind," more than the world, nature, and all that pertains thereto, is fulfilled when you patiently endure in your stillness. And the commandment that speaks of the love of neighbor is included within the former. Do you wish to acquire in your soul the love of your neighbor according to the commandment of the Gospel? *Separate yourself from him,* and then the heat and flame of the love of him will burn in you and you will rejoice over the sight of his countenance as though you beheld an angel of light. (220; my emphasis)

"Separate yourself from him," says St. Isaac, and "patiently endure in your stillness" until you behold your neighbor's face as "an angel of light": this movement constitutes the whole of our personhood. *Who we are* dwells in this spiritual sequence. And the end or fulfillment of it therefore vividly resembles that moment in Genesis when Jacob approaches his brother Esau after the long separation that had arisen from Jacob's having violently deceived Esau. Jacob thus anticipates retaliatory violence from his brother; but Esau, instead, embraces and kisses and weeps for his brother; and Jacob says, "I have seen thy face, as though I had seen the face of God" (Gen 33:10). Jacob's beholding of his brother's face perfectly expresses St. Isaac's *theoria*, a beholding that comes only after long separation, as if only so can Jacob see his brother apart from those old associational networks of mimetic envy and reciprocal violence. And in this encounter, each brother becomes both seed and ground to the other's fruitfulness. The vertical and horizontal dimensions of personhood thus meet in this moment of self-emptying love: and there personhood emerges.

IV

In this way, then, *The Ascetical Homilies* of St. Isaac worsen the human predicament as described in the Girardian discourse. For St. Isaac, the associational disaster extends to *every human contact*, even to those that seem not simply harmless but even actively good. For St. Isaac, the mimetic catastrophe is thus wider and deeper and more total than it seems for Girard. Yet on every page of *The Ascetical Homilies*, St. Isaac points to the one and only way out: the way of the Cross. In the final sentence of his 1996 interview, René Girard says this of his own work: "Mine is a search for the anthropology of the Cross, which turns out to rehabilitate orthodox theology" (*Reader*, 288). We have merely to capitalize Girard's "orthodox" in order to gain a superb insight into St. Isaac's solution to the disaster of envy: the anthropology of the Cross. If Girard's description of the disaster has not yet caught up to St. Isaac's, his instinct for the true resolution is unerringly right—with this one corrective: it is not that we must "rehabilitate" a ruined house; it is, rather, that we must in some way come to reinhabit the fully intact Orthodox theological home that Western culture abandoned—to its great grief—more than a thousand years ago.

Toward the end of Homily 74, St. Isaac writes this about the Cross:

> The cross is the door to mysteries. Through this door the intellect makes entrance into the knowledge of heavenly mysteries. The knowledge of the cross is concealed in the sufferings of the cross. And the more our participation in its sufferings, the greater the perception we gain through the cross. (364)

By *intellect*, St. Isaac means *nous*, the highest human faculty, whereby the person experiences *theoria*: which, again, is the direct spiritual apprehension of God or His creations. When we approach the Cross as "the door to mysteries," we can then enter into the *theoria* that is "the knowledge of the heavenly mysteries." In describing the Cross in this way, St. Isaac directly links the concept of personhood to Christ's experience of death and resurrection. We may express the link in this fashion: as we obey the injunction to flee all mimetic associations, we join Christ in His death to this world; as we arrive through *theoria* into that right relation to our neighbor wherein we behold his face as "an angel of light," we are joined to Christ's resurrection. The way of our personhood is therefore the way of the Cross—the Cross *enables* our personhood: such is St. Isaac's entire ascetical teaching in the *Homilies*. Along this way, St. Isaac says, "the man who lives in love reaps the fruit of life from God, and while yet in this world, he even now breathes the air of the resurrection" (46:224). The resurrection is an experience *in this world*: that is, the risen Christ walks and talks and eats food and both touches and is touched by others. Just so, the resurrectional life of relational love is an experience *in this world*: we begin to love others more fully precisely after the associational spins of envy begin to die in us. The air of the resurrection is already in our nose and mouth and lungs and heart. The way of personhood that is the way of the Cross is therefore—to use a key Orthodox word—a *substantial* way.

To best understand the *substantiality* of personhood in the Cross, we may turn (fittingly enough for monastic teachings) to the Psalter. In Psalm 88 (Septuagint numbering), the psalmist cries out to God: "Remember what my *substance* is" (l. 47; italics mine),[26] while in Psalm 138:15–16 we find this speech to God:

> My frame thou didst invisibly fashion was never hidden from thee, nor was my *substance* ever hidden in the earth's lowest depths. Thine eyes beheld me yet unformed; all men shall be written in thy book, they shall be fashioned continually when there are yet none of them. (My emphasis)

Now, the word for *substance* in the Septuagint Greek of the Psalms is *hypostasis*. In St. Isaac's lifetime in seventh-century Persia (roughly, modern Iran), there swirled an immense controversy about this word *hypostasis*. This controversy had its beginnings in the first Christian centuries when the early

Ecumenical Councils attempted to clarify certain matters about Jesus Christ, matters that had been raised in the sharp and dangerous form of heresy. In 451 AD the Council of Chalcedon fashioned the theology concerning the *two natures of Christ*, divine and human. The Chalcedonian theology aimed at resolving this fundamental question: how can we affirm as being a single Person *both* the eternal God who makes all things *and* the human being who lived and died in a specific time and place? How can Jesus possess *both* natures? To answer this essential question, Chalcedon borrowed a word from the ancient Greek philosophic tradition—*hypostasis*—to say this: the two natures together constitute His one Personhood (*hypostasis*), and this one Personhood is *substantial* (i.e., *enhypostatic*).

St. Isaac then beautifully articulates Chalcedon by saying that the way wherein the two natures are enhypostatically (substantially) one Personhood is, in spiritual fact, the way of the Cross. That is, each nature dies in love for the other; and this death and resurrection constitute the Personhood of Christ, His permanent *substantial* Personhood.

Yet, for St. Isaac, the crucial point is that the full knowledge of His Personhood is *concealed from us* in His sufferings on the Cross. The only way we may unveil this hidden knowledge, says St. Isaac, is by our participation in His sufferings, "and," he continues, "the more our participation . . . the greater the perception we gain" (*Homilies*, 74:364). And since the Cross is our personhood, we increase our participation in it precisely by becoming persons: that is, by dying to all our envious violence against others in order to be resurrected into that love wherein we willingly lay down our life for even the most violent of them. The door into this love stands open on every page of St. Isaac's great book.

V

Two questions may be put at this point. First, how can St. Isaac's injunction to flee all associations *make any sense at all* in terms of the actual lives we lead? Second, if all desire is mimetic, is all desire therefore *bad*? Let's take the second one first. If we engage another person in a relation wherein we extinguish every single one of our own envious impulses, then we shall be plunged into that ocean of desire the Gospels call love, an ocean whose every slightest current and tiniest motion *directly imitate Christ's love for all of us.* Mimetic desire is therefore good when we love other persons in the way they are loved by Christ—that is, when we imitate Christ. As Girard says, "A good model will make our mimesis good (Christ); a bad model will make our mimesis rivalrous" (*Reader*, 269). St. Isaac's injunction can thus be understood as the mimetic fulfillment of Christ's great commandment: "This is my commandment, that you love one another as I have loved you" (John 15:12).

But in saying this, am I allegorizing St. Isaac's texts, making them bear any interpretation I happen to devise? St. Isaac is not being merely figurative about the desert life; he really means it. Nor is he, on the other hand, being merely historical, that is, describing a set of ecclesiastical circumstances unique to seventh-century Persia. In fact, such "historicizing" stands condemned in the Gospels in that moment when the bystanders in the Nazareth temple, after hearing Jesus proclaim the start of His ministry, contemptuously dismiss Him by saying, "Is not this Joseph's son?" (Luke 4:22). And right on the heels of this contempt there occurs the first act of sacrificial collective violence recorded in Luke: "And all they in the synagogue . . . were filled with wrath, and rose up, and thrust him out of the city, and led him to the brow of the hill whereon their city was built, that they might cast him down headlong" (Luke 4:28–29). The point could not be clearer. The contempt contained within historical dismissals directly fuels collective violence against the reality of personhood.

If we set aside, then, both self-absorbed allegorizing and contemptuous historicizing, how can we possibly respond to both "Flee all associations" and "Love your neighbor"?

I have two related approaches to offer to this question, one ecclesiastical and the other literary. First, the Orthodox Church has always affirmed both of the two fundamental worlds of Christendom, the monastic and the parish. This affirmation is so central to the Orthodox heart that the relation between monastery and cathedral is as easily sustained as the relation between breathing in and breathing out. (But note well: this easily sustained relation does not mean that the relation is easy; often enough throughout Orthodox Church history, it has been wracked with tensions; but the relation has endured and, perhaps always, has borne fruit.) But—and this is the important point—it is not a relation that *logically* works; it is not a relation that can be reduced to fit the logic of an isolated, single set of propositions. Rather, this relation can only be *lived* within that community of relations that is the whole Church. And in this community, all the saints of all the ages *are experienced as living persons*. Such experience is not an idle allegory but an ongoing actuality. As a result, the relations between an Orthodox monastery and an Orthodox home can be—and often are—rich with a deep and reciprocal love.

And it is this rich reality that underlies much of the action in Dostoevsky's great novel *The Brothers Karamazov*. For in this novel, Alyosha Karamazov passes in and out of the monastery, all the while borne on currents as decisively life-sustaining as the act of breathing. At one moment, we see Alyosha with his fully illumined spiritual father, the Elder Zosima; at the next moment, we see him with his half-crazed biological father, Fyodor. These two worlds are for Alyosha vividly distinct; hence, they are not reducible to any single *logic*. Instead, the *relation* between Alyosha's monastic and biological homes is, in the textures, scenes, and speeches of the novel, a relation at once profound, substantial, inexhaustible, irreducible, and real. But the relation is almost never logically consistent.

Thus, we see Alyosha stand before his alcoholic father, Fyodor, and be mocked and jeered at and insulted by him. Yet because Alyosha never breaks relation with his spiritual father, he can stand before his abusive father and see him—indeed, *behold* him—as if this very mockery were a moment of *theoria* for them both. And then the miracle happens. For an instant, Fyodor himself is swept by a redemptive love for this incomprehensibly good son of his. Dostoevsky's great point is this: *Because* Alyosha sustains genuine relation to Fr. Zosima, he can therefore be a true son to Fyodor. The lived relation—not the logic—holds the transfigurative meaning.

Furthermore, in this transfigurative relation, Dostoevsky joins St. Isaac in absolutely rejecting the Messalian heresy. Now, this fifth-century heresy held that certain very special holy people could, *solely by the action of their own prayer*, reach (as the editor of the *Homilies* explains) "such a state of perfection and dispassion that they could walk about in cities and converse with all men without suffering spiritual harm or even distraction from prayer and peace of mind" (5). Such a teaching is heretical because it destroys the very matrix of personhood by replacing spiritually purposive relations with merely random occurrences. In this heresy, relation therefore vanishes, and the isolated self becomes the object of its own idolatry and the sole possessor of its own sanctity, a sanctity that is an imitative façade rather than a genuine participation in the divine energies.

In the character of Fr. Ferapont, Dostoevsky gives us the full picture of the spiritual disaster of such self-idolatry. Fr. Ferapont is so maddened by his violent envy of Fr. Zosima that, at the funeral service for Fr. Zosima, he attempts the supreme mimetic insanity: he tries to make everyone believe that Fr. Zosima had all along been possessed not by the Holy Spirit but by a demon. It is an extraordinary scene, and it raises the central question: Is it possible that Satan can cast out Satan? Dostoevsky's response in this scene is the same as Christ's in the Gospels: "He that shall blaspheme against the Holy Spirit—by saying that I have an unclean spirit—never has forgiveness but is in danger of eternal damnation" (Mark 3:29–30; my slight rearrangement). Fr. Ferapont's envy-driven violence is decisively defeated in this crucial scene. And in this defeat, Dostoevsky affirms the central meaning of St. Isaac's *Homilies*: only self-emptying love can still the violent madness of envy.

Reading St. Isaac in Dostoevsky's fine light, then, leads us to see that the sharp, binary opposition of our original question—reclusive stillness vs. relational purposiveness—is, in the end, a false opposition. For the opposition fades in the reality of personhood, fades in the way that the flame of a single candle fades in the full sunlight of a midsummer noon. For in the relational reality of a lived personhood, all oppositions become the occasion for a more substantial dimensionality. As a result, Alyosha Karamazov exceeds every logic: he is obedient novice, and ineffective helper, and prospective bridegroom, and anxious brother, and wonderful listener, and (momentarily) cynical sinner, and (by the end) spiritual teacher. And it is precisely into the reality of personhood that all of us are, at every moment of our lives, being called: into that profound, substantial, inexhaustible, and irreducible reality of personhood.

The question, then, is not how St. Isaac's *Ascetical Homilies* can make sense in our lives. The real question, perhaps, is how our personhood can become more fully present to St. Isaac.

VI

I began this essay on an autobiographical note; permit me to conclude the same way. But, first, some background. About a year ago, in October of 1996, several parishioners, a few friends, my wife, our then sixteen-year-old younger son, and I formed a study group to read Dostoevsky's final two novels, *Demons*[27] and *The Brothers Karamazov*. Every Monday evening that we could manage we have met, as few as four of us and as many as fifteen, for some three hours to discuss these astonishing works. I have worked as a university teacher since 1967, and I have been amazingly fortunate in having had so many gifted students. But I have never, in over thirty years, experienced as steadily *profound* a level of insight as in this study group. I use *profound* in the specific sense of a willingness, even eagerness, to follow Dostoevsky into any depth he wishes to go. Such willingness is, in my experience, very rare. For our usual habits as readers (including my own) are, in fact, envious habits. That is, we passionately assert our own comprehension as being in some way at least equal to and (usually) better than the author's comprehension. One usually says something that begins, "What [the author] *really* means here is . . ."—and the envious game is up and running.

But our study group—willy, nilly, without ever having become conscious of it—has somehow set aside a good deal of our habitual envy. And the result is, for me, unprecedented. We are rarely "brilliant" in the usual bad way of classroom brilliance; we have, in fact, become fairly good at bearing with—and forgiving—each other's attempts at such brilliance. What has happened, I think, is *relational* in nature. That is, we have deepened in our relation to each other *through* our shared listening to Dostoevsky's great texts. The demons of envy still swirl through our conversations—but often enough, other and better spirits also take hold and guide us, if only for a few seconds or brief minutes. These seconds and minutes are priceless. And we are just Orthodox enough to know from whose hands they flow—certainly not our own.

It was in such a moment, some months ago, while reading through Fr. Zosima's movingly beautiful discourse on the fires of hell that we suddenly heard another person's voice. Here is the opening passage we were reading that Monday; immediately after it is the penultimate paragraph of St. Isaac's Homily 28.

Fr. Zosima:

Fathers and teachers, I ask myself: "What is hell?" And I answer thus: "The suffering of being no longer able to love." Once in infinite existence a certain spiritual being, through his appearance on earth, was granted the ability to say to himself: "I am and I love." Once, once only, he was given a moment of active, *living* love, and for that he was given earthly life with its times and seasons. And what then? This fortunate being rejected the invaluable gift, did not value it, did not love it, looked upon it with scorn, and was left unmoved by it. This being, having departed the earth, sees Abraham's bosom, and talks with Abraham . . . and he beholds paradise, and could rise up to the Lord, but his torment is precisely to rise up to the Lord without having loved, to touch those who loved him—him who disdained their love. For he sees clearly and says to himself: "Now I have knowledge, and though I thirst to love, there will be no great deed in my love, no sacrifice, for my earthly life is over, and Abraham will not come with a drop of living water . . . to cool the flame of the thirst for spiritual love that is burning in me now, since I scorned it on earth; life is over, and time will be no more! Though I would gladly give my life for others, it is not possible now, for the life I could have sacrificed for love is gone, and there is now an abyss between that life and this existence." People speak of the material flames of hell. I do not explore this mystery, and I fear it, but I think that if there were material flames, truly people would be glad to have them, for, as I fancy, in material torment they might forget, at least for a moment, their far more terrible spiritual torment.

St. Isaac:

I also maintain that those who are punished in Gehenna are scourged by the scourge of love. Nay, what is so bitter and vehement as the torment of love? I mean that those who have become conscious that they have sinned against love suffer greater torment from this than from any fear of punishment. For the sorrow caused in the heart by sin against love is more poignant than any torment. It would be improper for a man to think that sinners in Gehenna are deprived of the love of God. Love is the offspring of knowledge of the truth which, as is commonly confessed, is given to all. The power of love works in two ways: it torments sinners, even as happens here when a friend suffers from a friend; but it becomes a source of joy for those who have observed its duties. Thus I say that this is the torment of Gehenna: bitter regret. But love inebriates the souls of the sons of Heaven by its delectability. (*Homilies*, 28, p. 141)

Between these two passages exists one of the most significant of all spiritual relationships: the relation of seed to fruit. So central is this relation to *The Brothers Karamazov* that Dostoevsky uses as an epigraph for the entire novel this great saying of Christ's: "Verily, verily, I say unto you, Except a corn of wheat fall unto the ground and die, it abideth alone: but if it die, it bringeth forth much fruit" (John 12:24). The full meaning of the Cross as the way of personhood is here revealed. Only as the seed willingly dies for the fruit—and that fruit, in turn, dies as seed for the next: only so does the torment of isolation, of "abiding alone," become transfigured into the joy of sustained relation. These two passages, taken together, exhibit precisely that joy, for St. Isaac's *Ascetical Homilies* are indeed the seed for Dostoevsky's "Talks and Homilies of the Elder Zosima."

As we glimpsed something of this transfigurative joy, we could hear the voice of St. Isaac within Fr. Zosima's lovely, pure voice: and both voices grew at once more fully distinct as they became more deeply related. In his letters, Dostoevsky speaks with something like awe when he tells of how his years of attempting—but failing—to articulate his comprehension of Orthodox spiritual truth became, all at once, fulfilled when he *incarnated his comprehension in the person of Fr. Zosima.* Such a flowering could only have occurred through another's voluntary dying for such a flowering. In other words, for a character in a novel to come to exhibit something like genuine personhood, another person in the actual world had to willingly give his own personhood as seed. Where, we wondered that Monday evening in March, does St. Isaac do this? It is spiritually one thing for an author to *appropriate* human personhood for his art; it is quite another thing—and something rarer and more beautiful—for someone to give himself for another's art.

Then a few weeks later, we came across this extraordinary passage from St. Isaac's Homily 23:

> For my own struggles I have not been vouchsafed to experience even one thousandth part of what I have written with my own hands, and especially in this homily which I now compose for the kindling and enlightenment of our souls, and of those who come across it, with the hope that, perchance, some might rouse themselves by reason of their desire for what I speak of, and endeavour to practise it. (115)

We knew at once that we were seeing revealed here the very heart of St. Isaac's reason for writing these *Homilies* some thirteen centuries ago. He intended that they become for us what they had become for Dostoevsky a century ago: the seed of our fruitfulness in Christ. Thus is the relational ground of the reality of personhood sustained in fruitfulness. We in our tiny study group here continue to be moved by the meaning of this relation.

Now, in his own life, Dostoevsky did not abandon the relational realities of his family, his art, or his nation when he encountered the person of St. Isaac. Instead, there began for him that profound Orthodox movement into and out of the monastic world. At nearly every significant event in the last decade of his life, Dostoevsky would visit the Optina monastery, there meeting the monastics who would also become—with St. Isaac—seeds for Fr. Zosima. Thus did he live *relationally* the essential and sustaining movement he would so beautifully bestow on Alyosha. And in all of his rich contacts with the monastery, Dostoevsky seemed to find and sustain that supreme grace of genuine relation: non-envious and self-emptying love.

Here, then, is perhaps the most significant guideline we have found in how to read St. Isaac's great work aright. Rather than entering into the rivalrous spirit of mimicking (i.e., outdoing) St. Isaac's reclusive life, we must in love let *The Ascetical Homilies* become seed in us. We must never make St. Isaac into a rival whom we are trying (God forbid!) to beat at his own game. We must instead humbly and actively love this great saint with the love with which the infinitely greater Christ is loving him and all of us: *in and as person.*

It is in the light of these discoveries this past summer that our study group has tried to read St. Isaac. It is therefore in this light that I say that our intellectual work has been not conceptual but *relational* in nature.

5

"The Spirit of God Moved Upon the Face of the Waters"
Orthodox Holiness and the Natural World[28]

I

n the Prima Vita of the nineteenth-century Russian saint known as Herman of Alaska, this passage occurs:

> In the middle of Spruce Island [a tiny island a few miles out to sea from Kodiak, Alaska] a little river runs from the mountain into the sea. There were always large logs of driftwood at the mouth of this river, continuously brought there by storms. In the springtime when the river fish would appear, the Elder would dig in the sand so that the river could pass by and the fish in the sea would hasten up the river. "It would happen that Apa would say: 'Go and get a fish from the river,'" said Aliaga. Father Herman used to feed birds with dried fish and they in great number would nest near his cell. Under his cell there lived ermines. This little animal, after giving birth to its litter, is unapproachable, yet the Elder would feed them with his own hands. "Wasn't that really a miracle we have seen!" said his disciple Ignatius. Father Herman was also seen feeding the bears. "With the death of the Elder both the birds and the beasts disappeared; even the garden would not give forth crop if someone were to care for it willingly," asserted Ignatius.[29]

Ignatius Aliaga's final assertion offers us our starting point. When St. Herman died, the birds and beasts suddenly vanished, and the garden became all at once and completely fruitless. What are we to make of this?

St. Herman Feeding the Ermine. Icon by Lasha Kintsurashvili of Georgia.

Panayiotis Nellas, in his magnificent book *Deification in Christ*, describes as our paradisical beginning: the bringing together of all things into the hands of man in order that man may then give all things back to God. "This," says Nellas, "is man's natural state in the image of God; this is his natural function, his natural work and goal."[30] From this perspective, we can say that, when the Elder feeds the otherwise unapproachable ermine and her newborns, or when he lifts up his hands with bits of dried fish in them and all the birds come, or when his fingers gently touch the bear's mouth, he is restoring to ermine and bear something like a paradisical glory: and in this moment the world of nature, simultaneously distinct and inseparable from that of man, becomes *icon* through the light of St. Herman's face.

The question, then, is *how*: How is the natural world made iconic? And how does the iconic face illumine the natural world?

Central to Orthodox asceticism is the work of opening space in ourselves between our desires and our actions. If every desire we have triggers an action we take—if, for example, every time I feel a touch of hunger I put something in my mouth—then two disastrous effects follow. First, our desires soon come to steer all our relations with the natural world in that the world becomes the materialization of all our desires and all our hungers—and, in that sense, the world is *dematerialized* into these desires and hungers. The second effect that follows when we fail to open space between our desires and our actions is that our selfhood becomes, in time, something like an entirely closed system of autonomous desire and autonomous satisfaction, a system wherein (once again) the natural world is dematerialized and unmade. The results of both effects are fear and depression: the fear born of the fact that our autonomous powers are indeed frail and crumbling; the depression born of the fact that we have willed our own desolation. Dostoevsky's portraits of such fear and depression in his novel *Demons* starkly depict the final goal of such states: suicide.

In the second century BC, the Septuagint translators came to the second verse of Genesis: "The spirit of God moved upon the face of the waters." The word they chose for the Hebrew *panēh* (face) was the Greek *prosopon*. This is the same word they used for the divine *countenance* of God. And a half-millennium later, this is also the word first used to mean the very *Person* of God: so essential is countenance to personhood.[31] In His movement of creatively self-emptying love, the Holy Spirit of God bestows countenance upon the waters. And when we enter into that conscious relation to the created world known as Orthodox ascetic practice, we also, "with open face, beholding as in a glass the glory of the Lord, are changed into the same image, from glory to glory, even as by the Spirit of the Lord" (2 Cor 3:17). And, entering ourselves into the likeness of God, we become able to bestow His countenance upon the created world in our creative relation to it. Thus we come to experience directly the way wherein the created world is an icon of God.

Quickened into being by the Holy Spirit of God, the true countenance of the natural world is thus *accomplished* and fulfilled by our exercise of our divinely given sovereignty over it. And our sovereignty over the natural world has, we may say, only one true expression: the action of self-giving love born of holy ascesis, an action by which each of us receives the likeness of God granted by the Holy Spirit. As Vladimir Lossky so beautifully tells us in his *Mystical Theology of the Eastern Church:*

> [T]he Holy Spirit effaces Himself, as Person, before the created persons to whom He will appropriate grace. In Him the will of God is no longer external to ourselves: it confers grace inwardly, manifesting itself within our very person in so far as our human will remains in accord with the divine will and co-operates with it in acquiring grace, in making it ours . . . [T]his divine Person, now unknown, not having His image in another Hypostasis, will manifest Himself in deified persons: for the multitude of the saints will be His image.[32]

In this Likeness, then, the sanctified human person confers something of grace on the natural world in his or her actions of sovereign ascetic love, thereby fulfilling the Divine Image in the natural world and restoring the creation to the Creator. For Lossky further tells us:

> [The] divine Persons do not themselves assert themselves, but one bears witness to another. It is for this reason that St. John Damascene said that "the Son is the image of the Father, and the Spirit the image of the Son." It follows that the third Hypostasis of the Trinity is the only one not having His image in another Person. The Holy Spirit, as person, remains unmanifested, hidden, concealing Himself in His very appearing." (*Mystical Theology*, 159–60)

That is, until the saints bear witness to Him.

St. Herman of Alaska. Icon by Father Luke Dingman.

What I am suggesting, then, is that, in the same way, we as persons must somehow, through our ascesis, conceal ourselves, remain hidden, so that the world we have been given to rule may bear witness to the Likeness in us, who are witnessing to the Holy Spirit. The natural world *will* bear witness to us whether we are trying to be holy or not; far better that we should try to be holy.

Now we may return to the final sentence in the passage from St. Herman's Prima Vita. When the birds and beasts vanish and the garden becomes fruitless, then we may say that, with the disappearance of St. Herman's deified and deifying countenance, the reality of Orthodox asceticism has— in this place, for this moment—been withdrawn. And the effect of such a withdrawal is to cease what Nellas calls the bringing together of all things in man so as to return all things to God. For only the human person possesses this capacity to restore the natural world to God.

Dostoevsky's *The Brothers Karamazov* beautifully explores this issue in the death of Fr. Zosima. But Dostoevsky is, in turn, drawing from an experience central to all Russian religious history: the death of St. Sergius of Radonezh.

▪   ▪   ▪

On the morning of September 25, 1392, at the age of 78, a very frail Fr. Sergius attended the Liturgy in the Monastery of the Holy Trinity that he had founded some twenty years earlier. After the Liturgy, he spoke a brief farewell in his cell to his fellow monks. And then he very peacefully died. The fourteenth-century account says that, at the moment of his death, his body gave off an intensely sweet fragrance that filled the cell and the whole hallway beyond. All hearts lifted, the account says, at the sweet intensity of this heavenly odor. Fr. Sergius was buried next to the church he had built, some of it with his own hands.

Then the miracles began. Many visiting his grave were healed of all kinds of afflictions and illnesses: the blind could see, the lame walked and danced. Some thirty years passed, and his body was exhumed by the Church in order that his bones might become relics. Then the great miracle was revealed. His body was perfectly preserved, dressed in the clothes he had been buried in, still fresh and intact. His body was then placed in the monastery church, where it remains to this day, still incorrupt. Here is the heart of Orthodox Russia.

What, then, are we to make of the incorrupt body of St. Sergius?

By way of approaching a response, I want to tell you of my visit, in August of 1988, to this place. I traveled to Russia as part of a small Orthodox group on pilgrimage to honor the first thousand years of Orthodoxy in Russia. The

Soviet regime would not fall until August 1991. Hence, in the summer of 1988, we were very much in the hands of the Soviet In-tourist Bureau, that branch of the Communist state which firmly controlled the activities of all tourists, especially U.S. citizens—and particularly U.S. citizens identified as Eastern Orthodox Christians. Our In-tourist guides thus assumed at every opportunity the right to speak to us about the sunny truths of atheism and the dark lies of religion. Even the tour-bus drivers never missed a moment of opportunity, raising their voices to carry to the back of the bus where I and my tour friend Elizabeth (whose Russian was better than mine) always sat, she quietly translating for me.

So it was that on August 23, 1988, we came by bus to what was then called Zagorsk. For the hour's drive from Moscow, the day's driver had been especially loud in his harsh laughter about the saint "who couldn't even rot right," that's how contemptible St. Sergius was. Our American guide and organizer, Masha Tkachuk, was a priest's wife and the daughter of one of the finest two or three Orthodox theologians in the twentieth century, Fr. Alexander Schmemann. Masha stopped our driver's stream of abuse with a single question: "Have you ever seen the inside of the church where St. Sergius' body lies?" "Well, no, of course not," he spluttered, brought up short. "Come in with us," Masha said quietly. For the final ten miles, he was silent, and as we all got off the bus, he would not look at any of us. Masha spoke to him once more: "Come," she said. He shook his head, a decided "No."

On that hot summer afternoon our little group joined the hundreds of pilgrims crowded in the church. It took me a minute to realize that everyone was silent, and in another minute I identified the faint sound of voices from the front of the church as the voices of Orthodox monks softly chanting words I was still too far away to catch, though I could now see them. People in twos and threes were exiting along the walls, and so we began to inch slowly forward, toward the point where the monks—two of them I now could see—were chanting in turns as they faced one another over the ends of a low table. In another few minutes, I would begin to catch the Slavonic forms of biblical names I knew from the Psalms.

Then it became clear. The monks were standing not at a low table but at the head and foot of a coffin, and over the entire coffin was placed a glass dome maybe ten inches high. Here was the body of St. Sergius of Radonezh. All the pilgrims were, one by one, going up three steps to the area where St. Sergius lay, kissing the dome above the saint, and then saying a brief prayer or petition. After a minute or so, another monk— not one of the chanters—would lightly touch the pilgrim's shoulder or arm, then help him or her to another set of three steps leading back down to the church floor. Already another pilgrim would be at the saint's tomb.

I wrote in my journal that night: "I will remember all my life the depth of the *presence* of St. Sergius; some dozen yards all around the casket there was a field of humming energy that was almost perceptible light." Today, nearly fourteen years later, I can still call to mind and heart the experience of "almost perceptible light" and almost audible sound.

When I came down the three exit steps, I was startled to see our tour-bus driver standing against the wall and watching. Then I came close to him, and I could see tears streaming down his face. He was softly shaking his head and saying something. I just caught his words: "I didn't understand, I didn't understand." His eyes were filled with the unshakable joy of beauty. That evening, in our Moscow hotel, he asked the priest in our group if he would baptize him, and our priest assented. He took the name Sergius as his Orthodox name.

I offer this experience as a tiny narrative icon of incorruptibility. Our driver had experienced in the monastery church that day the depth of the presence of St. Sergius. And this presence does not corrupt. For St. Sergius had, through long ascetic practice of fasting and prayer, so transfigured his body that he had restored the accord between man and nature that makes concrete the original relationship lost in Eden and restored only in ascetic practice: the harmony wherein the human presence ennobles everything and everyone in creation through the action of self-giving love. This is the strength that our tour-bus driver beautifully encountered that day in August 1988.[33]

II

In 1992, the American poet Nicholas Samaras published his award-winning first book of poems in the Yale Younger Poets Series, a book entitled *Hands of the Saddlemaker*. Early in the book there appears a remarkable poem called "Easter in the Cancer Ward." Here is the poem in its entirety:

> Because it has been years since my hands
> have dyed an egg or I've remembered
> my father with color in his beard,
> because my fingers have forgotten
> the feel of wax melting on my skin,
> the heat of paraffin warping air,
> because I prefer to view death politely from afar,
> I agree to visit the children's cancer ward.
>
> In her ballet-like butterfly slippers, Elaine pad-pads
> down the carpeted hall. I bring the bright bags,
> press down packets of powdered dye, repress my slight unease.
> She sweeps her hair from her volunteer's badge, leaves
> behind her own residents' ward for a few hours' release.
> The new wing's doors glide open onto great light. Everything is
> vibrant and clattered with color. Racing
> up, children converge, their green voices rising.
>
> What does one do with the embarrassment of staring
> at sickness? Suddenly, I don't know where to place
> my hands. Children with radiant faces
> reach out thinly, clamor for the expected bags, lead
> us to the Nurses' kitchen. Elaine introduces me and reads
> out a litany of names. Some of the youngest wear
> old expressions. The bald little boy loves Elaine's long mane of hair
> and holds the healthy thickness to his face, hearing
>
> her laugh as she pulls him close. "I'm dying,"
> he says, and Elaine tells him she is, too: too
> much iron silting her veins. I can never accept that truth

yet, in five months, she'll slip away in a September
night—leaving her parents and me to bow our heads, bury her
in a white wedding gown, our people's custom.
But right now, I don't know this. Right now, we're young,
still immortal, and the kids fidget, crying

out for their eggs. Elaine divides them into teams;
I lay out the tools for the operation.
I tell them all how painting Easter eggs used to be done
in the Old Country. Before easy dyes were common,
villagers boiled onion peels, ladled eggs
into pots so the shells wouldn't break.
They'd scoop them out, flushed a brownish-
red, and the elders would polish and polish

them with olive oil, singing hymns for the Holy Thursday hours.
The children laugh and boo when I try to sing. The boys swirl
speckles of color into hot water, while the girls
time the eggs. When a white-faced boy asks from nowhere
if I believe in Christ and living forever,
I stop stirring the mix, answer, "Yes, I do." I answer slowly
and when I speak, my own voice deafens me.
The simple truth blooms like these painted flowers

riding up the bright kitchen walls. I come
to belief. I know that much. Still, what a man may
do with belief demands more than what he says.
Now, the hot waters are stained a rich red. The eggs have
boiled and cooled. To each set of hands, Elaine gives
one towel, three eggs. I pass the pot of melted paraffin,
show these children how to take the eggs and dip them in
and out. While the wax hardens to an opaque film, we hum

Christos Anesti and the room bustles, ajabber
with speech. Holding pins firmly, we scratch out mad
designs where the color will fill. Small, flurried hands
etch and scrim the shells. Everyone's fingers whorl

and scratch in names, delicate and final.
Edging the hall's threshold, an April's allow-
ance of sun filters through tinted windows. Faces furrow
in solemn concentration. Looking to Elaine, my thoughts clamor

for what is redemptive in illness, for having
a Credo to hold these people to me. Etchings
done, everyone immerses the waxy eggs in the pooled
dye. We ooh together when transfigured eggs are spooned
out, wiped, and dried on the counters. Soft wax
is peeled gingerly, flecked away; more oohs for the tracks
of limned lines, testimonial names.
We burnish the shells with olive oil for a fine sheen.

For a moment, the cultivated, finished eggs hush
the room. Then, every child goes wild in a rush
to compare, to show the nurses, each
other. The bald boy taps my waist. Lined up and speechless, they present me with a bright autographed
egg, communally done. Elaine makes me close my eyes and laughs
when small limbs push at my back to follow
her. They shove my hands in the cool, wet, red dye. The hollow-

eyed girl squeals till tears streak from her laughing.
Another child cries, "You'll never get it off!"
And today, I don't want to. Today,
we've painted eggs a lively color, not caring
about the body's cells and the cells' incarceration.
I lift my arms to embrace Elaine, dab her nose and chin.
And my hands are vivid red. My hands
are bloody with resurrection

and we are laughing.34

Central to this beautiful poem is its *ascetic* drama. That is, the speaker is
in the cancer ward not because he wants to be; in fact, he much prefers "to
view death politely from afar." He is embarrassed, ill-at-ease, not knowing

"where to place" his hands. There is, if you will, an entire *inward clamor* of feeling of simply but powerfully not wanting to be there. Here is where all ascetic practice really begins: What do you *do* with this inward clamor of intense feeling?

The first stanza contains the Orthodox response: *Because* I don't want to go, *therefore* I agree to go. That is, precisely *because* the inward clamor is all shouting for one thing to happen, the speaker cuts to the root of that clamor by acting exactly in the opposite way. The first stanza constructs this ascetic cutting to the root as an action of *remembering* treasured things lost in the past: his hands with egg dye, his father's beard, the feel of wax. The point is beautifully made. Ascetic practice restores lost harmonies with the creation.

In stanzas 2 and 3, the first effects of this restored harmony emerge, effects primarily of intensified sensory reality: "Everything is / vibrant and clattered with color," he says in the second stanza. Even the thin, bald, and dying children have "radiant faces," "their green voices rising." As the speaker uproots his own inward clamor, the children's "clamor for the expected bags" rushes beautifully in. Despite the implacable context of cancer-ward death, the poem already expresses—just hints at—the undying incorruptibility of the Easter in its title.

But stanza 4 directly confronts the inevitable fact of Elaine's death "in five months," giving us moving details of Orthodox funeral customs. Samaras' point in doing so is at once plain and powerful: the resurrection into incorruptibility can occur solely because the crucifixion is actually real. "I'm dying," the boy says to Elaine, and she "tells him she is, too." Only in such affirmation can the reality of the incorrupt be made manifest.

By the poem's fifth stanza, the speaker has begun the process of coloring the Paschal eggs. This stanza—indeed, the rest of the poem—is rich with the details of the ancient Orthodox process of using onionskin dyes. The first stanza's hunger to remember is now beginning to be filled, for this descriptive richness everywhere exhibits in the poem a love for the created that restores something of the lost Edenic harmony between man and the natural world.

Then, in the sixth stanza—the poem's actual center—"a white-faced boy asks from nowhere / if I believe in Christ and living forever." This question centers the entire poem because, when answered affirmatively, the incorruptibility of the actual creation is assured. The speaker hesitates, for the boy's question is urgently real: if this man believes (the boy's heart is saying), then I can also believe, because my belief will then be grounded in the actual reality of another person. The boy's question thus registers the fully felt reality all ascetic practice seeks: the actual reality of the creation. The speaker says slowly: "Yes, I do" believe—and, he says, "my own voice deafens me." That is, these quiet words of Orthodox affirmation drown out with joy all of the speaker's initial inward clamor.

From this point, the poem moves toward a condition of increasingly outward joy. This movement into manifest joy is borne, in the poem's second half, on the wings of certainty that the ascetic extinguishing of one's own desire not to *be* there—not to *do* this—is being carried out for the sake of these dying children and their joy. Thus, by the eighth stanza the speaker and Elaine are humming the Paschal *Christos Anesti* (Christ Is Risen) while (the poem says) "the room bustles, ajabber / with speech." Samaras' point could not be clearer: precisely *because* the speaker and Elaine have ascetically died to their own desires, *therefore* the children are intensely alive in their happy words. In this sense, then, we can see how this moment in the poem may be said to harmonize with Christ's words in John 17: "these things I speak in the world, that they might have my joy fulfilled in themselves" (17:13). That is, just as every ascetic action is a tiny crucifixion, the result of such actions is always a tiny resurrection. And Paschal joy begins now to manifest itself.

For in the poem's final two stanzas, the speaker's once-nervous hands participate directly in the incorruptible resurrection of Christ through being plunged into the red dye. "And we are laughing," he says in the poem's final line, for such is the exuberance of all Paschal joy. And note above all: this supreme joy is *given to* the speaker by those for whom he has given himself ascetically. Elaine makes him close his eyes and the children delightedly push him, for such is the way of all genuine ascetic practice: in every ascetic action we take, we make ourselves voluntarily blind and directionless. Thus, in every ascetic action, we let go of all our own control—not because we know and see where we must go but because all our holding on has become a refusal of joy and a way of fear and depression. And as he dabs Elaine's laughing face with the bright Paschal dye, the speaker makes her dying face into an incorrupt countenance, incorrupt because now beyond (as he says) "the body's cells and the cells' incarceration." Such joy manifests the true Orthodox relation to the natural world: the action of a merciful heart.

What is a merciful heart? "It is," says St. Isaac the Syrian, "the heart's burning for the sake of the entire creation, for men, for birds, for animals, for demons, and for every created thing . . . And in like manner he even prays for the family of reptiles because of the great compassion that burns without measure in his heart in the likeness of God" (*Homilies*, 71:344–45). Here, in St. Isaac's words, we can discern an unmistakable icon of the face—better, the *countenance*—of St. Herman as he bends down to touch and feed the ermine and her newborns. His merciful heart burns with the great compassion that is in (as Isaac says) "the likeness of God," a likeness ascetically constructed from that totality of his empirical personalities called the image of God. Christ says in the Gospel: "Let your light so shine before all, that all may see your good works, and glorify your Father who is in heaven" (Matt 5:16). St. Herman's compassionate heart had, through a lifetime of Orthodox ascetic practice, become the beauty of his illumined face—better, his countenance. And when ermine and bear beheld this beauty, they were nourished—directly *fed*—by the works of his beauty. And such beauty does not die.

III

In late August 1994, my wife, Xenia, our son Rowan Benedict (then age 14), and I traveled to Kodiak, Alaska, to make a tiny pilgrimage to St. Herman's Spruce Island, in honor of the saint's arrival there in the autumn of 1794. Our national Church, the Orthodox Church in America (OCA), had organized a major pilgrimage in early August on the anniversary of the saint's canonization and the bicentennial of Orthodoxy's coming to America. But we had been unable to go then because of my summer teaching and administrative duties. So we came after everyone else, including Metropolitan Theodosius of the OCA and Patriarch Alexei of Moscow, as well as scores of clerics and several hundred pilgrims, had departed. By late August, the air in Kodiak was already cool with the coming winter, and in a few brief weeks the sun would begin its marked autumnal descent into the long winter darkness. Arriving, my wife, son, and I were if not somber at least sober at the sense of the fleeting time. Each of us wondered silently: Has all the joy fled?

We stayed at the Seminary in Kodiak, which had many rooms available, with the pilgrims now gone and the students not yet back. We asked the administrator: Is there any way to reach Spruce Island? "Today?" he asked (it was now past noon), shaking his head. "I doubt it, but I'll go see." Mostly silently, we began to unpack our few things and to arrange our icons. We had come six thousand miles. "Perhaps tomorrow we can find a way over," we said.

Then a sharp knock on the door. A small but stocky Aleut man stood there. "Do you want to go see Father Herman?" he asked. Our hearts lifted.

Down at the water, two short blocks away, his little craft was beached. It was maybe seventeen feet long, with a fifty-horsepower outboard motor. Spruce Island was visible some five miles over now calm ocean. Our guide—named Herman [of blessed memory],[35] as we might have expected, after the saint—pointed out across the water. "Look at that! Father Herman wants you to come, he's made the water all calm." We clambered into the boat, and Herman shoved us off and then started the motor.

The ride across was lovely. Herman pointed to the left of the ten-mile island now looming up. "There's the town, down at that end." He pointed right. "We're heading to that end, where Father lived." He gestured between the island's two ends. "All that's the woods, that's where the animals all live." He smiled. "We're at one end, Father's at the other."

The boat throttled down as we nosed into a small lagoon—Monk's Lagoon it's called. I looked down. The bottom was rising toward us. Herman said, "I got to drop anchor pretty soon now." A few seconds later the concrete-block anchor splashed into maybe twenty inches of water. The boat's prow was nearly three yards from the shore.

"We got to jump to shore," said Herman. "From up there on the deck," waving us up.

Our fourteen-year-old son went first, jumping the gap gracefully—but, as his foot touched the shore, he stumbled a brief moment, and then righted himself. Then my wife jumped: and her very strong jump carried her just to the shore. But her stumble was more serious than our son's, and she went down to hands and knees—but all on dry land.

Then I climbed up on the deck. And all at once I felt every one of my fifty-four years and all the gracelessness of my academic life. Then I heard Herman's voice on my left side. He was standing in water above his knees next to the boat. He said, "Come on, get on my back, I'll carry you."

I flushed, embarrassed. "Oh, no, I weigh over 170 pounds."

"Oh, come on," he said, "I carry packs heavier than you."

So I settled myself onto Herman's back. Not since my two sons had, at different points in their childhood, tried to carry me had I been actually carried by someone.

Herman strode through the water easily. "Oh, heck," he said, "I could carry you clear up to the woods there." But he set me down on the shore by my wife and son.

Weeks later, telling my priest about this moment, he would smile. "It's always so. Whenever you visit a holy place, God arranges for a surprise. The real miracle is that you let yourself be carried." I had traveled six thousand miles in order to be carried by someone for the final three yards. It is always so: in every ascetic action we must let go of all our own control.

We then made our way up the beach and into the woods. The path led us to the tiny wooden skete or kellia of Fr. Gerasim, who had lived here for thirty years, until his death in 1969, on the very site where once had stood St. Herman's wooden skete. Herman unlocked the door.

Inside the skete, a sense of peaceful Orthodox devotion and practice pervaded even the very air, a peace that seemed to breathe from the very desk, books, and single chair—and above all, from the icon corner where Herman now stood. "Here's where Father Gerasim prayed all night, storms beating, snow flying, he'd keep on praying."

Herman pointed out the one window. "The church is up there. We'd get across the island after every big snow, and we'd dig our way to here, and Father he'd be smiling to see us."

We asked if we could see the church. "Oh, sure, let's go there now."

We stepped out the door. Our son went ahead, then Herman, and my wife and I a little behind them. Then it came to us, to both of us at once: an indescribably sweet odor at once powerful and gentle, an odor like nothing in this world. Our eyes quickly scanned the forest of

Monk's Rock, Spruce Island, Alaska, where St. Herman often prayed.
Photo: Fr. Joseph Huneycutt.

Monk's Lagoon, Spruce Island, Alaska. Photo: Patrick Barnes.

The path from the beach, Spruce Island, Alaska. Photo: Patrick Barnes.

Fr. Gerasim's kellia, where he lived as a hermit, tending to St. Herman's home and relics. Photo: Patrick Barnes.

Fr. Gerasim's icon corner. Photo: Patrick Barnes.

moss-covered evergreen and found nothing in bloom. Then we turned to one another. On my wife's face I read perfect joy.

Herman had stopped. "You coming?"

"What's that amazing odor?" I asked, filled with a trembling delight.

"Oh," said Herman, stepping back toward us, his dark-gold face lit in smiling. "That's Father Herman, some people notice it, that's the land remembering him."

Incorruptibly remembering.

Since that August moment in 1994, Herman's response has come to hold for me much of what the Orthodox Church knows as imperishable joy in the creation, a joy that is grounded in the liturgy itself. For in every Orthodox Divine Liturgy we are called to enter into the sweet and shocking contact with the mind and countenance and very body and blood of Christ. The priest chants, "Peace be unto all," and the choir sings, "And to your spirit." Then the priest chants: "Let us love one another, that with one mind we may confess"—an incomplete sentence; confess *what?* The choir sings the sentence's completion: "Father, Son, and Holy Spirit, the Trinity, one in essence and undivided." The deacon then intones: "The doors, the doors!"— meaning, keep the doors that are now opening between heaven and earth free from every attack, human or demonic—and the deacon then chants: "In wisdom, let us attend." Then we all sing the Creed.[36]

And then, taking the only way in the world to sustain the intimate contact that Christ calls us into—the way of Orthodox ascetic practice that St. Herman of Alaska so beautifully shows, the way of giving oneself entirely to and for another in the sovereign action of ascetic love, the way into the undying heart of all creation—we begin the approach to Holy Communion: "Take, eat, this is My body . . . Drink, this is My blood."

6

The Way of Beauty and Stillness
Shakespeare's *Winter's Tale*[37]

E arly in J. D. Salinger's novella *Franny and Zooey*, the college-age Franny tries to tell her disastrous boyfriend Lane about a book she is reading called *The Way of a Pilgrim*.[38] Written in the first person, this book is an anonymous nineteenth-century Russian text about a peasant who wants to know what it means in the Epistle to the Thessalonians when St. Paul says: "Pray without ceasing" (1 Thess 5:12). Sitting in the restaurant having dinner, Franny tells Lane about the pilgrim: "So he starts out walking all over Russia, looking for someone who can tell him *how* to pray unceasingly. And what you should say if you do" (*Franny*, 33). Lane plainly cares nothing about what Franny is saying to him, but she continues on: "Then he meets this person called a starets—some sort of terribly advanced religious person—and the starets tells him about a book called the 'Philokalia.' Which apparently was written by a group of terribly advanced monks who sort of advocate this really incredible method of praying" (33–34).

Against Lane's massive indifference, Franny then asks: "Do you want to hear what the special method of praying was that the starets told him about? . . . It's really sort of interesting, in a way." Barely concealing his boredom, Lane says, "Sure, sure." Franny goes on: "Well, the starets tells him about the Jesus Prayer first of all. 'Lord Jesus Christ, have mercy on me.' I mean that's what it is. And he explains to him that those are the best words to use when you pray" (36).

Now, Salinger's use of this prayer in his extraordinary fiction is—for my purpose here—not the point. My point, quite apart from the story, is this. Early in the 1950s, Salinger introduced into American literary culture something very like the living heart of Eastern Orthodox Christianity: the way of beauty and stillness.

In November 1993, the Abbot of Iveron Monastery at Mount Athos in Greece, Father Archimandrite Vasileios, gave a talk entitled "Beauty and Hesychia in Athonite Life."[39] Father Vasileios opens his lecture by describing his recent return to Mount Athos, the thirty-five-mile-long peninsula in northern Greece where some twenty Orthodox monasteries have existed since the ninth century. After a brief two sentences, he says this:

> The sun was setting; the sea was still. The mountain of Athos seemed like a crimson-tinged emerald, entirely heavenly lit. The Athonite peninsula itself sparkled in the same dazzling way with a slightly purplish hue. The monasteries were shining white along the sea shore. This was no mere external visual spectacle nor the type of beauty which is perceived only by the physical senses. It wasn't just a peaceful moment.

A half page further on, Fr. Vasileios says this:

> To die, to be buried, to depart. Not to trouble anyone, not to interrupt anyone when they are speaking, not to usurp their position no matter what that might be. And yet to have lived and died in such a way that your presence, discretely and from a distance as if a fragrance from someone absent, can give others the possibility to breathe divine fragrance! To grant someone else the possibility of living, of being invigorated, of having the nausea dispelled; to give another the ability to love life, to acquire self-confidence and stand on his own two feet, so that from within him there arises spontaneously a "Glory to Thee, O God!" Just such a gift of divine beauty and discerning love envelops a person on the Holy Mountain. (7–9)

What Franny is offering Lane—without either one really knowing it—is precisely this gift of divine beauty. In her hands—put there by J. D. Salinger—is the priceless gift of the Orthodox way of beauty and stillness. As Salinger's story unfolds, Franny herself (let alone Lane) seems wholly unable to accept this gift—unable, that is, until she has the magnificent final conversation on the telephone with her brother Zooey, a conversation wherein she receives from her brother the very gift which she had poorly understood in her conversation with Lane and which he had so boorishly rejected. This final conversation thus moves in the very light that Father Vasileios describes as "no mere external visual spectacle," a light of beauty that isn't "just a peaceful moment." For Zooey gives his sister—in Fr. Vasileios' words—"the possibility of living, of having the nausea dispelled," "the ability to love life, to acquire self-confidence . . ." Here, then, is the key to the Orthodox way of beauty and stillness: "To die, to be buried, to depart," in order "to give to another the possibility to breathe divine fragrance!"

■   ■   ■

And here, then, is our approach to Shakespeare's play *The Winter's Tale*. Now, the action of this astonishing play is initiated by the Sicilian King Leontes' violent verbal attack on his wife, Queen Hermione. He accuses her of adultery with King Polixenes of Bohemia, his friend since childhood. Crucial to the play is the rock-solid fact that Leontes' charges against Hermione are entirely groundless, fueled entirely by his own sick fantasies that have not even the least thread of connection to any reality. And in dizzying fashion this very groundlessness becomes for Leontes proof of his wife's guilt. He says this early in Act I:

> There have been,
> Or I am much deceived, cuckolds ere now;
> And many a man there is, even at this present,
> Now while I speak this, holds his wife by the arm,
> That little thinks she has been sluiced in's absence
> And his pond fish'd by his next neighbour, by
> Sir Smile, his neighbour: nay, there's comfort in't
> Whiles other men have gates and those gates open'd,
> As mine, against their will. Should all despair
> That have revolted wives, the tenth of mankind
> Would hang themselves. Physic for't there is none;
> It is a bawdy planet, that will strike
> Where 'tis predominant; and 'tis powerful, think it,
> From east, west, north and south: be it concluded,
> No barricado for a belly; know't;
> It will let in and out the enemy
> With bag and baggage: many thousand on's
> Have the disease, and feel't not.[40]

This is an extraordinary speech. The husband who "little thinks" his wife "has been sluiced in's absence" is one of the many thousands, says Leontes, who "Have the disease, and feel't not." To be sick without any perceptible symptoms is to construe disease in such a way that the apparent presence of perfect health becomes the very proof of real sickness. The result is, of course, that there can be no cure. "Physic for 't there's none." The sexual intensities in Leontes' final lines—"It will let in and out the enemy, / With bag and baggage"— serve to increase his conviction that he sees his wife rightly. This terrifying state of mind must be fully seen: the extent and depth of his mental and emotional disturbances guarantee for him that these disturbances are based in truth. I am vastly upset; therefore, my wife is deeply unfaithful. A bit earlier in the scene, in an aside, Leontes says this about intense passion: "Thy intention stabs the center" (I, ii:138). Your purpose, O my passion, pierces to the center of my world, my heart, revealing the objective truth of what is happening in the world and in my heart.

His trusted servant and loyal confidant Camillo—to whom King Leontes gives this vicious speech—objects to his master, saying that these charges against Hermione are entirely groundless, mere nothings. Leontes responds this way:

> Is whispering nothing?
> Is leaning cheek to cheek? is meeting noses?
> Kissing with inside lip? stopping the career
> Of laughing with a sigh?—a note infallible
> Of breaking honesty—horsing foot on foot?
> Skulking in corners? wishing clocks more swift?
> Hours, minutes? noon, midnight? and all eyes
> Blind with the pin and web but theirs, theirs only,
> That would unseen be wicked? is this nothing?
> Why, then the world and all that's in't is nothing;
> The covering sky is nothing; Bohemia nothing;
> My wife is nothing; nor nothing have these nothings,
> If this be nothing. (I, ii:284–96)

This is an astonishing list. We must understand that all these charges against Hermione *have nothing to do* with reality. But in the logic of the speech, the intensity of Leontes' feeling fills the nothingness with this very vivid content. The eyes of all others who do not see these things are, says Leontes, blind "with pin and web" (i.e., with cataracts) compared to the strength with which Leontes' eyes see these nothings now become (for him) actual visual facts. This is what we can call emotional ontology, the false fullness of real nothingness.

In Act II of *The Winter's Tale*, King Leontes puts his wife, Hermione, on public trial, charging her both with adultery in the marriage and conspiracy against his kingdom—both charges validated for Leontes by the fact of Polixenes' having fled Sicily and returned to his own kingdom, Bohemia. Part of Leontes' proof against his wife is that the beginning of her present pregnancy—just now arriving at the moment of birthgiving—coincided with the arrival of King Polixenes at the Sicilian court nine months earlier. The newborn baby girl is therefore a bastard, and Leontes orders that the infant be killed by being left in the wilderness; he says, angrily, "I'll not rear / Another's issue" (I, iii:284). The newborn child is taken away, and Leontes' and Hermione's ten-year-old son, Mamillius, flees the courtroom, shattered with grief. The trial of Hermione then begins.

Now, Hermione cannot defend herself against any of her husband's charges, because (as she puts it) "mine integrity / Being counted falsehood, shall as I express it, / Be so received" (III, ii:23–25). She can offer no defense because the ontological ground of her honesty is seen as falsehood. This ontological ground of honesty is, of course, her very personhood. It is therefore less *what* she may have done that is on trial and more *who she is* as a person. And in the teeth of ontological violence against personhood there can be no defense.

Events move rapidly in Act III, scene ii, the trial. Hermione responds to her husband's charges and is, of course, denounced by him. But then Leontes' messengers to the oracle at Delphi return to reveal the truth: "Hermione is chaste, Polixenes blameless, . . . Leontes a jealous tyrant" (III, ii:130ff.). Leontes instantly says, "There is not truth at all i'th' oracle, / The sessions shall proceed; this is mere falsehood" (III, ii:136–37). At that instant, a servant enters to say that Mamillius, their young son, in agony and terror at his mother's plight, "is gone." Stunned, Leontes says, "How? Gone?" The servant answers, "Is dead" (III, ii:141–42). Leontes reverses ground suddenly and completely: "Apollo's angry, and the heavens themselves / Do strike at my injustice" (III, ii:143–44).

Hermione faints and is carried away, and Leontes pleads for pardon from Apollo. Then Paulina—Queen Hermione's trusted servant and loyal confidante—reappears on stage to tell Leontes that the Queen herself has just died. Wife and son are now both dead, and the newborn baby girl has been taken into the wilderness to die. The proclamation from the Delphic oracle concludes: "the King shall live without an heir, if that which is lost [that is, the newborn child] be not found" (III, ii:144–46). Death is the overwhelming consequence of ontological violence.

In Acts IV and V, Shakespeare constructs what may well be his most intricate storyline. Hermione is not dead but is hidden away by Paulina for sixteen years while Leontes grieves the loss of his wife and repents of his sins in causing her and their son's deaths and the baby girl's loss. But we learn (as Act IV unfolds) the infant girl does not die and is found in the Bohemian wilderness by shepherds, having been taken to Bohemia (Polixenes' kingdom) by Leontes' servant and left there with much gold and a brief letter naming her *Perdita* (meaning "the lost girl"). This servant is killed by a bear while leaving the baby (producing what may be Shakespeare's most interesting stage direction: "Exit, pursued by a bear"— III, iii:56), and the ship that carried the servant from Sicily to Bohemia is wrecked in a storm, with the result that no one in Bohemia knows the baby's true heritage. The girl grows up to become a beautiful sixteen-year-old shepherd's daughter. And in Act IV, King Polixenes' son, Prince Florizel, meets Perdita in the forest and falls in love with her. Polixenes opposes this liaison between his royal son and this shepherd's daughter, threatening to disfigure the face of the beautiful girl and to disinherit his son unless he renounces Perdita. Then Camillo—once Leontes' confidant and now advisor to Polixenes—counsels the young couple to flee Bohemia and to put themselves under the protection of the now fully repentant King Leontes. They agree to Camillo's plan because—as was the case with Leontes' attack against Hermione—there can be no defense against ontological violence.

Then we come to Act V. At this point in the play, no one knows that Hermione still lives—except Paulina; and no one knows that Perdita is the lost daughter of Hermione and Leontes—except the audience. In this final act, Shakespeare brings together all the play's intricate plot lines. In the first two scenes, we learn from various court figures that King Leontes has welcomed the young couple and has also reconciled them to Polixenes when it is learned that this lovely girl Perdita is indeed his lost daughter, the Bohemian shepherd who raised her having kept the letter and its handwriting having been recognized—as well as by recognizing Queen Hermione's mantle and jewel also left with the baby sixteen years before. Polixenes welcomes this news with great joy, and he blesses his son, Florizel, and Leontes' daughter, Perdita, while he and Leontes greet one another with still greater joy.

Then, in the play's final scene, Paulina invites all four of them to her house to view a recently completed statue of Queen Hermione, and all four go: the now reconciled friends Leontes and Polixenes, both now fully beyond their acts of ontological violence (Leontes' against his wife, Polixenes' against his son and Perdita), as well as the young couple, Prince Florizel and Princess Perdita, blessed by both fathers. Camillo also attends, recognized again by both kings as good, true, and wise in all his counsels.

The statue of Hermione is, of course, the very Queen herself. But—very significantly—Paulina invites Leontes to respond as if it were a statue, saying:

> I like your silence; it the more shows off
> Your wonder; but yet speak, first you, my liege.
> Comes it not something near? (V, iii:30–32)

In commending Leontes for the silence of his awestruck wonder, Paulina sounds the theological note that gives shape to this final scene and the entire play. She does so by sustaining the fiction that the Hermione before them is a statue, a work of art: "Comes it not something near?" Leontes responds that the statue possesses his departed wife's "natural posture," even saying to it: "indeed / Thou art Hermione" herself. "But yet," he continues to Paulina, "Hermione was not so much wrinkled, nothing / So agèd as this seems" (V, iii:27–29). Paulina answers:

> So much the more our carver's excellence,
> Which lets go by some sixteen years, and makes her
> As [if] she lived now. (V, iii:39–40)

By thus keeping Hermione fictional, Paulina is making her become for Leontes what the Eastern Orthodox icon is for the Orthodox believer: an image that reveals the likeness of God by being on the very boundary where this world touches the heavenly kingdom.

One usually thinks of a boundary as that which merely divides and separates one realm from another. But the Orthodox believer thinks of the boundary disclosed by the icon as that which *simultaneously* separates and reconciles two distinct realms. That is, the icon can never be mistaken for its prototype, for the two are forever distinct. Yet the icon forever reconciles image to prototype by revealing in full earthly materiality the heavenly reality of the prototype. The icon thus *joins* the two worlds at the very moment it distinguishes them.

In this way, the Orthodox icon becomes crucial to the believer's penitential action, for it invites the believer into the realm it reveals at the very moment it rebukes the believer for his not yet having attained in himself full likeness to God. This simultaneous action of invitation and rebuke creates in the believer still deeper yearning for a still fuller reconciliation with God. In other words, the Orthodox icon is the call into the fullness of self-emptying love, the love wherein one remembers all one's own violent sins against one's beloved at the very moment the beloved is bringing to one the fullness of love in an ecstatic relation.

As Leontes gazes at the statue, he says:

> I am ashamed: does not the stone rebuke me
> For being more stone than it? O royal piece,
> There's magic in thy majesty, which has
> My evils conjured to remembrance and
> From thy admiring daughter took the spirits,
> Standing like stone with thee. (V, iii:48–51)

This is an extraordinary moment. Leontes finds all his sins "conjured to remembrance" as he draws always nearer to the ecstasy of direct contact with the image's living prototype. He glances at his daughter to see that she, too, is not "like stone," that she, too, has now entered the state of awestruck wonder the Orthodox believer always enters when standing before the Orthodox icon. When Perdita seeks to cross the boundary and kiss the statue's hand, Paulina once more intervenes to sustain the iconic stillness of the moment: "O, Patience! / The statue is but newly fixed, the color's / Not dry" (V, iii:46–48).

Now Paulina begins to move the scene—and whole play—into the fullness of its revelatory power, saying:

> Either forbear,
> Quit presently the chapel, or resolve you
> For more amazement. If you can behold it,
> I'll make the statue move indeed, descend
> And take you by the hand; but then you'll think—
> Which I protest against—I am assisted
> By wicked powers. (V, iii:85–91)

The question is thus raised: Is Paulina a necromancer, conjuring a ghost from the grave? For the characters in the play—as for us, the audience—Hermione has been dead for sixteen years. But in a few moments, she will step down from the pedestal, fully alive, to greet her husband and daughter, as she tells them (and us) that, with Paulina's guidance and help, she had hidden herself away these sixteen years in hopes that her husband would learn repentance and her daughter be finally found.

But the revelatory moment is held off by Paulina so that Leontes and Perdita can deepen into the stillness of awestruck wonder. "Shall I draw the curtain?" Paulina asks, and Leontes responds, "No, not these twenty years," while Perdita echoes her father: "So long could I / Stand by, a looker-on." Shakespeare's point is magnificently clear. By sustaining the iconic significance of Hermione, Paulina is increasing for both husband and daughter the way of beauty and stillness.

Then the revelatory moment arrives. Paulina says:

> It is required
> You do awake your faith. Then all stand still;
> On those that think it is unlawful business
> I am about, let them depart. (V, iii:95–97)

Leontes says, "Proceed. / No foot shall stir" (V, iii:97–98). Paulina then says:

> Music, awake her; strike.
> 'Tis time; descend; be stone no more; approach;

> Strike all that look upon with marvel. Come,
> I'll fill your grave up: stir, nay, come away,
> Bequeath to death your numbness, for from him
> Dear life redeems you. You perceive she stirs:
> [*Hermione comes down.*]
> Start not; her actions shall be holy as
> You hear my spell is lawful . . . (V, iii:98–105)

St. Isaac the Syrian, the seventh-century Orthodox saint whose writings on the way of stillness have shaped the Orthodox understanding of prayer for thirteen centuries, says: "If you love repentance, love stillness also," adding that stillness is "the mother of repentance" (*Homilies*, 64:316). Paulina's command—"all stand still"—is precisely the call into the way of penitential resurrection, in which the penitent dies to his sinfulness in order to resurrect into aliveness in God. When Paulina calls Hermione to awaken from fictional stoniness—"be stone no more"—she is also calling Leontes to end that stony-heartedness in himself that had produced his violence against Hermione. Paulina says to Leontes and Perdita (and to us), "Start not"—that is, do not abandon the way of awestruck stillness now descending upon all of you *in* and *as* this moment. For in sustaining such stillness, the way of genuine aliveness opens.

■　■　■

In the final conversation between Franny and Zooey in Salinger's story, they remember how their older (now deceased) brother Seymour had told both of them, at different times in their childhood, about the Fat Lady, encouraging them both to be good and generous and loving for the Fat Lady—for someone, that is, neither of them had ever seen but whom both of them came to imagine vividly. Zooey says to his sister: "This terribly clear, clear picture of the Fat Lady formed in my mind. I had her sitting on this porch all day, swatting flies, with her radio going full-blast from morning till night" (200).

Franny adds to her brother's image: "I didn't ever picture her on a porch, but with very—you know—very thick legs, very veiny. I had her in an *awful* wicker chair. She had cancer, *too*, though, and she had the radio going full-blast all day! Mine did, too!" (201).

In other words, the Fat Lady has become fully iconic, for in her fictional materiality, she brings Franny and Zooey into fullest contact with heavenly love. And in this sense, the ending of Salinger's story parallels perfectly the ending of Shakespeare's play. The result, in both works, is beautifully articulated by Paulina when she tells Leontes and Hermione, Florizel and Perdita, to share their joy with everyone: "your exultation / Partake to every one" (V, iii:131–32).

Similarly, Franny listens to the dial tone after her brother hangs up, saying, "I can't talk anymore, buddy" (202)—finding the dial tone, says Salinger, "extraordinarily beautiful to listen to, rather as if it were the best possible substitute for the primordial silence itself" (ibid.). This silence is precisely that expressed by St. Isaac in two brief sentences: "True wisdom is gazing at God. Gazing at God is silence of the thoughts" (*Homilies*, 64:306).

Salinger continues: "But she seemed to know, too, when to stop listening to it, as if all of what little or much wisdom in the world were suddenly hers" (202). This wisdom is above all *iconic,* for it reveals to the beholder— both to Franny and to Leontes—the way of beauty and stillness.

In both Salinger and Shakespeare, this way opens through death: the death of Hermione and the death of Seymour. For in both, death becomes the way in which both Hermione and Seymour can become iconic, and in so doing, they can become for Leontes and Franny the transforming experience of the boundary, that place between the worlds that simultaneously separates and reconciles. As Father Vasileios puts it: "To die, to be buried, to depart" so as "to give another the ability to love life" (*Beauty,* 9). Here is the light of beauty and stillness that shines in late Shakespeare and Salinger.

■   ■   ■

Toward the end of his November 1993 talk, Father Vasileios tells of the death of a fellow monk some six years earlier, a monk named Father Hesychios."I saw him before he died," says Father Vasileios, continuing:

> I saw him as he was dying, wasting away from cancer and becoming bare bones, yet having no complaint about it, nor about anything else in his life . . . I saw him thanking everyone

for the care they had given him . . . His face shone. He spoke in silence . . . We wanted him to say something to us and he spoke in his own way: "Now leave me be. I thank you for what you have done for me; I don't need anything any more. I am still with you but in another way. The Master of the house has arrived; life has begun . . ." (15)

Father Vasileios adds, "And he told us everything clearly with a silence which could speak and by the resplendent joy on his face"; concluding: "What the departure of Father Hesychios says to us is the same message which the Holy Mountain has given perpetually with all its existence: 'A Beauty exists which abolishes death; a Stillness exists which abounds with eternal blessedness and splendour for all of us'" (16–17).

7

"Shall Thy Wonders Be Known in the Dark?"
Robert Frost and Personhood[41]

An Old Man's Winter Night
Robert Frost

All out-of-doors looked darkly in at him
Through the thin frost, almost in separate stars,
That gathers on the pane in empty rooms.
What kept his eyes from giving back the gaze
Was the lamp tilted near them in his hand.
What kept him from remembering what it was
That brought him to that creaking room was age.
He stood with barrels round him—at a loss.
And having scared the cellar under him
In clomping there, he scared it once again
In clomping off; —and scared the outer night,
Which has its sounds, familiar, like the roar
Of trees and crack of branches, common things,
But nothing so like beating on a box.
A light he was to no one but himself
Where now he sat, concerned with he knew what,
A quiet light, and then not even that.
He consigned to the moon, such as she was,
So late-arising, to the broken moon
As better than the sun in any case
For such a charge, his snow upon the roof,
His icicles along the wall to keep;
And slept. The log that shifted with a jolt
Once in the stove, disturbed him and he shifted,
And eased his heavy breathing, but still slept.

One aged man—one man—can't keep a house,

A farm, a countryside, or if he can,

It's thus he does it of a winter night.[42]

In a crucial essay on Robert Frost some fifty years ago, poet Randall Jarrell remarked on Frost's 1923 lyric "An Old Man's Winter Night." How could any lyric poem, says Jarrell, be "more grotesquely and subtly and mercilessly disenchanting than the tender 'An Old Man's Winter Night'"? Such a poem, he continues, expresses "an attitude that makes pessimism seem a hopeful evasion." He says it begins "with a flat and terrible reproduction of the evil in the world and [ends] by saying: It's so; and there's nothing you can do about it, and if there were, would *you* ever do it? The limits which existence approaches and falls back from have seldom been stated with such bare composure."[43]

Jarrell's great service to readers of Frost's poems was—and still is—to extricate from the apparently banal optimism of Frost's public persona that "other Frost" (a title Jarrell gives one of his Frost essays), that poet of terrifying darkness and pervasive despair.

But Jarrell's success in defining this "other Frost" can, I think, also be understood as Jarrell's limitation. That is—to put the matter as a question— what, in this great poem, is the *relation* (and not merely the *distinction*) between the public persona and the private darkness? For I want to suggest precisely that such a relation exists; that it is in fact a *coherent* relation; and that this relation actively helps to shape what is finest and most moving about the poem. These matters may be best understood by asking this simple question: In this poem, what is Frost's relation to darkness? What does darkness *mean*?

The poem's first line is: "All out-of-doors looked darkly in at him." The darkness is animate, possessing a gaze that can therefore be returned if one turns out the lights at hand. For by line 4, it is the lights that prevent the old man from returning the gaze. Next, in lines 6 and 7, these lights are interestingly associated with growing old, an association established almost entirely by syntactic parallelism: "what kept his eyes from giving back the gaze . . . / What kept him from remembering what it was . . ."

The lights at hand keep him from returning the gaze of darkness; his age keeps him from remembering why he had come in "to that creaking room."

And just as the lights get turned off, so too the old man consigns to the moon "As better than the sun" the task of keeping intact the snow on his roof, presumably as insulation against the winter cold. The failing memory of old age is thus associated with having only a slender light. Yet clearly: if the light must be turned off so as to return the gaze of darkness, so, too, failing memory must be extinguished so as to keep rightly one's own house. The poem concludes:

> One aged man—one man—can't keep a house,
> A farm, a countryside, or if he can,
> It's thus he does it of a winter night.

The slenderness of the man's resources—the little lamp, the fading memory—serves to emphasize the vast power of the winter's darkness. And, the poem implies, we have to forego even this slender resource if we are to keep our houses, farms, and whole countries. Thus I ask: what is this darkness?

To approach a response, I shall propose a starting point well outside the usual range of reference to Frost's poetry. My starting point is the sixth-century AD text called *The Mystical Theology*.[44] This text is attributed to the first-century person named Dionysius the Areopagite, a man mentioned in the biblical Acts of the Apostles as one of the first in Athens to believe in Christ after listening to St. Paul. The text was later attributed by scholars to an anonymous monk in the late fifth or early sixth century; however, the name of Dionysius has stayed with it, modified by nineteenth-century scholarship to Pseudo-Dionysius. I shall use the ancient name, Dionysius the Areopagite.

Now, this very brief text—some six pages of Greek—has had an extraordinary impact on all Christian theology for fourteen centuries. Eastern Orthodoxy and Western Catholicism, as well as Lutheran and all later forms of Protestantism, have all drawn directly from this text. I think it safe to say that Frost's Swedenborgian mother Isabelle would likely have known something of this text, it being one very much to her strongly mystical tastes in religion. And so I think it also not inconceivable that she would have instructed her bookish son Rob in certain key aspects of it during their years of home schooling. The text is very difficult, its Greek prose at once perplexing, lyrical, cryptic, and assured.

Let me give some indications of its nature. Toward the end of chapter one, St. Dionysius tells of how Moses, in ascending Mt. Sinai to receive the Commandments from God, breaks "away from what sees and is seen, and he plunges into the truly mysterious darkness of unknowing" (137). Dionysius continues: By renouncing everything the mind can conceive, Moses can belong "completely to him who is beyond everything" (ibid.); that is, Moses can belong to God by deliberately turning out all the lights. Dionysius then says: "Here, being neither oneself nor someone else, one is supremely united by a completely unknowing inactivity of all knowledge, and knows beyond the mind by knowing nothing" (ibid.). That is, by completely turning out all the lights of seeing and knowing things—including the seeing and knowing of oneself—one approaches unity with God. So concludes chapter one.

Then the brief second chapter develops this concluding point. Here is chapter two in its entirety:

> I pray we could come to this darkness so far above light! If only we lacked sight and knowledge so as to see, so as to know, unseeing and unknowing, that which lies beyond all vision and knowledge. For this would be really to see and to know: to praise the Transcendent One in a transcending way, namely through the denial of all beings. We would be like sculptors who set out to carve a statue. They remove every obstacle to the pure view of the hidden image, and simply by this act of clearing aside they show up the beauty which is hidden.
>
> Now it seems to me that we should praise the denials quite differently than we do the assertions. When we made assertions we began with the first things, moved down through intermediate terms until we reached the last things. But now as we climb from the last things up to the most primary we deny all things so that we may unhiddenly know that unknowing which itself is hidden from all those possessed of knowing amid all beings, so that we may see above being that darkness concealed from all the light among beings. (Ibid., ch. 2)

I shall start at the center of this passage, with the metaphor of the sculptor. The sculptor slowly chips material away from the block of stone, and slowly the image that had been hidden in the stone comes into view. The chipping of the stone is like the denial of assertions about knowing. In this way, the denial of assertions is like the turning out of lights. The famously—if not notoriously—difficult final sentence contains the essence of Dionysius' point. Let me paraphrase the final sentence this way: We are seeking to know openly ("unhiddenly") that form of knowing we can enter into only when we deliberately turn out the lights of all our knowing. That is, we say: "God is not this, He is not that, nor is He this, nor that, nor is He anything we can ever see or say or think about or point at"—in other words, we can know Him only through not knowing. And the reason this is so is that God is *hidden* from all creatures who, like ourselves, possess the capacity to know. Then, turning out the lights of all our knowings, we can enter into that darkness that is concealed from us by all these various lights: and this darkness is fully alive, fully aware, fully creative.

When we see Frost's lyric from this perspective, two interesting aspects become clear. First, his use of negations in the poem—"A light he was to no one . . . and then not even that . . . one man—can't keep a house, a farm"— can be understood as a kind of reverse affirmation, one in which powerlessness becomes a kind of potential strength. Second, this strength—at first hypothetical ("*if* he can")—becomes actualized in the final line: "It's thus he does it of a winter night."

In the third chapter of *The Mystical Theology*, Dionysius says that when one begins with a single denial and then proceeds to deny all denials, one also is thereby making an assertion that is beyond every assertion. That is, the denial of all denials of course asserts that something *is*. But such an assertion is beyond every other assertion in the sense that every other assertion must *depend upon* this one; it is "beyond" in the sense of "prior to" and "higher than." This movement of Dionysius' thought parallels the movement of Frost's lyric.

So seen, "An Old Man's Winter Night" goes the way of negation so as to achieve affirmation; it goes the way of deliberately turning out the lights so as to find the way of keeping a whole countryside. As Dionysius tells us to do, the poem goes into darkness to encounter that which illumines beyond

all the false lights. And the central fact of this darkness is—as I have said—
that it is fully alive, fully aware, fully creative.

In his essay, Randall Jarrell calls Frost's public persona the "Skeleton on
the Doorstep." He says this:

> Just as a star will have, sometimes, a dark companion, so Frost has
> a pigheaded one, a shadowy self that grows longer and darker as
> the sun gets lower. I am speaking of that other self that might
> be called the Grey Eminence of Robert Taft, or the Peter Pan of
> the National Association of Manufacturers, or any such thing—
> this public self incarnates all the institutionalized complacency
> that Frost once mocked at and fled from, and later pretended to
> become a part of and became a part of. (*Poetry*, 40)

Jarrell is quite right, I think, in this characterization of Frost's public
persona. It is indeed a dark shadow, a Grey Eminence. But—following
Dionysius—I want to suggest an alternative reading. This persona can be
seen as a deliberate turning out of all the lights of false knowing, a voluntary
darkening of selfhood, in order to behold—in Dionysius' astonishing
words—"that darkness concealed from all the light among beings" (138).
His public persona may indeed (as Jarrell claims) shed no light on his poems;
indeed, it may have darkened them. It *may* have. But, with Dionysius' help,
we may also ask whether the shadowy opacity of that persona has, in fact,
done something quite otherwise.

▪   ▪   ▪

In the spring of 1961, I was a junior at the University of Florida in
Gainesville, majoring in English, when Robert Frost came to campus to give a
reading. I had, of course, known that Frost owned a house in Gainesville. But I
had never seen him, nor had I tried to. My tastes in contemporary poetry ran,
at that point, to T. S. Eliot, Ezra Pound, and (above all) Wallace Stevens—and
not to Frost. But when I heard about the reading I instantly decided I'd go.

It was a Florida-warm April evening, and the hall was packed with over
three hundred people. Someone introduced Frost (I forget who). Then
Frost walked to the lectern amidst thunderous applause. A fleeting thought
crossed my mind at that instant: would Wallace Stevens be applauded this

way? Then we hushed into silence as Frost leaned on the lectern and—with no books or papers—began to say his poems, in that low, strong, measured, and gravelly voice of his, pausing between each poem to offer a brief comment. He spoke his poems for more than an hour, and then he asked us if there were poems any of us wanted especially to hear, or to hear again. There were, and so he spoke those. All of us were enchanted.

Remembering back nearly forty-five years to that evening—and the memory remains for me very vivid—I want to tell you now my strongest, most lasting impression: Frost as a person was at once completely opaque and completely intimate. None of us that evening could "read" him or in any way "see into" him. Yet every one of us felt deeply that he was speaking directly and uniquely to each of us singly. Darkness and closeness were entirely at one, both in the poems and in the person of Robert Frost. In my nearly thirty years as director of The Frost Place in Franconia, New Hampshire, I have attended more poetry readings than I can count. None of these readings, wonderful as they have been, have had this unique blending of opacity and intimacy that I saw and heard in Frost in 1961.

This opacity and intimacy in Frost thus together constitute what I want to call the *personhood* of Robert Frost. Personhood is a reality entirely distinct from either a public persona or private personality—in the same way that an ocean is a reality entirely distinct from either a *picture* of an ocean or a private swimming pool. Now, swimming pools and pictures are clearly *related to* oceans: but such relationships can never obliterate for us the reality of the ocean. In fact (to use Dionysius' language), in order to *know* the personhood of another, we must *unknow* both the persona and the personality: we must let these lights go out. Again and again, in his finest poems, Robert Frost accomplishes precisely this unknowing, the deliberate extinguishing of all the false light, and a welcoming-in of the darkness in which true personhood can shine forth. And true personhood is, always, genuinely beautiful.

I think what moves us so deeply about the poem "An Old Man's Winter Night" is Frost's evocation of genuine personhood in the old man. The old man in Frost's poem is not a persona nor a personality; he is, genuinely, a *person*. And as the lights go out in the poem, the more beautifully and movingly his personhood emerges. One vivid detail: when the log in the stove shifts with a jolt, we, too, are jolted into a deeper intimacy with the old man, an intimacy that gains in power because of the darkness.

■   ■   ■

Poet Sydney Lea's book *Ghost Pain* has a poem toward the end called "Wonder: Red Beans and Ricely."[45] In it, Lea tells of an experience, some forty years earlier, when he and his cousin and their girlfriends attend a concert in a large tent, called The Sunny Brook Ballroom, in East Jesus, PA, where the famed Louis Armstrong blows the four-note opening phrase to "West End Blues"—and then pauses, a "long long pin-drop pause," says Lea, "the moment . . . knocked even us in the know-it-all chops," a moment so powerful, he says, that it "lingered strong, beginning to end, through the blues that followed."

What is this astonishing moment? It is a moment entirely empty of any and every conceivable sound as everyone, Lea says, sits absolutely still and "rapt," and even the stars in the night sky stop blinking, and the "cows and great-eyed deer" in the surrounding fields and woods are "stock-still." St. Dionysius would say of this moment (we can *just* hear his voice): all the false light of every earthly sound has gone absolutely out, so that we can "unhearing-ly" hear the sound that is beyond all sounds.

The poem continues with the younger Lea, after Armstrong's sound ends, standing to tell his cousin and girlfriends: "I'll get his autograph." And in the fourth stanza, he goes out behind the tent to open the exactly right door where Armstrong sits at a desk, and he stammers his request for an autograph, Then:

> it was all
> one simple motion, the way he reached into a drawer,
> drew out a jug of Johnny Walker, sucked it down
> to the label, squared before him a sheet of paper, ready
> for me, it seemed, flourished a fountain pen and wrote:
> Red Beans and Ricely Yours at Sunny Brook Ballroom. Pops.

"And what remains from then?" Lea asks. "Not the paper, long since lost," nor the cousin, who died years ago, nor the girlfriends, not even that "stunningly blessed younger I" remains; all is gone, he says, including "the heavenstruck beasts and the trees and the moon and the sky." Then the poem's beautiful final line tells what does remain: "Just a handful of opening notes from a horn which are there forever."

In Dionysian terms, all the false lights go out in the poem so that the poem's speaker (and we with him) can enter something very like the place—and these words of Dionysius' occur very near the start of *The Mystical Theology*—"where the mysteries of God's Word / lie simple, absolute and unchangeable / in the brilliant darkness of a hidden silence" (135). Dionysius' comprehension of the absolute simplicity and unfading brilliance of this opaque silence is very much at one with Lea's understanding of the "handful of notes . . . which are there forever" in the "long long pin-drop pause" of absolute stillness. And St. Dionysius and Sydney Lea, in turn, perfectly illumine the old man's winter night in Frost's great poem.

■ ■ ■

What brings together these three—Dionysius, Frost, and Lea—is the reality of personhood: a reality beyond all the false lights of personality and persona, a reality at once forever hidden in darkness yet simultaneously shining in an eternally radiant beauty. This is the beauty of personhood, a beauty that never fades.

One final poem will perhaps help us comprehend more fully this beauty and its creation. Here is Psalm 87 (LXX numbering)—a poem that is arguably the darkest text in all the vast entirety of biblical literature.

1 O Lord God of my salvation, I have cried out day and night before thee.

2 Let my prayer come before thee; incline thine ear, O Lord, to my supplication.

3 For my soul was filled with troubles and my life drew close to Hades.

4 I am counted among those who go down into the pit, like a man no one would help, like a man free among the dead,

5 Like mangled men lying in graves whom thou rememberest no more, like those snatched from thy hand.

6 They have laid me in the lowest pit, in dark places, in death's shadow.

7 Thy wrath leaned heavy on me, thy waves all crashed down on me.

8 My friends thou hast taken from me, I was made
loathsome to them; betrayed, I could not escape.

9 My eye weakened with great poverty, O Lord, all day I
cried out to thee, to thee I stretched out my hands.

10 Wilt thou work miracles for the dead? Can physicians
really resurrect them to proclaim thy praises to thee? *Selah*

11 Shall anyone in the grave give an account of thy mercy?
Or thy truthfulness in a ruined place?

12 Shall thy wonders be known in the dark? Thy
righteousness in oblivion's land?

13 But I, O Lord, I cried out to thee, and in the morning my
prayer shall draw very near to thee.

14 Why, O Lord, dost thou cast away my soul? Why turnest
thou thy face from me?

15 I am poor and troubled since childhood; briefly raised up,
I was brought down into the depths of bewilderment.

16 Thy furies have swept through me, thy terrors have
utterly unmade me,

17 Swirling around me daily like waters, surrounding me
from every side.

18 Thou hast taken loved ones and friends far from me, even
anyone who knew me, because of my misery.

I begin with two points. First, the terrible affliction here described as "death's shadow" is the psalmic metaphor for what we would call depression. In Psalm 141, this place is termed a "hidden . . . snare," and the psalmist says this: "I looked on my right, and I saw that no one had recognized me, that all flight had failed me, that no one saw deeply my soul" (Ps 141:4). Here is the complete wreckage of all relational reality in and through psalmic depression: *no one* sees deeply his soul, *all* flight fails him, *no one* even recognizes him. And in the next psalm (Ps 142), the action of the psalmic enemy is described as directly causing the deepest of depression:

For the enemy has tormented my soul, he has laid low my life
to the earth, making me dwell in dark places like one who has
been long dead,
And my spirit has fallen into depression, my heart deeply
troubled within me. (Ps 142:3–4)

The psalmic meaning is abundantly clear. The depressive state can be best characterized as that place of completely immobilizing darkness, as the dark and unrelenting place of a very long death. In Psalm 87, this merciless darkness is likened to "mangled men lying in graves" (87:5), a "wrecked place" (87:11), "oblivion's land" (87:12). So seen, this psalmic place can be viewed as analogous to the (implied) inner darkness of the old man in Frost's great lyric—a darkness that deepens as the poem unfolds:

> [He] scared the outer night,
> Which has its sounds, familiar, like the roar
> Of trees and crack of branches . . .
> A light he was to no one but himself
> Where now he sat, concerned with he knew what,
> A quiet light, and then not even that.

As the lights go out in the poem, the beauty of personhood grows always stronger. The old man is *not at all* an image of depression; but the darkness of the poem is plainly a Dionysian darkness, carrying a light that is beyond all other lights.

My second point about Psalm 87 is that this dark place of massive depression is understood by the psalmist as directly given by God. Consequently, it is a place where "my prayer shall draw very near to" God Himself. And yet (and this cannot be overemphasized) the drawing-near to God does not at all lift the depression; if anything, it deepens it. Hence, the darkness of this pit, with its fury and terror, can be truly understood as a *Dionysian* darkness: as, in Dionysius' words, "that darkness . . . beyond intellect" where "we . . . find ourselves not simply running short of words but actually speechless and unknowing," that place where "language falters" and then "turn[s] silent completely" because the one falling mute is now becoming "at one with him [i.e., with God] who is indescribable" (*Mystical Theology,* 139).

As a result, when Psalm 87 calls this depressive state the place of *ptocheia,* "extreme poverty" (Lust II, 411b), the psalm is also saying that it is a place of extreme richness: the place, that is, where the psalmist's prayer is drawing very near to God. There is an astonishing moment in Psalm 138 that perfectly articulates this paradox:

> I thought darkness would surely kill me, but to my delight even
> the night shall shine,

> For darkness shall never be dark with thee, the night shall be bright
> as day, darkness and light one and the same. (Ps 138:11–12)

Here is the key to St. Dionysius: the darkness and light are "one and the same." And it is not that the psalms are Dionysian; it is, rather, that Dionysius is deeply psalmic. The extreme poverty of depression thus becomes one with God's abundant bounty.

One final point about this extraordinary psalm. It is *not* that the depression *causes* the drawing-near to God. Rather, it is that the psalmist's prayer is being answered in the very midst of the depressive darkness. Sixth-century AD St. John Climacus, in his book *The Ladder of Divine Ascent*, offers a remarkable insight: "when there is no psalmody [i.e., the daily practice of praying the Psalms], then despondency [i.e., depression] does not make its appearance."[46] The psalmody does not *cause* the depression; instead, it perfectly discloses the depression in its full demonic catastrophe. Thus, when psalmody ceases, the demonic triumph becomes complete. *And yet*, even in the depths of the pit, "my prayer shall draw very near to thee"; in this sense, then, the swirling waters of fury and terror are entirely God's direct actions. "It made no sense," says Sydney Lea in his poem, "except it did."

■ ■ ■

Poet Christopher Merrill once gave a talk at The Frost Place. At the very start, Merrill said this: "It is not possible to imagine poetry in any Western tongue without the imagery, insights, and ideas of the Psalms, the ground of our inheritance."[47] Merrill went on to discuss the poems of several significant poets in modern world literature (including Christopher Smart, Walt Whitman, St. John Perse, and Czeslaw Milosz), all of whose texts beautifully illumine the psalmic "ground of our inheritance." And a very strong part of that ancestral ground can be rightly, I think, seen in the extraordinary light of St. Dionysius' *Mystical Theology*: As Sydney Lea's younger self goes unerringly to the one right door—and as Frost's old man turns to the moon "As better than the sun"—so, too, some of our finest poets have come to the bright darkness of the Psalms: that darkness wherein all the false lights are extinguished, and where we can thereby behold the light "concealed from all the light among beings" (130).

It's thus it happens.

8

The Action of a Merciful Heart
Wisdom, Depression, and the Ascetical Life[48]

P salm 118 is the longest psalm in the Psalter. The poem is 176 lines
long, and it is organized into twenty-two eight-line stanzas. The
twenty-two stanzas are sequenced according to the twenty-two letters of the
Hebrew alphabet. Also, each stanza employs—in each of its eight lines—an
initial word that begins with that letter of the alphabet. That is, every line
of the first stanza starts with a word that begins with Aleph, the first letter
of the Hebrew alphabet; every line in the second stanza begins with Beth,
the second letter; and so on, through twenty-two stanzas in alphabetical
order. One of the effects of this pattern is that it creates a sense of antiphony
between change and corruption: the psalmist moves in his prayer always in
relation to a structure that never corrupts or changes. The *Zohar* (a medieval
Jewish mystical treatise) says that the sequence of the Hebrew alphabet
is the sequence in which God created heaven and earth. So the psalmist
dances with God.

When in the second or third century BC the Hebrew Scriptures were
translated into Greek, the anonymous translators faced the question of
how to register a Hebrew verse pattern that is entirely untranslatable into
any language. What the LXX scholar-poets did was *not* to reproduce the
alphabetic stanza. Instead, they created from each single Hebrew line a
two-part Greek line, and established in every line a relationship between
the two parts that is simultaneously very clear and very surprising. The
relation is clear because the second part of the line *always directly responds*
to the first. The relation is surprising because the first *never directly causes* the
second; instead, the second part is always a freely chosen responsiveness
and is never something compelled. Thus clarity and surprise are everywhere
sustained in Greek throughout the entire psalm by this formal property.

Here is my version of the fourth stanza of Psalm 118:

25 My soul lies prostrate on the earth,
    Quicken me according to thy word.
26 I declared my ways, and thou didst hear me,
    Teach me thy statutes.
27 Make me comprehend the way of thy statutes,
    I shall ponder thy wondrous works.
28 My soul has fainted from depression,
    Strengthen me with thy words.
29 Put the unjust way far from me,
    With thy law have mercy on me.
30 I have chosen the way of truth,
    I have never forgotten thy judgments.
31 I have clung to thy testimonies,
    O Lord, put me not to shame.
32 I have run the way of thy commandments
    When thou didst enlarge my heart.[49]

I offer two points about my version. First, as the Greek does, my version breaks each line into two short ones. I do so because I am seeking to create something like the Greek's balletic movements between call and response, and counter-call and counter-response. Second, I am attempting here to use first and second-person pronouns—"I" of the psalmic speaker and "thou" of the divine presence—in ways that recall something of the Hebrew alphabetic repetitions. Thus, the effect I am after is this: the "I" defers to the "thou" only to have the "thou" then bow gracefully to the "I" in a way that prompts the "I" to further response. In so moving this way, the "I" can be seen as entering into direct participation in the movements of "thou," while the "thou" can be seen as moving toward the "I." In this way, the divine moves toward incarnation while the human moves toward deification.

What this pattern is used for in Psalm 118 is to focus the poem's psychic and spiritual intensities. In this stanza, these intensities are best approached through the first half of verse 28: "My soul has fainted from depression." The Greek word I here translate *depression* is *accidie*, while the Hebrew word behind it is *tugah*. For *accidie*, the lexicon for LXX Greek gives "apathy, indifference, exhaustion," while the Hebrew lexicon says *tugah* means "grief, sorrow." There is plainly the merest step in these definitions to what we mean by the word *depression*.

■ ■ ■

Poet Jane Kenyon's "Having It Out with Melancholy," published in 1993, is one of the most extraordinary explorations we have into depression.[50]

Here is the first of the poem's nine sections, entitled "From the Nursery":

> When I was born, you waited
> behind a pile of linen in the nursery,
> and when we were alone, you lay down
> on top of me, pressing
> the bile of desolation into every pore.
> And from that day on
> everything under the sun and moon
> made me sad—even the yellow
> wooden beads that slid and spun
> along a spindle on my crib.
> You taught me to exist without gratitude.
> You ruined my manners toward God:
> "We're here simply to wait for death;
> the pleasures of earth are overrated."
> I only appeared to belong to my mother,
> to live among blocks and cotton undershirts
> with snaps; among red tin lunch boxes
> and report cards in ugly brown slipcases.
> I was already yours—the anti-urge,
> The mutilator of souls.

Two points are at once very clear. First, depression is absolutely total: "the bile of desolation [presses] into every pore" of the baby's body, and as a result, everything, she says, "made me sad." Second, this totality strikes at the psychic core of personhood, as depression becomes "the mutilator of souls," the destroyer of the psychic capacity to experience the urgencies of joy—"the anti-urge," Kenyon calls it.

Here, then, is a central meaning of what the psalms call *accidie*. Kenyon conceives this affliction as so profound that it ruins her "manners toward God," a ruination she expresses this way: "We're here simply to wait for death; / the pleasures of earth are overrated."

In seeing depression this way, Kenyon is concurring with Psalms in understanding depression as fundamentally a spiritual affliction that has profound psychological effects. In ruining our "manners toward God," depression unmakes our relation to the created world as well in such a way that "the pleasures of earth" become empty and meaningless, "overrated." The spiritual antidote to depression is spiritual *joy*: that experience of the created world that reveals it to us to be the direct work of an entirely loving creator, one who is unceasingly responsive and steadily calling us to yet deeper responding. Depression, says Kenyon, destroys in us the capacity for such experiences of spiritual joy. And consequently depression leaves in its wake a hatred of actual existence so thorough and systemic that there is in it, finally, little or no psychic heat. She says in section seven that she is "tired / beyond measure," exhausted and apathetic. This is the central meaning of *accidie*, both for the stanza from Psalm 118 and for Kenyon's terrifying poem. And the primary psychic consequence in both texts is the experience of *corruption*. The whole of creation begins to disintegrate as the psyche seeks—not the bright reality of the created world—but the numbing darkness of sleep.

Here is Kenyon's fourth section, entitled "Often":

> Often I go to bed as soon after dinner
> as seems adult
> (I mean I try to wait for dark)
> in order to push away
> from the massive pain in sleep's
> frail wicker coracle.

This section can be seen as commentary on the line from Psalm 118: "My soul has fainted from depression." The Greek verb indeed means to go into a slumber, into a semi-sleep. The point of such sleep is—as Kenyon brilliantly sees—entirely narcotic, "to push away / from the massive pain." The pain that is thus drugged is the psychic agony of corruption, an agony so frightful that even this frailest of drugs is sought. How are we to understand this agony of corruption?

In the Eastern Orthodox tradition there is a stunning long prayer written by the priest Protopresbyter Gregory Petrov shortly before his death in

1940 in a Soviet prison camp.[51] In the midst of the most terrible suffering, Fr. Gregory prays this:

> I was born a weak, defenceless child, but Your angel spread his wings over my cradle to defend me. From birth until now Your love has illumined my path . . . from birth until now the generous gifts of Your providence have been marvellously showered upon me . . . You have brought me into life as if into an enchanted paradise. We have seen the sky like a chalice of deepest blue, where in the azure heights the birds are singing. We have listened to the soothing murmur of the forest and the melodious music of the streams. We have tasted fruit of fine flavour and the sweet-scented honey. We can live very well on your earth. It is a pleasure to be Your guest . . . How great and how close You are in the powerful track of the storm! How mighty in the blinding flash of lightning! How awesome is Your majesty! The voice of the Lord fills the fields, it speaks in the rustling of the trees. The voice of the Lord is in the thunder and the downpour. The voice of the Lord is heard above the waters . . . When the lightning flash has lit up the camp dining-hall, how feeble seems the light from the lamp. Thus do You, like lightning, unexpectedly light up my heart with flashes of intense joy.

In this sense, then, incorruptibility is the love of the Creator discerned in His creation. And as such, it is the antidote to depression's hatred of creation. The experience of incorruption is the experience of joy: which is what the tour-bus driver experienced that August day at Holy Trinity monastery church, in the presence of St. Sergius—experienced so directly that he chose to be baptized that day and to take the name of Sergius as his own name.[52]

In the final section of her poem, Jane Kenyon describes an extraordinary experience. Here is the section, entitled "Wood Thrush":

> High on Nardil and June light
> I wake at four,
> waiting greedily for the first
> notes of the wood thrush. Easeful air

presses through the screen
with the wild, complex song
of the bird, and I am overcome
by ordinary contentment.
What hurt me so terribly
all my life until this moment?
How I love the small, swiftly
beating heart of the bird
singing in the great maples;
its bright, unequivocal eye.

Kenyon is here "overcome / by ordinary contentment," an entry into joy. This "wild, complex song" of the thrush presses through the screen as direct counterpoint to depression "pressing / the bile of desolation into every pore." The result is for her an onrush of joyful love for the singing bird. And in loving completely this song, Kenyon also loves the whole of creation: suddenly and entirely loves. This love is what Orthodox ascetic teaching understands to be our one right relation to the natural world: the action of a merciful heart.

Similarly, in another recent poem by another New England poet—the long poem "Phases," by poet Sydney Lea (published in 2000)—we read these extraordinary lines:

Praise Zoloft, bringing back not only moon but also ambient woods
    and bird sound, such as the nesting raven's cluck-cry
        today, which for guests I identified, happy I hadn't forgot.
One pill a day regives, in brief, a nerve that once governed this my life,
    so that I don't sit fat in the fat corner chair in dull regard of limbs
        refusing to move, nor willfully stop the lift of these eyes
            when firstest brisk wind of firstest autumn slams
Hard down on the pond, the ragged white pine hedge, while just overhead
    a fish hawk hen fights hard to gather yards of hurtled air and then
        plunges entirely and thrillingly true to her target in water
            —trout or dace—with a fractional adjustment of wing.[53]

In these lines, Sydney Lea finds beautifully the love of the created world, a love as exact and passionate and powerful as the dive of the fish hawk he here sees and perfectly articulates. Again, this is the action of the merciful heart: a tiny, fractional adjustment of the whole way of going.

The seventh-century writer St. Isaac the Syrian composed a collection of essays entitled *The Ascetical Homilies*. This book has played an important part in Orthodox teaching for thirteen centuries, and Dostoevsky considered it to be his greatest spiritual teacher. In Homily 71, St. Isaac asks the question, What is a merciful heart? and then he answers: "It is the heart burning for the sake of the entire creation, for men, for birds, for animals, . . . and for every created thing" (344–45).

In "Wood Thrush," Kenyon experiences precisely this action of the merciful heart, moved by love for the bird's complex song, its "swiftly / beating heart," and "its bright, unequivocal eye." The eye is unequivocal in the sense that its brightness is entirely uncorrupted by the "bile of desolation" that is depression. And her merciful love is so vivid that she achieves full participation in this bird's song and brightness. The depression is transfigured.

Now it is essential that she is at this moment "High on Nardil" as well as on "June light." The previous section begins: "Pharmaceutical wonders are at work." Yet, she says, "I believe only in this moment / of well-being." She *chooses* the reality of what she calls "ordinary contentment" at the very moment she knows her capacity to choose that reality is a gift she is being given, in part by the drugs and the doctors as instrumentalities she does not herself command. In this sense, the Nardil signals the cessation of a certain self-will and the beginning of genuine joy. It is not that the drugs are God for her. Rather, the drugs are restoring her ability to choose the reality of God's creation. And the gift that is given her is therefore not the Nardil but the thrush's "wild, complex song" and her great joy. In this way, then, she is here re-articulating what the psalmist says in the final line of our stanza: "I have run the way of thy commandments / When thou didst enlarge my heart" (Ps 118:32). This is not a drug effect but a genuine experience. And depression is transformed by what St. Isaac calls "the strong and vehement mercy which grips [the] heart."

In Homily 71, shortly after he asks and answers the question, What is a merciful heart? St. Isaac the Syrian asks, How can man acquire humility? He answers his question this way:

> By unceasing remembrance of transgressions; by anticipation of oncoming death; by inexpensive clothing; by always preferring the last place; by always running to do the tasks that are the most insignificant and disdainful; by not being disobedient; by unceasing silence; by dislike of gatherings; by desiring to be unknown and of no account; by never possessing anything at all through self-will; by shunning conversation with numerous persons; by abhorrence of material gain; and after these things, by raising the mind above the reproach and accusation of every man and above zealotry; by not being a man whose hand is against everyone and against whom is everyone's hand, but rather one who remains alone, occupied with his own affairs; by having no concern for anyone in the world save himself. But in brief: exile, poverty, and a solitary life give birth to humility and cleanse the heart. (345)

Many of these phrases of St. Isaac's perfectly summarize much of the content of Kenyon's poem. She, too, remembers unceasingly her crimes against love that the demon Melancholy has provoked in her; she, too, anticipates death, over and over; she, too, shuns gatherings and conversations; she, too, focuses solely on herself. It seems as though St. Isaac's practice of humility resembles very much Kenyon's effects of depression. "Exile, poverty, and a solitary life": Are these actively to be sought as the way to cleanse our hearts, or are these the devastating effects of "the bile of desolation"? Is St. Isaac's humility a proven way of spiritual wisdom, or is it a guaranteed recipe for clinical depression?

It is in the light of these questions that I want to reflect on St. Isaac's extraordinary Homily 14. Here is the text in its entirety:

> I shall tell you something, and do not laugh, for I speak the truth; neither doubt my words, for they who have handed them

down to me are true. Though you should suspend yourself by
your eyelids before God, do not think you have attained to
anything by the manner of life which you lead until you have
attained to tears. For until then, your hidden self is in the service
of the world; that is, you are leading the life of those who dwell
in the world, and do the work of God with the outward man.
But the inward man is still without fruit, for his fruit begins with
tears.

When you attain to the region of tears, then know that your
mind has left the prison of this world and has set its foot on the
roadway of the new age, and has begun to breathe that other air,
new and wonderful. And at the same moment it begins to shed
tears, since the birth pangs of the spiritual infant are at hand. For
grace, the common mother of all, makes haste mystically to give
birth in the soul to the Divine image for the light of the age to
come. But when the time of its delivery is arrived, simultaneously
the mind begins to be stirred by something of that other age, just
like the subtle breath the babe draws inside the body wherein it
is nurtured. And since the mind cannot bear what is not usual for
it, it suddenly begins to set the body to wail, a wailing mingled
with the sweetness of honey. And as much as the inward babe
is raised, by just so much is there an increase in tears. But this
order of tears, the one of which I have been speaking, is not
the one that also at intervals comes over hesychasts. Because
this consolation, which appears from time to time, is every
man's who dwells in stillness with God. Sometimes it comes to
him when he finds himself in the divine vision of his mind, and
sometimes through the words of the Scriptures, and sometimes
in the converse of prayer. But I am rather speaking of that order
which belongs to him who sheds tears unceasingly both night
and day.

Whoever has found the reality of these things truly and
accurately has found it in stillness. The eyes of such a man
become like fountains of water for two years' time or even
more (that is, during the time of transition: I mean, of mystical

transition). But afterwards he enters into peace of thought; and from this peace of thought he enters into the rest of which Saint Paul has spoken, only in part, however, and to the extent that nature can contain it. From that peaceful rest his intellect begins to behold mysteries. And thereupon the Holy Spirit begins to reveal heavenly things to him, and God dwells within him, and raises up the fruit of the Spirit in him. And from this he perceives, dimly somehow, and in a figure, as it were, the change nature is going to receive at the renewal of all things.

These things I have written down as a reminder and source of profit for myself, and for every man who comes upon this book, according to what I have understood from both the divine vision of the Scriptures and from true mouths, and a little from experience itself, in order that they might be a help to me through the prayers of those who are profited by them. For I have taken no little trouble to set these things down.

But again, hear also what I am about to tell you; it is something I learned from a mouth that does not lie. When you enter into that region which is peace of the thoughts, then the multitude of tears is taken away from you, and afterwards tears come to you in due measure and at the appropriate time. This is, in all exactness, the truth of the matter as told in brief, and it is believed by the whole Church and by Her eminent men and front-line warriors. (82–83)

Isaac is very clear. The one "who sheds tears unceasingly both night and day" is the one whose "mind has left the prison of this world and has set its foot on the roadway of the new age, and has begun to breathe that other air, new and wonderful." In Homily 37, Isaac says this: "So let us entreat the Lord with an unrelenting mind to grant us mourning. For if we are granted this free grace, which is more excellent and surpasses every other gift, then with its help we shall enter into purity" (178). Mourning is a grace that "surpasses every other gift." And in this way, Homily 14 can be seen as an extended commentary on the line in the Beatitudes: "Blessed are those who mourn, for they shall be comforted" (Matt 5:4)—that is: Those who shed tears unceasingly shall be given the Comforter, the Holy Spirit.

So again the great question arises. How can this condition of constant tears that Isaac describes as greatly blessed be distinguished plainly from what we call extreme depression? A response can be found in a single sentence midway in Homily 14: "Whoever has found the reality of these things truly and accurately has found it in stillness" (83). For Isaac—and, indeed, for all Eastern Orthodox ascetic teaching—stillness can be defined as the voluntary practice of separating oneself from every anxiety, both one's own and others'. Now, as one astute recent commentator on Isaac says: "The state of stillness of mind is not acquired by human effort but is a gift." Isaac says: "No one is so stupid as to want to find this by means of struggle and the strength of his own will; for this is the gift of the revelation to the intellect, and it is not . . . a matter of the will." [54] And yet—here is the key—you must be attentive, even expectant, that the gift of stillness truly exists in God's hands and that He greatly wishes to give it to you. You cannot *will* the gift of stillness. But you must choose actively to await its giving.

And here is where Jane Kenyon's lovely poem can shed light for us. As I noted earlier, the drugs she takes are *not* God for her. Instead, they restore her ability to *choose* the reality of God's creation. What Isaac says about the gift of stillness, so, too, Jane Kenyon is saying about "the first / notes of the wood thrush [and its] wild, complex song": you cannot *will* the song, but you can most assuredly choose to await eagerly—her word is "greedily"— the gift of that song. To paraphrase the psalmist in line 32 from Psalm 118: You, O Lord, have enlarged my heart so that I may then choose to go on the paths You commanded for me. "I have chosen the way of truth," the psalmist says in line 30. *I* have chosen the way; but the way lies in obedience to God.

Just so for Isaac: stillness is a gift that is actively, indeed urgently, sought for. Thus, both our seeking the gift and God's giving of it may be best seen as the dance of relationship that is the life of prayer.

The way such a life of prayer always takes, Isaac says, is the way of humility. In Homily 71, Isaac vividly describes what a life of humility actually looks like—a description that seems to resemble what we might call a life of depression:

Humility is accompanied by modesty and self-collectedness;
that is, chastity of the senses; a moderated voice; mean speech;

self-belittlement; poor raiment; a gait that is not pompous; a gaze directed toward the earth; superabundant mercy; easily flowing tears; a solitary soul; a contrite heart; imperturbability to anger; undistracted senses; few possessions; moderation in every need; endurance; patience; fearlessness; manliness of heart born of a hatred for this temporal life; patient endurance of trials; deliberations that are ponderous, not light; extinction of thoughts; guarding of the mysteries of chastity; modesty; reverence; and above all, continually to be still and always to claim ignorance. (349)

Yet, what distinguishes this description of humility from clinical depression? What Isaac's ceaseless crying plainly implies is that such tears—when connected to the incorrupt—are completely blessed.

In this light, then, let us return once more to Isaac's central metaphor in Homily 14. When the tears start in us, our spiritual infancy begins. Then as we begin to grow spiritually, our tears increase; and when we become fully mature, our tears will flow without ceasing "for [in Isaac's words] two years' time or even more" (14:83). Finally, he says, we "enter into that region which is peace of the thoughts, . . . and afterwards tears come . . . in due measure" (ibid.).

The child grows up, and yet the adult always remembers the child he or she once was and always will be; and this adult memory is best understood as the full understanding of the child. Two movements may thus be discerned in Isaac's metaphor. The first is the movement from beginning tears to recurrent weeping and then to ceaseless crying, and then finally to measured tears. The second movement is from infancy to adolescence and then adulthood, and finally to fullest maturity. What holds these two movements in a single focus is memory and prophecy. That is, what remains as a kind of visual memory in the face of someone even extremely old is the face of the child she or he once was. Just so, you can see very plainly even in a small infant's face the image and shape of that face's fullest maturity. The elderly face recalls vividly the child; and the childish face prophesies clearly the elderly face. Memory and prophecy together focus for us an icon of what never corrupts—the permanent person.

In this way, then, the infant's first tears of (in Isaac's words) "wailing mingled with the sweetness of honey" prophesy both the ceaseless tears of spiritual maturity and the proportionate tears of the fully purified heart. Thus, though they plainly differ—and Isaac notes the difference in many passages—these two orders of tears are often seen by him as two sides of the same reality. As Metropolitan Alfeyev says in his book on Isaac: "Isaac does not always distinguish between the bitter tears of repentance and the sweet tears of compunction. The two types of tears are as two sides of a single coin, two aspects of one and the same experience" (142). This single coin, this one experience, constitutes what I am here calling the icon of the incorrupt.

In the stanza from Psalm 118 that we began with, the psalmic "I" defers to the divine "thou" in a sustained gracefulness of call/response, counter-call/counter-response. And as I said, this gracefulness seeks always to incarnate the divine and to deify the human. In the entire 176 lines of this immense psalm, only the first four lines do *not* have both "I" and "thou" actively present: for this grace of relationship between the human and the divine is the whole poem's clear pattern. The significance of this pattern is, at every moment, equally clear: the pattern teaches us the way of stillness. The way in which the psalm accomplishes this can be best suggested by noting this: what instantly unmakes in us any practice of stillness we may attempt is the way our minds *cling to*—and incessantly replay—our resentments and angers and grievances, imagined or real. The pattern of relationship that every stanza of the twenty-two in this poem sustains, directly teaches the way to surrender our mind's clinging to its angers and resentments. And once again: we can enter into that dance of blessedness *only* when we voluntarily choose to walk in the law of the Lord, to search more deeply into His testimonies, and to seek Him with our whole heart.

In the first stanza of Psalm 118, the psalmist says: "I shall keep Thy statutes, / Do not utterly forsake me" (l. 8). Now, as we move through the 176 lines of this poem, we see affirmed the truth that God never has and never will utterly abandon anyone, *never.* He is always moving toward us in every way possible. What is necessary is that we move also and always toward Him. In this eighth line, the psalmist promises to keep God's statutes, then he turns toward God in prayer: "Do not utterly forsake me." But God has not forsaken him, nor will He; yet the psalmist must take his own step in the dance—keeping God's statutes, turning to God in prayer—in order to meet God already coming toward him, not forsaking him, never having forsaken him. Watch now how the pattern of the dance moves through these lines:

> Blessed art thou, O Lord,
> Teach me thy statutes. (l. 12)
> I am a stranger on the earth,
> Hide not thy commandments from me. (l. 19)
> My soul lies prostrate on the earth,
> Quicken me according to thy word. (l. 25)
> I declared my ways, and thou didst hear me,
> Teach me thy statutes. (l. 26)
> My soul has fainted from depression,
> Strengthen me with thy words. (l. 28)
> I have clung to thy testimonies,
> O Lord, put me not to shame. (l. 31)
> Behold, I have longed for thy commandments,
> Quicken me in thy righteousness. (l. 40)

This pattern by no means exhausts what is going on in this complex psalm, but it defines a basic step in the psalmist's relation with God. We move in our lives, we turn that movement toward God, we enter into intimate relation with Him through prayer, and we find that He is always already moving toward us to carry us up into His dance of salvation. But we must make these first movements ourselves in order to know and experience this. It is not enough to remain prostrate on the ground, fainted from depression, alien on the earth, or even to cling to His testimonies or long for His commandments; we must take the next step of inviting Him into intimate relationship with us through prayer. And when we do, we find ourselves already quickened, strengthened, taught. (It is for this reason that the Orthodox Church sings and chants so much of its liturgy antiphonally—two voices each calling out to and answering the other; or the priest's prayer alternating with the "Lord have mercy" of the people—to remind us of the dance in which we move in partnership, call-and-response, with God.)

In the same way, our depression can move into the dance with God's wisdom. Whenever we can turn our tears of depression toward God—or our anger or fear or even our joy; indeed, all that we do or think or feel or say— then we meet Him coming toward us in mercy, in teaching, in opening our eyes, in gracious judgment, in quickening, in strengthening, in enlarging our hearts, in bestowing wisdom and hope and genuine stillness. And then our self-pitying tears of depression—that is, tears not yet penitential and still far from compunctionate—can begin to become our penitential tears of the dance.

In the tradition of the Orthodox Church, this turning toward God is called in Greek *metanoia*, which means the turning-around of consciousness, translated in English by the word *repentance*. We turn to face God, right where we are, even in the midst of our tears of pain and self-pity, and He receives us into His dance and transfigures us. But if we seek to do the dance by ourselves, without Him—seeking not His glory but our own; seeking happiness, success, love, creative inspiration, whatever our ruling passion may be, rather than God—we will find ourselves in a solo dance that God cannot enter, because He has made us free and He will not invade our dance unless we will it. It is instead we who must turn and invite Him into our dance, and by so doing we enter into His—which is never solo, always growing in beauty and grace. Whereas ours alone is a dance of entropy eventually sinking into deep depression and death.

And so we can say this: even in the depths of our depression—in Jane Kenyon's words, that "bile of desolation" that presses into every pore—God never abandons us. For our depression can indeed offer us a look-alike for the ascetical life, that icon that can lead us to the stillness of wisdom. It is perhaps even a gift given to remind us to seek God and to show us something of the blessed life that willingly seeks the lowest places and finds the King of Glory revealed on the Cross. For even in the blackest depression, we need only turn around, not looking for a way out into happiness, but, instead, seeking always God, the divine Creator who awaits always our invitation so that He may dance with us. And only the slightest turn in the darkness brings us very close to Him—a turn much slighter indeed than the one we must make from the pinnacle of self-willed self-empowerment and the admiring applause of others.

■　■　■

I want to say something further about this resemblance between depression and the ascetical life before I end, lest we make too much of it; for it is clear that something altogether different motivates the ascetical life. When Isaac urges us to flee all associations (see Homily 44), to renounce the world and take to the desert in solitary existence—when he tells us over and over to have "no concern for anyone in the world save [ourself]" (71:345)—he is telling us to disentangle our minds and to set free our hearts from the restless turmoil of unstill resentments on which depression dwells. Only a brief scan of words and phrases of unstillness in Psalm 118 is enough to unmask the reality of the depressive eye: "workers of iniquity," "be ashamed," "the proudly arrogant that reject thy commandments," "the unjust way," "sinners have ensnared me with cords," "reproach and contempt," "shame," "endless desirings," "my scorn," "those who taunt me," "I was humbled, I transgressed," "disgraced," "I am shriveled like a wineskin," "my tormentors." They are the merest accentuating of one small piece of the great dance, and hence a terrible distortion of it. But this is exactly how depression works, and still the dance goes on. The only way the immense freedom of the ascetic way—the way of stillness—can come to us is by our willingly entering into the dance of divine relation that Psalm 118 so magnificently describes, neither discounting the dark places (for there we will meet God if we look for Him) nor dwelling in them.

In early August 1992, I was hosting a poetry reading at The Robert Frost Place in Franconia, New Hampshire. Jane Kenyon was the reader, and she read that night for the first time in public the not-yet-published "Having It Out with Melancholy." When she began the second section, "Bottles," she had to stop after the first four or five names—"Elavil, Ludiomil, Doxepin, / Norpramin, Prozac"—because she was weeping and could not continue, and we—seventy or so of us—waited the long minute or more of silence, and then she went on. After the reading she asked me, "Why was it just the *names* that so upset me?" Ten summers ago I did not know what to answer. But I now say this: Your tears, dear friend, are blessed tears of repentance, the tears of someone engaged in turning away from every unstillness, every false hope, and turning entirely to God. Later that summer, when I visited her and her husband, Donald Hall, at their home, Jane would weep easily for the sufferings of others, almost never for her own. She was, I now understand, entering into a wondrous dance with God.

Thus, even in Psalm 87—in what is perhaps the darkest of all psalms—when the psalmist cries out—"Why, O Lord, dost thou cast away my soul? Why turnest thou thy face from me?" (l. 14)—and when (as Jane Kenyon also does) he tells us that he has been "poor and troubled since childhood" (l. 15) by unceasing misery: even so, he says, "in the morning my prayer shall draw very near to thee" (l. 13). In Psalm 118's final line, the psalmist says to God:

> I have gone astray like a lost sheep,
> Seek out thy servant,
> I have never forgotten thy commandments.

And thus the dance is sustained.

In the very affliction's depths can be opened the way to the great blessing: here is the central fact about depression that we must never forget, that we must always re-grasp more deeply and fully. For the depression is—*can be, must be*—a call into the dance that God wishes most ardently for us. *This does not mean that when we answer that call the depression will go away, or even that the drugs we take to survive it or protect others from it can or should be thrown out.* Indeed, in the sense that the ascetic way described by St. Isaac—the way of withdrawal from the marketplace, remembrance of one's own transgressions, anticipation of oncoming death, preferring the last and lowest place, desiring to be unknown and of no account, abhorring material gain—in the sense that this way is the true face of depression and the way into relationship with God, then we *must* not abandon it.

Our release from the suffering of depression can bring an enlargement of the heart toward God as described in Psalm 118. It can also bring renewed creativity, expansion, and joviality—or that modern cure-all, self-esteem. If we run free and heedless in celebration of our liberation (which is a very different thing from gratitude, because here we quickly forget that the return of joy has been a gift), we risk losing all that we might have gained through our suffering. This is why Christ always told those He healed not to shout their blessing from the rooftops but instead to return to the Temple and quietly offer thanks.

A great modern saint, Silouan of Athos, has put this very simply: "Keep your mind in hell, and do not despair."[55] In this way, in time, our engagement with hell, in the form of depression, will most certainly be transfigured and blessed, and it will become the very way by which we enter into transfiguration and blessing. St. Silouan says in another place: "It is impossible to escape tribulation in this world, but the man who is given over to the will of God bears tribulation easily, seeing it but putting his trust in the Lord, and so his tribulations pass." And he prays, "O Lord, grant me tears to shed for myself, and for the whole universe," explaining that "the man who has learned love from the Holy Spirit sorrows all his life over those who are not saved, and sheds abundant tears for the people, and the grace of God gives him strength to love his enemies."[56]

Here, then, is my concluding point: If you would transfigure all your depression into the way of all wisdom, you would do very well to study and love Isaac's *Ascetical Homilies* as you pray and love without ceasing the great and wondrous 118th psalm. Our right relation to the Creator and to all the creation may well depend on doing just this.

PART TWO

Orthodox Poetics and the Great Psalm

The Septuagint (LXX) is the oldest Greek translation of a lost Hebrew text of what Christians call the Old Testament.[57] Tradition has it that seventy-two scholars, six from each of the twelve tribes of Israel, were assembled by the Pharaoh Ptolemy in Alexandria sometime in the second or third century BC to produce a Greek version of the Hebrew Scriptures, Greek being at that time the *lingua franca* of the empire, and Hebrew dying out. They worked for forty days, the legend goes, in separate tents, producing in the end a translation that agreed in every word. It is called the translation of the Seventy (hence LXX).

Following the destruction of Jerusalem in 70 AD, all Hebrew texts were lost, until, much later (between the seventh and tenth centuries), the Masoretes assembled what had survived and, combined with oral tradition, refashioned a Hebrew Bible (*Tanakh*). It is this Masoretic text that most English Bibles are based on, while the Greek Septuagint represents a considerably older tradition. My Hebrew teacher at Dartmouth College, visiting from Hebrew University in Jerusalem, told me once that, "Of course we correct the Hebrew from the Greek."

My many years as a university teacher of both ancient and modern lyric poetry, along with my work of reading, writing, and translating poetry—both privately and professionally—guided me in my Psalms translation to see that each psalm in the Psalter possessed a unique *cadential shape* in every line as well as in each whole poem. I soon discovered something of what Mother Maria had found in translating the Hebrew Psalter: that every psalm has a unique face; that is, each psalm possesses something very like personhood.[58] I found the lexical meanings of the Greek words would therefore illumine the musical shape of my translation just as the English cadences would help reveal to me more fully the Greek meanings.

I also consulted the Hebrew text in working on the Greek, thereby gaining a growing awareness of and insight into the remarkable achievement of the LXX translators. For in measuring the arc from Biblical Hebrew to LXX Greek—from, for example, the rich, oceanic, grandeur of sonic movement in the Hebrew to the light, almost balletic, grace of movement in the Greek—I understood more clearly the relational work every translation must accomplish. I saw that the Hebrew was, at every moment, being uprooted and replanted by and in the Greek, at once completely changing the living personhood of every psalm and yet truly deepening that personhood. It was being completely changed in the sense that any plant is changed by being uprooted from the soil where it has grown to fruitfulness. Yet this very same Hebrew personhood was being truly deepened in the sense that the psalm's unique shape was unalterably recognizable in the new Greek soil.

I thus came to see the relational reality of the LXX psalms. The Greek was simultaneously giving itself wholly to the Hebrew at the same moment—and at the same depth—it was reconfiguring the Hebrew in and as LXX Greek. It was breathtaking to behold. I would find myself altering a word—very often a syllable—of my English to reflect more fully something of the relational reality existing between LXX Greek and Biblical Hebrew.

Hence, my constant hope was that my work on English cadential shape and Greek lexical meaning would help bring my versions closer to the beautiful soil wherein the LXX translators had established that living relationship between their psalms and the Hebrew originals, thereby giving richer shape and deeper meaning to my English. Such was my deepest hope for my translation; such, indeed, was my prayer.[59]

■   ■   ■

In making our approach to the subject of psalmic poetics, three points are important at the outset: First, psalmic poetics are aural and oral—in the ear and mouth—sung (chanted), not silently read. Second, psalmic poetics are communal, holding the meaning of the entire Israelite community. Third, psalmic poetics are actions of blessedness, actions that secure whole communities from demonic human violence: "God is . . . working salvation in the midst of the earth" (Ps 73:12). I once read a story about a Polish village during World War II in which an old man chanted psalms continuously. For some reason the German army had never touched that village, though others all around it fell. Then the man died and that night the village priest learned from an angel in a dream that the village had been spared because of the old man's prayer. The following day the Germans invaded the village.

Rabbinic scholars—and Eastern Orthodox Christendom—agree with rock-solid assurance that David is the author of all 150 psalms. At the same moment, they also concur that ten other poets are present in the Psalter. Taken together, these two assurances are, to our eyes, meaningless and (possibly) delusory; at the very least, they are disturbing. But all Hebrew poetics is founded upon these two assurances: *How?* How can unified authorship be understood in terms of eleven distinct names?

The answer is, of course, prophecy. Psalmic poetics everywhere assumes the literal reality of the prophetic mode. In this mode, what we might call the creative personality is permeable to other voices, especially angelic and divine voices. And this prophetic permeability is essential to the multiple yet unitary poet of the Psalms: this poet is at once David *and* the other ten: a permeability that simultaneously keeps the ten poets firmly distinct from and yet deeply related to the one poet, David, and all of them to the one Poet (Gr. *Poietes*, "Maker") of poets and of all Creation.

A related point is that psalmic poetics everywhere presupposes the active reality of distinct yet related *voices*: the voices of the psalmists (at once David's and another of the ten poets) and the divine voice of God. The shape each psalm takes, then, is determined by the action of voices. That is, each verse sentence in every psalm follows the rhythms of the actual speaking voice; and the sense of syntactic shape arises directly from these spoken rhythms.

My experience in praying the Psalms may be understood, then, as an experience in shape. For what both Rabbinic and Eastern Orthodox writers say is that a life in the Psalms means, first of all, a life given entirely *into* the text of the Psalms: into the very words and voices and events of the poems. And the unceasing substance of this experience is indeed *shape*. Here, for example, is Psalm 97:5 (98:5 in Hebrew numbering), first in transliterated Hebrew:

> *Zammeru lihvoh bekinnor, bekinnor vekol zemirah*

The sonic shape here is densely interwoven. The first and final sounds rhyme exactly, being forms of the same word, while the second and penultimate words—*lihvoh* and *vekol*—neatly reverse their sonic sequences at the same time they semantically "rhyme" reversely (*lihvoh* is God's voice, *vekol* is the psalmist's voice). The middle pair of words is the exactly identical prepositional phrase. So tightly woven are the sonic patterns these six words make that any attempt to translate them to another language is an exercise in despairing loss.

Now look at the Septuagint Greek:

> ψάλατε τῷ Κυρίῳ ἐν κιθάρᾳ ἐν κιθάρᾳ καὶ φωνῇ ψαλμοῦ
> *psalate to Kyrio en kithara, en kithara kai phone psalmou*

I have translated the line from Greek this way:

> Sing psalms to the Lord on a lyre, on a lyre and in psalmic voice

Note, first, how exactly the Greek word sequence follows the Hebrew. Here is the primary quality of the LXX: its willingness to give itself entirely over to the Hebrew, producing a syntactic movement that is more Hebraic than it is Hellenic (especially Classical). This Greek rhythmic shape transforms—

perhaps better: transfigures—Hebrew rhythm in that it makes the Hebrew's rhythm—a rhythm like quiet waves slowly coming onto a beach, then slowly withdrawing—into a sonic shape that is quick, light, and balletic. This Greek shape is very beautiful in its performance, at once deferentially attentive to the Hebrew and fully alert to its own inner movement. Yet—and here's the point—the Greek loses nearly all the Hebrew sonic density by (as it were) "freezing" the Hebrew movement in speech the same way we can say that a dancer "freezes" the ocean when she or he is dancing oceanically.

The *inevitability* of such devastating losses—that is, the fact that LXX Greek can move in no other way than it does; nor can the English—creates what might best be called the cadential necessity of psalmic shape. That is, the Greek *must* transfigure the Hebrew cadence, fully attentive to the Hebrew dance while *simultaneously* affirming its own way of moving: and in this simultaneous attentiveness, the Greek establishes a duality of cadential shape. And this cadential duality of translation both parallels the Hebrew original's multiplicity of voices and exactly translates that multiplicity. For, just as in every psalm David is at once fully distinct from yet deeply related to one of the ten psalmic poets, so, too, in every psalm, the sonic shape of each verse-sentence simultaneously, in every translation, arises from its own linguistic ground and is also rooted in the rich soil of Biblical Hebrew. This duality of cadential shape forms the basis of all psalmic poetics, in Hebrew, in Greek, and in all other languages.

It is in this light of cadential duality that I want to discuss (briefly) Psalm 87, the darkest psalm in the entire Psalter.

1 O Lord God of my salvation, I have cried out day and night before thee.

2 Let my prayer come before thee; incline thine ear, O Lord, to my supplication.

3 For my soul was filled with troubles and my life drew close to Hades.

4 I am counted among those who go down into the pit, like a man no one would help, like a man free among the dead,

5 Like mangled men lying in graves whom thou rememberest no more, like those snatched from thy hand.

6 They have laid me in the lowest pit, in dark places, in death's shadow.

7 Thy wrath leaned heavy on me, thy waves all crashed down on me.

8   My friends thou hast taken from me, I was made loathsome to them; betrayed, I could not escape.

9   My eye weakened with great poverty, O Lord, all day I cried out to thee, to thee I stretched out my hands.

10 Wilt thou work miracles for the dead? Can physicians really resurrect them to proclaim thy praises to thee? *Selah*

11 Shall anyone in the grave give an account of thy mercy? Or thy truthfulness in a ruined place?

12 Shall thy wonders be known in the dark? Thy righteousness in oblivion's land?

13 But I, O Lord, I cried out to thee, and in the morning my prayer shall draw very near to thee.

14 Why, O Lord, dost thou cast away my soul? Why turnest thou thy face from me?

15 I am poor and troubled since childhood; briefly raised up, I was brought down into the depths of bewilderment.

16 Thy furies have swept through me, thy terrors have utterly unmade me,

17 Swirling around me daily like waters, surrounding me from every side.

18 Thou hast taken loved ones and friends far from me, even anyone who knew me, because of my misery.

I offer two points here about this psalm. First, terrible affliction (here: massive depression; Heb. *Sheol*, the pit) is understood as directly given by God. Second, one can become more directly intimate with God *through* the affliction (l. 13): "my prayer shall draw very near to thee." Yet, this drawing-near *does not lift* the affliction; if anything, it deepens it. Thus, Psalm 87 can be seen as a poem of deepest courage: the courage to enter the darkest places of earth—and, there, to suffer the abandonment that draws you closer and closer to God as the experience of His fury and terror utterly unmakes you.

Psalmic courage is therefore profoundly dual in operation: for courage draws you into the very intimacy that will unmake you in the same way that all psalmic poetics are grounded in two languages at once. The Hebrew unmakes every translation; yet every translation since LXX Greek is drawn into that intimacy. Every translator of Psalms therefore comes, at some point, to discover what can be called candlelight courage: that late night moment when you see and hear (and touch and taste and smell) the Hebrew voices—and are unmade by them at the moment you are drawn to them, like moths hurrying toward their fiery deaths by candlelight.

■   ■   ■

A great question now opens before us. How are we to understand the spiritual significance of psalmic technique? Or—to put the same question another way— how does the mind of the psalmist or the reader of Psalms become through Psalms the mind of Christ?[60] It is a process with three dimensions. The first is *chiastic patterning*. Fr. John Breck's seminal book *The Shape of Biblical Language* elucidates chiastic structures in biblical texts in ways both richly significant and immediately comprehensible. Chiasmus, says Breck, is that pattern which trains us "to read from the center outward and from the extremities toward the center."[61] So deep and widespread is the use of this pattern in all ancient literary cultures, Breck continues, that "writers in antiquity drew upon it almost instinctively" (*Shape*, 34). Perhaps Breck's greatest insight into biblical chiastic pattern is his discussion of the pattern's double movement: (1) the movement from the passage's midpoint forward and back to its two extremities (i.e., its first and final lines), combined with (2) the movement from the passage's narrative start to its narrative conclusion. When these two movements are combined, the result is a situation wherein the forward narrative movement constantly *doubles back* to earlier points— but always at a higher, more intense, and more comprehensive point. Yet each doubling back is necessarily *moving away* from the passage's midpoint; hence, each doubling back can be seen to *ascend* from this midpoint. Equally, and at the same time, the movement toward this midpoint can be seen to *descend* toward it. These two distinct movements thus interlock and cohere.

Chiastic patterning in turn shapes and is shaped by the *experience of antinomy*. Antinomy is the experience of disjunction. It is the experience wherein human discursive rationality breaks helplessly apart in the face of—better, *in the teeth of*—dissonant, often harsh realities.[62] Such realities are the very ground of all biblical (indeed, all *human*) experience. The agony of forced exile is, at the same moment, the way of redemptive joy; the created world is simultaneously completely good, completely fallen, and completely redeemed; Christ is at once fully divine and fully human. There is no direct way wherein human rationality alone can reconcile the disjunctive elements in these experiences; equally, there is no way whereby any element can be eliminated without radically falsifying the experience. Our fallen reason simply breaks down when it directly confronts such antinomies as these. And chiastic pattern in the Psalms is thus the literary structure that most perfectly fits the experience of antinomy, for the contrastive structure firmly and directly holds all of antinomy's jarring contradictions.[63]

But psalmic antinomy has a deeper significance: it contains its own reconciliations. The mind of David is continually broken on the reefs of all the world's most dreadful antinomies. Psalm 87 says: "Thy furies have swept through me, thy terrors have utterly unmade me" (l. 16). I am overwhelmed with terror and fury; and yet I am blessed, because God—the "God of my salvation" (l. 1)—is Himself steering the agony: *"thy* furies" and *"thy* terrors." What merely human rationality could even survive, let alone master, such antinomy? The fallen reason thus breaks open. Yet once so broken—and it is broken in the action of every psalm—the mind of David can then be *lyricized by God*—enlarged, made new, illumined, by David's love for God and God's for him. Now, amidst the very brokenness, he can begin to sing that wholeness and healing which God Himself is singing: "O Lord, thou shalt open my lips and my mouth shall declare thy praise" (Ps 50:15). By singing the psalm, the Davidic mind heals itself and all the world.

The second dimension of psalmic technique arises from the first: the dimension of *blessedness*. St. Gregory of Nyssa sees the "aim of the entire Psalter in the first word of the Book of Psalms":[64] *"Blessed* is the man who walks not in the counsel of the ungodly." Each of the over sixty subsequent occurrences of the word in Psalms gathers in each prior experience, deepening and intensifying its significance as the antinomies grow sharper and more dire and the mind of the psalmist grows correspondingly more illumined. This way toward the experience of blessedness is beautifully registered in the longest psalm, LXX 118, which gives us in its first stanza: "I shall keep Thy statutes; do not utterly forsake me" (l. 8). For as we move through the poem, we see affirmed the truth that God never has and never will utterly abandon anyone, *never*. He is always moving toward us in every way possible. When we turn to face Him, right where we are, He receives us into His dance and transfigures us. This is blessednesss.

The third dimension of psalmic technique gathers in the first two and becomes their shared ground. For as the mind of David draws near to God, first in love and then in blessedness, psalmic technique then reveals its most perfective dimension: the dimension of *memory*. In its antinomical movements throughout the Psalter, the mind of David *remembers* and *is remembered by* the active presence of God. The fulfillment of all desires in the Psalms occurs always as perfect memory: "I shall never forget thy statutes, in them thou hast quickened me to life" (118:93). *To not forget God is to be given actual life.* In this way, memory may be best understood as the generative, or creative, principle of all psalmic thought.

▪ ▪ ▪

All of what we have said is preparation for our approach toward the Great Psalm, LXX 118, the perfect model of the way of union of the psalmist with

God. As we have seen,[65] the twenty-two alphabetically sequenced eight-line stanzas of Psalm 118 create a pattern of call and response between the psalmist and God, an antiphony between change and incorruption: the psalmist moves in his prayer always in relation to a structure that never corrupts or changes. He dances with God: the psalmist in the changing cadences of his love for God; God unchangeable in his love for the psalmist.

By way of entering into our analysis of the poetics of Psalm 118, let us look for a moment at how this dance moves and what its effects are. In nearly every line of Psalm 118—194 times—we find one or more of nine different words for divine law (all expressive of God's love): commandments, statutes, law, word, testimonies, teaching, judgments, way, and path (see Chapters I–III). Taken together, these nine words are an *entire system* of spiritual life-givingness that acts to transmit divine energies to the human person. This transmission of energies has two closely related consequences: First, it fulfills every human potential for achieving *blessedness* (the psalmic word for healing), and second, this achievement of blessedness leads to what is signified by the word *theosis* (full spiritual health, akin to sanctity).

I read recently, in an article about medical decision-making, that "classic literature in medical decision-making would have you believe that everyone [practicing medicine] generates a hypothesis and then follows a pathway with decision points . . . But no one really works that way."[66] What really occurs is this: a practitioner responds simultaneously—or fails to respond—to a complex set of actual and potential disintegrations and traumas. Hence, the healing response is one that is more spatial than temporal: that is, it is occurring on many fronts at once, each aspect or plane of the presenting disintegrative set touching—in ways that are often dynamically shifting at every instant—every other aspect in the set. Therefore, the healing response is best characterized as *asymmetrical*—moving this way here, that way there, following signals and guidelines sometimes vivid, at other times faint: signals and guidelines always only *faintly patterned* at any given instant. Thus, a decision at one moment is wholly reversed in the next, modified in a third moment, and then joined in a still newer shape to yet another decision: the whole set never once assuming a fixed or symmetrical pattern. This asymmetricality in the medical crisis is therefore always dynamic, possessing vivid aliveness in its disintegrative state. For this reason, then, the healing (or integrative) response to this asymmetricality must itself always sustain a dynamically comparable asymmetricality.

Continuing within the metaphor of this useful understanding, we can say that *theosis* is the integrative system of divine energies of Psalm 118's nine words that heals our own "complex set of actual and potential disintegrations and traumas." It is a system so deeply (i.e., divinely) patterned as to be, in our experience, dynamically asymmetrical in relation to us.

It is of great moment, therefore, to ask: Where in Psalm 118 does the greatest asymmetricality occur, signaling the integrative center of the poem? A central fact of the poem is that at every line the poem is "over" in the sense of completely having articulated everything about God's ways in the creation; yet every line is also adding to a continuously deeper and fuller revelation of God's ways in the creation. Thus, the Psalm at every moment is at once perfectly complete and always entering into a still greater perfection: the perfection of achieving pure *perfectiveness;* that is, the purity of state wherein the poem *brings about perfection in its readers*. It is always over and always ongoing.

This central antinomy sustains, at every moment, the poem's asymmetric-ality—and, at every moment, it bestows upon the poem the dynamism of that asymmetricality. That is, the antinomy of being simultaneously complete and incomplete—an antinomy in which neither the poem's completeness nor its incompleteness can ever diminish, abolish, or dominate the other—this antinomy is the engine that is being steadily fueled by the nine words. And the asymmetricality of the poem—that is, its ninefold healing response to the crisis of complex disintegration—establishes the poem's central (*Lamed* or twelfth) stanza, the first stanza in the poem's second half, as a fulcrum of all its meaning.[67]

> 89 Unto all eternity, O Lord,
> Thy word endures in heaven,
> 90 Thy truth unto generations of generations,
> Thou didst found the earth and it endures.
> 91 By thine ordering, each day endures,
> For all earthly things are thy servants.
> 92 If thy law had not been my meditation,
> I would have perished in my affliction.
> 93 I shall never forget thy statutes,
> In them thou hast quickened me to life.
> 94 I am thine, O Lord, save me,
> For I have sought thy statutes.
> 95 Sinners lurked for me to kill me,
> But I comprehended thy testimonies.
> 96 I have seen the limits of all achievements,
> But thy commandment is immensely spacious.

The stanza is one of the poem's least symmetrical in a number of ways: First, the poem's numerical halfway point is line 88, which concludes the previous stanza. However, the force of the *Lamed* stanza's pivotal role confers on its own turning point, line 93, the generative position in the whole poem; that is, this line is the heart of the stanza that is itself the heart of the poem, and it is therefore considered by the Orthodox to be Psalm 118's *mese* or midpoint.[68] Two further asymmetries in the stanza may be seen in lines 90 and 91, which interrupt the deep symmetry of the poem's otherwise unceasing use of the nine words by using none of them; and line 96, which uses the most frequently occurring word, *entolai* ("commandments"), in the singular form (a usage occurring only twice in the whole poem). The lines effect this interruption so as to emphasize that logically impossible fact that Psalm 118 is everywhere asserting: All earthly incarnation of the divine is raising all earthly things up, *and into*, direct participation in God through the asymmetry of His immeasurable love for us.

The key word in line 93—"statutes"—translates the LXX word *dikaiomata*, itself translating the Hebrew *piggudim*, "precepts," one of seven instances in Psalm 118 wherein the Hebrew "precepts" is being absorbed by the Greek "statutes" (see Chapters I and II below). The semantic significance of this absorption, as we will see, is that the specific acts of Hebrew obedience to the divine word (the "precepts") are, in the LXX, becoming incarnate as and in the divine patterns of the whole creation (the "statutes").[69] For you to "never forget" the statutes is to obey fully the divine patterns in and as the way of your own life.

As the human mind enters into unceasing meditation on God's law, it is slowly and deeply *transfigured* through its meditation into the very end of all its studies: the mind of God. And this transfiguration of the human mind is radically—and unchangeably—asymmetrical in that the divine mind immensely exceeds every human action of comprehension. And yet (and here is the great point) the divine mind is always and forever "quickening" the human mind into an unceasing aliveness: a quickening that never obliterates the human mind but is, instead, always deepening it into being always more fully alive: for this is the foundational asymmetry of God's love for us.

The asymmetry of the central stanza, then, focused in this central line—"I shall never forget thy statutes, / In them thou hast quickened me to life"—arises directly from the antinomy of the way wherein the divine "thou" and the human "I" approach and, in effect, enter into one another. As this central stanza "breaks" the Psalm's alphabetic symmetry, it opens deeply the way into psalmic poetics.

I give you now the Great Psalm.

THE GREAT PSALM
LXX Psalm 118[70]

Aleph

1 Blessed are the blameless in the way,
   Who walk in the law of the Lord.
2 Blessed be those searching his testimonies,
   Who seek him with the whole heart.
3 For the workers of iniquity
   Have never walked in his ways.
4 Thou hast charged that thy commandments
   Be kept most diligently.
5 O that my ways be all directed
   To the keeping of thy statutes.
6 Then I shall not be ashamed
   When I behold all thy commandments.
7 I shall praise thee with upright heart
   As I learn thy righteous judgments.
8 I shall keep thy statutes,
   Do not utterly forsake me.

Beth

9 How shall a young man make straight his way?
   In the keeping of thy words.
10 I have sought thee with my whole heart,
   Let me not stray from thy commandments.
11 In my heart I have hidden thy teachings,
   That I might not sin against thee.
12 Blessed art thou, O Lord,
   Teach me thy statutes.
13 With my lips I have declared
   All the judgments of thy mouth.
14 I delight in the way of thy testimonies
   As much as in every kind of wealth.
15 I shall deeply ponder thy commandments,
   I shall comprehend thy ways.
16 I shall meditate in thy statutes,
   I shall never forget thy words.

Gimel

17 Give thy servant this reward:
   That I shall live and keep thy words.

18 Take away the veil from my eyes
   That I may see the wonders in thy law.

19 I am a stranger on the earth,
   Hide not thy commandments from me.

20 My soul has always longed to desire
   Thy judgments at every moment.

21 Thou didst rebuke the proudly arrogant,
   Cursed be they that reject thy commandments.

22 Take from me reproach and contempt
   For I have sought thy testimonies.

23 For princes sat and spoke against me,
   But thy servant pondered on thy statutes.

24 Thy testimonies are my meditation,
   Thy statutes my counselors.

Daleth

25 My soul lies prostrate on the earth,
   Quicken me according to thy word.

26 I declared my ways, and thou didst hear me,
   Teach me thy statutes.

27 Make me comprehend the way of thy statutes,
   I shall ponder thy wondrous works.

28 My soul has fainted from depression,
   Strengthen me with thy words.

29 Put the unjust way far from me,
   With thy law have mercy on me.

30 I have chosen the way of truth,
   I have never forgotten thy judgments.

31 I have clung to thy testimonies,
   O Lord, put me not to shame.

32 I have run the way of thy commandments
   When thou didst enlarge my heart.

He

33 Give me as law, O Lord, the way of thy statutes,
   And I shall seek it out always.

34 Give me wisdom to search deeply thy law,
 I shall keep it with my whole heart.

35 Guide me on the path of thy commandments
 For I have desired this.

36 Incline my heart to thy testimonies
 And not to endless desirings.

37 Turn away my eyes from empty things,
 Quicken me to live in thy way.

38 Establish thy teaching in thy servant
 That I may be rooted in fear of thee.

39 Take away my scorn, which I dread,
 For thy judgments are gracious.

40 Behold, I have longed for thy commandments,
 Quicken me in thy righteousness.

Waw

41 Let thy mercy, O Lord, come upon me,
 Thy salvation according to thy teaching.

42 I shall answer those who taunt me,
 For I have hoped on thy words.

43 Take not the word of truth
 Completely from my mouth
 For I have hoped in thy judgments.

44 So I shall keep forever thy law,
 Always and unto ages of ages.

45 I kept on walking in spaciousness,
 For I sought always thy commandments.

46 I kept on speaking of thy testimonies
 Even to kings, never once ashamed.

47 I kept on meditating in thy commandments
 For I have deeply loved them.

48 With upraised hands, I loved thy commandments,
 And I kept on pondering thy statutes.

Zayin

49 Remember thy word to thy servant
 By which thou hast given me hope.

50 This comforted me in my affliction
 For thy teaching has given me life.

51 The arrogant have greatly transgressed,
    But I have never swerved from thy law.

52 I remember thine eternal judgments,
    O Lord, I have been comforted.

53 Depression has seized me seeing the sinners
    Who everywhere abandon thy law.

54 Thy statutes have been my songs
    In the house of my pilgrimage.

55 In the night I remembered thy name,
    O Lord, and I kept thy law.

56 All this has happened to me
    Because I have searched deeply thy statutes.

Heth

57 Thou, O Lord, art my inheritance,
    I said I would keep thy word.

58 I pleaded before thy countenance
    With all my heart: Have mercy on me
    According to thy teaching.

59 I gave my reason over to thy ways,
    I turned my feet over to thy testimonies.

60 Untroubled, I have made myself ready
    In the keeping of thy commandments.

61 Sinners have ensnared me with cords,
    But I have never forgotten thy law.

62 At midnight I rose to give thee thanks
    For the righteousness of thy judgments.

63 I am companion of those fearing thee,
    Of those keeping thy commandments.

64 Thy mercy, O Lord, fills all the earth,
    Teach me thy statutes.

Teth

65 With grace thou hast dealt with thy servant,
    O Lord, according to thy word.

66 Teach me goodness, discipline and knowledge,
    For I have believed thy commandments.

67 Before I was humbled, I transgressed,
    Therefore I have kept thy teaching.

68 Thou art good, O Lord, and in thy goodness,
   Teach me thy statutes.
69 The wickedness of the arrogant
   Has multiplied against me,
   But with my whole heart
   I shall search deeply thy commandments.
70 Their heart has gone sour like milk,
   But I have meditated in thy law.
71 It is good thou hast humbled me,
   That I might learn thy statutes.
72 The law of thy mouth is better to me
   Than thousands of gold and silver.

Yod

73 Thy hands formed and fashioned me,
   Teach me to know thy commandments.
74 Those fearing thee will rejoice seeing me
   Because I have hoped in thy words.
75 I know, O Lord, thy judgments are righteous,
   That with truth thou hast humbled me.
76 Let now thy mercy be for my comfort,
   According to thy teaching to thy servant.
77 Let thy compassions rest upon me,
   Then I shall live,
   For thy law is my meditation.
78 Let the proud be disgraced,
   Who have transgressed against me unjustly,
   But I shall meditate in thy commandments.
79 Let those fearing thee turn to me,
   Those who know thy testimonies.
80 Let my heart be blameless in thy statutes,
   That I may never be disgraced.

Kaph

81 My soul faints for thy salvation,
   I have hoped in thy word.
82 My eyes dimmed in awaiting thy teaching,
   Saying: When wilt thou comfort me?

83 I am shriveled like a wineskin in frost,
    Yet I have never forgotten thy statutes.

84 How many are the days of thy servant?
    When wilt thou judge my tormentors?

85 Transgressors have spread stories about me,
    But they are far from thy law.

86 All thy commandments are truth,
    Help me: I am unjustly persecuted.

87 They almost ended my life on earth,
    But I never once forgot thy commandments.

88 Quicken me to live by thy mercy,
    I shall keep the testimonies of thy mouth.

Lamed

89 Unto all eternity, O Lord,
    Thy word endures in heaven,

90 Thy truth unto generations of generations,
    Thou didst found the earth and it endures.

91 By thine ordering, each day endures,
    For all earthly things are thy servants.

92 If thy law had not been my meditation,
    I would have perished in my affliction.

93 I shall never forget thy statutes,
    In them thou hast quickened me to life.

                                    midpoint[71]

94 I am thine, O Lord, save me,
    For I have sought thy statutes.

95 Sinners lurked for me to kill me,
    But I comprehended thy testimonies.

96 I have seen the limits of all achievements,
    But thy commandment is immensely spacious.

Mem

97 How I have loved, O Lord, thy law,
    It is my meditation all the day long.

98 Thou hast made me wise in thy commandment
    Above my enemies, and forever it is mine.

99 I comprehended more than all my teachers,
    For thy testimonies are my meditation.

100 I comprehended more than the elders,
　　Because I sought always thy commandments.

101 I restrained my feet from every evil way
　　That I might keep thy word.

102 I have never rejected thy judgments,
　　For thou hast established law for me.

103 How sweet to my taste are thy teachings,
　　Sweeter than honey in my mouth.

104 From thy commandments I won comprehension,
　　Therefore I hated every false way.

Nun

105 Thy word is a lamp to my feet
　　And a light to my paths.

106 I swore an oath and confirmed it,
　　To keep the judgments of thy righteousness.

107 I have been deeply humbled, O Lord,
　　Quicken me according to thy word.

108 Receive, O Lord, my mouth's free tribute,
　　And teach me thy judgments.

109 My soul is always in thy hands,
　　I have never forgotten thy law.

110 The wicked have set snares for me,
　　But I never strayed from thy commandments.

111 I have inherited thy testimonies forever,
　　They are my heart's rejoicing.

112 I set my heart to do thy statutes
　　Forever, as a recompense.

Samek

113 Transgressors I have hated,
　　But I have loved thy law.

114 Thou art my helper and protector,
　　I have placed my hope in thy word.

115 Depart from me, you evildoers,
　　I shall search deeply my God's commandments.

116 Uphold me according to thy teaching,
　　And I shall live,
　　Do not disgrace my expectation.

117 Sustain me and I shall be saved,
    I shall meditate always in thy statutes.

118 Thou despisest all who spurn thy statutes,
    For their inward thought is wicked.

119 I counted as transgressors all of earth's sinners,
    I have always loved thy testimonies.

120 Pierce my flesh with fear of thee,
    For I have feared thy judgments.

Ayin

121 I have done judgment and righteousness,
    Do not deliver me to my tormentors.

122 Vouch for thy servant's goodness,
    Let not the arrogant falsely accuse me.

123 My eyes dimmed in awaiting thy salvation,
    The teaching of thy righteousness.

124 Deal with thy servant in thy mercy,
    And teach me thy statutes.

125 I am thy servant, make me comprehend,
    And I shall know thy testimonies.

126 It is time for the Lord to act,
    They have shattered thy law.

127 I have therefore loved thy commandments
    More than gold and precious stone.

128 Therefore I have been guided rightly
    Into keeping all thy commandments,
    And I have hated every false way.

Pe

129 Wondrous are thy testimonies,
    My soul therefore deeply searched them.

130 The revelation of thy words illumines,
    And even infants comprehend.

131 I opened my mouth, I drew in my breath,
    I longed for thy commandments.

132 Look upon me and have mercy on me,
    According to the judgment
    Of those who love thy name.

133 Direct my steps by thy teaching,
   And let no iniquity rule over me.

134 Set me free from every man's slander
   And I will keep thy commandments.

135 Make thy countenance shine upon thy servant
   And teach me thy statutes.

136 My eyes have poured streams of tears
   Because men have not kept thy law.

Tsadde

137 Righteous art thou, O Lord,
   And upright is thy judgment.

138 The testimonies thou hast commanded
   Are vast righteousness and truth.

139 The zeal of thy house has consumed me,
   For my enemies have forgotten thy words.

140 Thy teaching is purified in fire,
   Thy servant has deeply loved it.

141 I am small and counted as nothing,
   But I have never forgotten thy statutes.

142 Thy righteousness is everlasting righteousness
   And thy law is the truth.

143 Affliction and anguish have found me,
   But thy commandments are my meditation.

144 Thy testimonies are forever righteousness,
   Give me comprehension, and I shall live.

Qoph

145 I cried with my whole heart:
   Hear me, O Lord,
   I shall search deeply thy statutes.

146 I cried out to thee: Save me,
   I shall keep thy testimonies.

147 I have arisen in the night's depths,
   Crying: In thy words I have hoped.

148 My eyes awoke before the dawn
   To meditate in thy teachings.

149 Hear my voice, O Lord, in thy mercy,
   Quicken me in thy judgment.

150 Those wrongly hounding me draw near,
   Having drawn far from thy law.

151 How very near thou art, O Lord,
   All thy commandments are truth,

152 And long have I known from thy testimonies
   That thou hast founded them forever.

Resh

153 Behold my humiliation and rescue me,
   For I have never forgotten thy law.

154 Plead my cause and redeem me,
   Quicken me according to thy word.

155 Salvation is far from all sinners,
   They never searched deeply thy statutes.

156 Many are thy compassions, O Lord,
   Quicken me according to thy judgment.

157 Many are those who pursue and afflict me
   But never have I swerved from thy testimonies.

158 I beheld those indifferent to God,
   And I wasted away,
   They have never kept thy teachings.

159 I have loved deeply thy commandments,
   Quicken me, O Lord, in thy mercy.

160 The beginning of thy words is truth,
   The judgments of thy righteousness
   Endure for all ages.

Shin

161 Princes have pursued me for no cause,
   But my heart feared only thy words.

162 I shall rejoice in thy teachings
   Like one finding great treasure.

163 Injustice I have hated and abhorred,
   Thy law I have deeply loved.

164 Seven times a day I have praised thee
   For the judgments of thy righteousness.

165 Great peace have all those
   Who keep on loving thy law,
   There is no stumbling block for them.

166 I have longed for thy salvation, O Lord,
     I have deeply loved thy commandments.
167 My soul has kept thy testimonies,
     I have loved them very deeply.
168 I kept thy commandments and testimonies,
     For all my ways are before thee.

Taw

169 Let my cry come near thee, O Lord:
     Make me comprehend fully thy teaching.
170 Let my petition come before thee:
     According to thy teaching, rescue me.
171 My lips shall overflow in song
     When thou teachest me thy statutes.
172 My tongue shall speak of thy teaching,
     For all thy commandments are righteousness.
173 Let thy hand be there to save me,
     For I have chosen thy commandments.
174 O Lord, I have longed for thy salvation
     And thy law is my meditation.
175 My soul shall live and praise thee,
     And thy judgments shall help me.
176 I have gone astray like a lost sheep,
     Seek out thy servant,

     I have never forgotten thy commandments.

The Poetics of the Resurrection

M y thesis about the LXX text of Psalm 118 rests on two assertions: (1) that the Orthodox placement of this psalm, in its entirety, in the Matins for Holy Saturday—as well as in Lazarus Saturday—reveals the *resurrectional meaning* of the psalm; and (2) that the LXX retention of the twenty-two letters of the Hebrew alphabet as "titles" for the poem's twenty-two stanzas reveals the *resurrectional movement* of the psalm.[72]

Taken together, these two assertions can help us approach Psalm 118 as a text unique in all Scripture. For I wish to suggest here that it is a text being composed by Christ Himself as He lies in the tomb between death and resurrection. In fact—and here is my thesis about Psalm 118—the poem is actively helping Christ's death become His resurrection, and its artistic techniques can therefore be best understood as the poetics of the resurrection.

Now, far from asserting that the Psalm itself somehow raises Christ, I am proposing that the Holy Trinity—Father, Son, and Holy Spirit—acts in and through the psalm—in a way similar to that in which Christ worked in and through his own words of command, "Lazarus, come forth!" when He raised Lazarus from the dead—composing it in and as the Lord's own mind (given long ago to the prophet David[73]) to restore life to His immolated flesh. Or, to continue the metaphor from our introduction, as Christ prays the psalm, the nine words for God's life-giving law (themselves infused with that law) act as an asymmetrically dynamic response to the physical death inflicted by the Crucifixion, permeating His broken body and infusing Him with Holy Resurrection. And they do this also for us, for He is the Way, the Truth, and the Life (John 14:6).

■   ■   ■

We may begin our reading at the psalm's central line—at the line, that is, that Orthodox Christendom has for many centuries called (in Greek) the *mese*: a line, as we have noted, occurring not at the poem's arithmetic midpoint (l. 88) but five lines further on, at line 93:

> I shall never forget thy statutes,
> In them thou hast quickened me to life.[74]

The key to this line lies in the LXX verb "to quicken" (*zoein*), a verb often used to signify the first felt movement of the baby in the mother's womb. Here, at line 93 (and throughout Ps 118), the agent of this quickening is the divine word made incarnate on earth: *the statutes.*

We may note, here at the start, that Psalm 118 uses nine terms to signify divine law: commandments, statutes, law, word, testimonies, teaching, judgments, way, and path. These nine Greek words translate ten Hebrew terms, with LXX "commandments" and "statutes" together absorbing the Hebrew word *mitzvot*, rendered in English as "precepts." This Hebrew word for "precepts" is best understood as signifying specific actions of self-emptying love. These actions are wonderfully explained by a Rabbinic parable from *Perek Shira*:[75]

> When David completed the Book of Psalms he was uplifted with satisfaction. He said to God, "Does there exist any creature which You created anywhere in the entire universe which sings songs and praises which surpass mine?" At that moment a frog passed and said, "David, do not be uplifted with pride, for I sing songs and praises which surpass yours! . . . Not only that, but I also perform a mitzvah [an ascetic obedience]. On the seashore there is a creature which draws its sustenance from the sea. When that creature is hungry it takes me and eats me. That is my ascetic obedience." . . . The song of the frog is: "Blessed be the name of the glory of His Kingdom forever and ever." (xlviii–xlvix)

As the frog gives himself wholly so that the other creature may live, he sings of divine glory with the full weight of all his existence—a weight we can feel in every line of the Psalter and especially (I would say) in every line of Psalm 118. Now, when the Septuagint absorbs the Hebrew *mitzvah*, "precepts," into the Greek "commandments" and "statutes," we can understand that the latter two words are *directly incarnating* the former—with the result, in Psalm 118, that the LXX "statutes" and "commandments" fully register total psalmic obedience to the experience of death and resurrection.

Thus (to return to l. 93 of Ps 118), the statutes *quicken* the psalmist into the resurrected life. And the immediate consequence of this quickening, in line 93, is what Orthodox Christendom has come to call Memory Eternal: "I shall never forget thy statutes."

The two primary emphases, then, in line 93, lie, first, on the statutes' life-bestowing powers and, second, on the eternality of their effects. When heard as words spoken by Christ in the tomb, these two emphases in line 93 touch the listener—any listener, anywhere and always—with the same perfective consequences: we are made whole and beautiful in and by them. The fluidity with which, in Orthodox practice, the psalm's speaker can be seen now as Christ, now as the crucified thief (and therefore as all other persons in the New Testament), and now as ourselves—this fluidity is central to the resurrectional poetics of Psalm 118: blessed life-giving-ness is flowing into and through and from the poem. Here, then, is the *resurrectional meaning* of Psalm 118: life is flowing everywhere within it.

The *resurrectional movement* of Psalm 118 is shaped by the sequence of the Hebrew alphabet. The alphabetic sequence is meaningful in the sense we signify when we say, "from A to Z"—that is, as signifying the totality of all things, visible and invisible. And specifically in the Hebrew of Psalm 118, the alphabetic sequence (from *aleph* to *taw*) enacts the creation of Adam in Paradise, the sequence wherein God first fashioned man from the earth and then breathed life into that fashioning. This sequence is strongly emphasized in Psalm 118 by having each of its twenty-two eight-line stanzas employ—in every line—an initial word that begins with the appropriate letter of the alphabet. That is, every line in the first Hebrew stanza starts with a word that begins with *Aleph*, the first letter of the Hebrew alphabet; all eight lines in the second Hebrew stanza begin with *Beth*, the second letter; and so on, through twenty-two stanzas in Hebrew alphabetical order. Thus, every stanza of Psalm 118 can be seen as a distinct moment in the Adamic creation and thus the alphabet can be understood as providing the DNA of this creation—that is, as providing the flow of the poem's creative movement. And it is this flow that the anonymous LXX poet-translator registers in Greek by using the twenty-two names of the Hebrew letters as sequential "titles" for the poem's twenty-two stanzas.

An important moment in understanding this flow occurs in line 131 of Psalm 118:

> I opened my mouth, I drew in my breath,
> I longed for thy commandments.

The first two of these three actions—opening the mouth and drawing in the breath—are the actions God performs in His breathing of life into the creation; they are also the actions a singer performs in beginning to sing. But the third action in line 131—longing for God's commandments—sharply distinguishes the psalmist from God breathing life into Adam. Yet—and here is a crucial point—these distinct actions also connect to each other while sustaining their distinction: for just as God gives life to His creation by His breathing into it, so, too, the singer's longing makes the divine commandments become alive in his psalmic song. And becoming alive is what defines the resurrectional movement of Psalm 118, an aliveness that infuses meaning into the psalm's ongoing alphabetic flow. And I suggest that it is this flow of aliveness that helped lead Orthodox Holy Tradition to discern the creation of Adam in the resurrection of Christ: and thereby to place the whole of Psalm 118 in the Matins of Holy Saturday.

From this perspective, then, we may approach the very heart of resurrectional poetics in Psalm 118: the subject of psalmic music. I shall use two starting points to approach this important subject. The first is Rabbinic, from the *Yalkut Shimoni*: "Portions of the Torah were purposely recorded without proper sequence, because, had they been in order, whoever read them would have had the power to revive the dead and to perform miracles. Therefore, the true order is concealed from man and known only to the Lord."[76] A contemporary Jewish scholar thus adds: "Our mission and challenge is to toil over [the true psalmic order] in an effort to achieve understanding [of it]. If these vital formulae were spelled out clearly and unambiguously, then anyone could know the secret of producing life and manipulating nature" (ibid.).

Here, then, is our first starting point: psalmic music is both deeply hidden and highly potent, a phenomenon possessing the power to resurrect the dead, a power whose true order can work miracles and yet remain hidden from our eyes, a power that Psalm 118 nevertheless calls us to comprehend always more finely, more fully, more exactly.

The second starting point for understanding psalmic music arises from the final line of the entire Psalter: "Let every breath praise the Lord" (Ps 150:6). Now, the LXX Greek word for "breath," *pnoe*, is, in Hebrew, *neshamah* (BDB 675b). This Hebrew word embraces a complex set of biblical significances, ranging from the breath of God as a hot wind kindling a flame (Isa 3:33), to a destroying wind (Ps 17:16), to a cold wind producing ice (Job 38:29), to a wind as the divine breathing of life into man (Gen 2:7). Hence, *neshamah* comes to signify in Biblical Hebrew the human soul, or psyche; and as such, *neshamah* occupies the middle stage of what Rabbinic tradition sees as the five progressive stages of the soul's earthly movement.

It is therefore crucial, in our approach to psalmic music, to understand these five stages of the soul's progress on earth. The first stage is called *nephesh*, and it signifies the divine spark infused in the embryo to be joined to human flesh; *nephesh* is thus the incarnation of the soul; as such, it corresponds (say the Rabbis) to the book of Genesis, wherein is described the birthing of all the worlds.

The second stage begins at actual birth, when the baby is released from the womb to begin its devotion to God; and this stage, called *ruach* in Hebrew (BDB 1112b), corresponds to the book of Exodus, as the text of freeing the soul to enter a new kingdom. The third stage, *neshamah*, begins when the baby starts to nurse. Here, the Rabbis say, "an entirely new world begins to unfold—the cycle of nourishment" (*Tehillim*, IV, 1238).

Neshamah thus corresponds to the book of Leviticus, where all the details of nourishment, prayer, and fasting are fully elaborated. The soul's fourth stage on earth, called *havah* (BDB 3106), begins, say the Rabbis, when the soul first discovers in childhood that it is involved in a lifetime of spiritual warfare against dangerous enemies, both earthly and demonic; and this stage is completed when the soul at last sees that every demonic and earthly evil will inevitably be conquered (ibid.).

And in so seeing, this fourth stage of the soul corresponds to the book of Numbers, where the triumph over demonic evil is described. The fifth and final stage of the soul's progress, called *yehidah* (BDB 402b), happens when the soul enters into earthly death and is thereby released to participate fully in God's joy. This fifth stage, explicitly resurrectional, corresponds to Deuteronomy, where the last days and the prophetic death of Moses are vividly depicted. The Hebrew word *yehidah* literally means, say the Biblical Hebrew lexicographers, "the one unique and only one," and signifies "the one unique and priceless possession which can never be replaced" (BDB 402b).

Now, these five stages of the soul's life on earth correspond, the fourth-century Gregory of Nyssa believes, not only to the five books of Torah but also to the five "books" (or divisions) of the Psalter. St. Gregory divides the five books of the Psalter in this way: (1) Psalms 1–40, (2) Psalms 41–71, (3) Psalms 72–88, (4) Psalms 89–105, (5) Psalms 106–150. And the aim of the Psalter, he asserts, is entirely musical: the Psalter enacts a movement into that blessedness of music wherein "every breath praise[s] the Lord" (Ps 150:6). This is a singing, he says, in which our earthly "nature reflects on itself . . . and heals itself," adding that psalmic singing "is a cure of nature."[77]

St. Gregory continues: As we in prayer move in the musical sequence from Psalm 1 to Psalm 150, Christ is formed in us: "[B]y means of the forms of virtue, [the Psalter] forms Christ in us, in accordance with whose image we existed in the beginning, and in accordance with which we again come to exist" (Heine, 164).

"The order of the psalms," he says, "is harmonious"—and as the soul moves through the Psalter's five books it is restored to its original and unfallen nature, one in full harmony with angelic nature. "[T]he grace we look for," Gregory says, "is a certain return to the first life, bringing back again to Paradise him who was cast out from it" (51), a return wherein we sing again with the angels. In so asserting, St. Gregory follows perfectly our Lord's direct teaching; for those who are resurrected from the dead, Christ says, "are equal to angels and are the children of God, being the children of the resurrection" (Lk 20:35–36). Here is the Gospel basis for the poetics of the resurrection. Here also is the musical importance, in Psalm 118, of the Hebrew alphabet: the alphabetic sequence of the Adamic creation is the musical sequence of our angelic resurrection with— *and into*—Christ Himself.

St. Gregory also cites, from Psalm 150, the line just before "Let every breath praise the Lord": "Praise him with resounding cymbals, praise him with triumphant cymbals" (Ps 150:5). St. Gregory says of this line:

> I take this [clashing of two cymbals in Ps 150] to mean the union of our nature with the angels . . . For such a combination, I mean of the angelic with the human, when human nature is again exalted to its original condition, will produce that sweet sound of thanksgiving through their meeting with one another. And through one another and with one another, they [—this harmonic] combination of the angelic with the human nature [—] will sing a hymn of thanksgiving to God for his love for humanity which will be heard throughout the universe. For the coming together of *cymbal* with *cymbal* shows this. . . . (Heine, 121)

Psalmic music, in other words, brings about *in us* a renewed spiritual harmony between our nature and the angelic nature. And thus, psalmic music may be accurately said to be a poetics of the resurrection.

And now we may see why Rabbinic tradition asserts that the "true order" of psalmic music will remain something always concealed from us and yet, simultaneously, must be actively sought by us. For were psalmic music to be openly seized by us, we would at once debase it into necromancy and false-miracle working: such is our fallen nature. But were we to approach that music the way the frog, in the parable, approaches *his* songs, we would instead be giving ourselves to psalmic music so that it could live again through us *and in us*: and so make the world *live* again.

Now, too, we can see how the Rabbinic five stages of the soul are, in fact, moments in a *musical* progression of self-emptying love. That is, the baby in embryo (*nephesh*) incarnates the divine spark but is entirely *un-self-willful* in doing so; and at birth (*ruach*), the baby draws in breath *instinctively*—and *not* willfully—

and thereby enters into a new kingdom. Similarly, when the baby begins to nurse (*neshamah*), this new cycle of nourishment can be characterized as entirely obedient and deeply loving, an obedience and a love fueled by the sharpest intensity of longing but *not* with even the least hunger for willful domination. The fourth stage (*havah*), when in childhood the soul enters spiritual warfare, and the fifth stage (*yehidah*), when the soul at death is resurrected into God's joy: these two final stages are, again, entirely obedient and *un-self-willfully* loving. As such, the five stages exhibit the same musical progression that St. Gregory sees the five books of the Psalter exhibiting: a progression that restores harmonic relationship between the human race and the angelic orders.

And in this restored harmony—this resurrectional music—the statutes of God become, here on earth, the songs of the psalmist in Psalm 118.

> Thy statutes have become my songs
> In the house of my pilgrimage. (l. 54)

The statutes become songs in the same way that the printed sheet of music becomes living harmonic sound. As the incarnate singing voice gives itself entirely to the progression of written notes—and does so without imposing its own domination but, instead, gives itself entirely to comprehending the music—the song is again resurrected, once again the song *lives*. Thus, with St. Gregory's immense help, we may see that to sing the songs of God's statutes (in Ps 118) is to become, ourselves, *re-musicalized*. Such are the psalmic poetics of the resurrection. And in the light of this resurrectional poetics we can see why it is that, in the Orthodox monastic practice that begins on Saturday evening with Psalm 1 and concludes the following Saturday morning, the concluding text is always Psalm 118 as the highest goal of all psalmic prayer.[78]

The final stanza of Psalm 118 begins this way:

> Let my cry come near thee, O Lord:
> Make me comprehend fully thy teaching. (Ps 118:169)

This was my prayer for my twin brother during the long illness that ended in his death in March 2007. To comprehend fully God's teaching in Psalm 118 is to enter, with Christ, the darkness of the tomb.

At the end of 2003, I visited Mt. Athos with my two sons and a friend. There the deputy abbot of Vatopaidi Monastery, Fr. Arsenios, spoke to us about St. John Climacus' book, *The Ladder of Divine Ascent*, especially emphasizing Step 7, entitled "On Joy Making Mourning." Father said that everything one needs for salvation in Christ can be found in this section of *The Ladder*. There, St.

John says: "When I consider the actual nature of compunction, I am amazed at how that which is called mourning and grief should contain joy and gladness interwoven within it, like honey in the comb . . . which, like a child, at once both whimpers to itself and shouts happily" (7:49, 54).

Called *katanyxis* in the *Philokalia*, this joy-making mourning occurs in us when we (as the glossary of the *Philokalia* puts it) become "conscious of [our] own sinfulness and [simultaneously] of the forgiveness extended to [us] by God" (IV:428). Just as mourning possesses joy, so, too, in Psalm 118's final line: the cry becomes deepest comprehension as the speaker sees that he has "gone astray like a lost sheep" and yet he has "never forgotten thy commandments" (Ps 118:176).

In this context, then, I shall approach one more crucial insight into psalmic poetics from St. Gregory of Nyssa's beautiful treatise on Psalms. Contrasting the lyric poetry of classical Greek culture with the poetry of the LXX Psalter, St. Gregory says that the Psalms "have not been composed in the manner of lyric poets who are outside our wisdom" (Heine, 92). "For," St. Gregory continues, "the music [of the LXX Psalms] does not lie in the pitch of the words . . . by a certain combination of pitch modulation" (ibid.). Now, St. Gregory is here referring to the fact that classical Greek poetry (which he knew well) possessed five distinct pitch-levels when spoken aloud; and the skill greatly admired in classical culture was the poet's ability to modulate these pitches into rhythmic patterns of rising and falling, longer and shorter sounds. No, says St. Gregory, "David . . . [instead] entwined . . . the ordering of pitch in relation to the term"—or, in other words, the LXX Psalms connected pitch to meaning—and *not* to rhythmic pattern.

The significance of St. Gregory's insight cannot be overstated. For he has here described the way wherein, in Psalm 118, the statutes of God become the psalmist's songs. This way could perhaps be expressed as the freeing of pitch from the bonds of rhythmic pattern out into the bright sunlight of somatic spaciousness (see Ps 118:45: "I kept on walking in spaciousness, / For I sought always thy commandments"): that is, the way of resurrectional poetics. Every line in Psalm 118 sheds light on this resurrectional way; for every line exhibits the boundless intensity of loving God's holy word—an intensity that runs always wider and deeper in spiritual meaning: always more *spacious*.

This intensity of loving is in LXX psalmic poetics because it is first in the Hebrew psalmic shapes and sounds. This intensity is therefore plainest, of course, in the Hebrew. But it is also fully realized in LXX Greek—and (here is an essential point) the musical consequences of this intensity are *fully translatable into any other language on earth.* In other words, the loving practitioner of psalmic prayer working solely, say, with English or German or Russian or Aleut, has open before him the fullness of what I shall call the *breathing* of psalmic poetics: the steady musical *ison* of the Psalms. Just as there is no moment in the Gospels after which Jesus of Nazareth ceases being a Jew—that is, Jesus of the Gospels is steadily and entirely engaged in a process wherein Messianic Judaism is becoming *fully translated* (indeed, *transfigured*) into His Personhood— just so: there is nothing of psalmic music that cannot be made to breathe fully and beautifully in any other earthly language—provided, of course, that the translator has searched deeply both the Hebrew and the LXX music in forming the music of his or her own Aleut or Russian or English. "Every breath praises[s] the Lord" (Ps 150:6). Such is the astonishing consequence of (in St. Gregory's description) resurrecting the pitch of LXX Greek from the tomb of rhythm in such a way that death is translated into life.

And this is the context in which I wish to tell you about a miracle that (Holy Orthodox Tradition tells us) my name-saint, Donatos, performed: the calling forth of a recently dead man from his coffin. As a fourth-century hierarch of Epirus in Euboea, Bishop Donatos in his episcopacy had undoubtedly had to settle countless disputes among his flock. Once (the story goes), a man had died suddenly; and at the funeral service, the man's brother—in grief and anger—cried out that his brother had died owing him a considerable debt, his whole life's savings. Calming the raging brother, St. Donatos stood before the open coffin and made the sign of the cross over it. The dead man sat up and told his brother where, in his house, he had hidden the money, asked his brother's forgiveness, then lay back down in the coffin, again dead. The man forgave his brother in the joy of compunction.

This story calls our attention to the sign of the cross. In making the sign of the cross, St. Donatos created the spiritual reality in which genuine joy could be resurrected from darkest anger and mourning. And this is the spiritual reality in which we can best comprehend the whole of Psalm 118.

Fairly early in the poem, the psalmist says:

> This comforted me in my affliction
> For thy teaching has given me life. (Ps 118:50)

Now, the LXX Greek word here for "affliction" is *tapeinos*, a word also meaning "humility" in Patristic texts (see Lampe). In Step 7 of *The Ladder*, St. John Climacus says that those who have made considerable progress in attaining the blessings of "joy-making mourning" are characterized by "humility, thirst for dishonours, voluntary craving for involuntary afflictions, non-condemnation of sinners, compassion even beyond one's strength" (7:4). In every line of Psalm 118, we can see and hear all these qualities—and we do so because we see and hear them in every word Christ speaks in the Gospels.

And by coming to Psalm 118 in this way, we can come fully to affirm St. Ignatius Brianchaninov's remarkable insight in his book *The Arena*. In discussing what Orthodox monks know as vigilant sobriety, St. Ignatius calls it a "constant activity."[79] The practice of this sobriety, he tells us, leads us to a singularly crucial awareness: "When in Christ the veil that lies on their spiritual eyes is [lifted], even a Jew becomes a Christian. Then the Old Testament acquires the same significance for the reader as the New" (131).

This bears repeating: The Old Testament acquires the same significance as the Gospels: and this is especially the case, I feel, with Psalm 118. For when it begins to acquire such significance, then Psalm 118 can affirm for us what the psalmist says late in the poem:

> Thy word is a lamp to my feet
> And a light to my paths. (Ps 118:105)

We go not only by a very narrow path (St. Ignatius says), we travel solely by night (*Arena*, 133). This night is, St. John Climacus says, the night of endless dishonor and unceasing affliction, joined to the deepest compassion for every-one—a "compassion even beyond one's strength." We travel, in other words, the way of Christ's cross—which is the way of psalmic music and the poetics of the resurrection. This is the way of Psalm 118.

11

The Nine Words for the Law

I wish here to raise two issues about the nine words for the Divine Law in the LXX text of Psalm 118. The first issue is the LXX absorption of the Hebrew *mitzvot* (sing. *mitzvah*) into two Greek terms: *entolai* and *dikaiomata;* an absorption that reduces the original ten Hebrew words to the LXX Greek nine. The second issue is St. Gregory of Nyssa's interpretation of the LXX *diapsalma* (Hebrew *selah*). My point is that these two issues are, in Psalm 118, connected.

Let us take the second issue first. In his magnificent (if unfinished) *Treatise on the Inscriptions [or Titles] of the Psalms*, St. Gregory devotes an entire chapter to the meaning of *diapsalma* in the Psalter. He says this: "*diapsalma* is a pause which occurs suddenly in the midst of the singing of a psalm in order to receive an additional thought which is being introduced by God. Or, one might rather define it as follows. *Diapsalma* is a teaching from the Spirit which occurs in a mysterious manner in the soul when the attention given to this (new) thought impedes the continuity of the song" (Heine, 158).

But (St. Gregory immediately adds), lest anyone misinterpret him by holding that he is saying that the Holy Spirit had *forsaken* the psalmist just prior to the *diapsalma:* "the Holy Spirit was always in the [psalmist's] soul [and] was always speaking in [the psalmist], but his speech paused, and the [LXX] translators called this pause *diapsalma*" (ibid.). *Diapsalma*, then, is a definitive factor in the shape of any psalm it occurs in; hence, we may see *diapsalma* as key to what we may call the poetics of the Psalms: that is, the compositional theory of poetry that underlies and nurtures the actual practice of psalmic poetry.

St. Gregory gives a compelling and elegant simile for this interpretation of *diapsalma:* "It often happens that, if people who are walking together or conversing with one another at banquets or meetings should suddenly hear a sound from somewhere, they stop their discourse and give their full attention to the sound, so that in the silence they may hear and know the meaning of the sound. Then when the noise has ceased they again take up their discussion with one another" (ibid.).

David, he continues, "submitted to the Spirit who was making the hearing of his soul resound and stopped the music, and when he was filled with these thoughts he related these matters, again entwining [the words] with the melody" (ibid.). Note carefully what St. Gregory is saying here. Each pause consists of three elements: (1) the psalmist interrupts his music by hearing "his soul resound" with *diapsalma;* (2) the silence-producing *diapsalma* nevertheless fully sustains connection with the ongoing music, which has now become, for the *diapsalmic* moment, an *inward* connection; and (3) after the moment ends, the psalmist takes up the discussion once more, now *entwining* (St. Gregory's word; Greek *eneiro;* Lampe, 470a) the newly arrived meanings with the ongoing psalmic music. *Silence* thus possesses the power to give shape to psalmic music. These three elements—the interruption of the psalmic music; the going inward of that music; the renewing of the music with new content—together define *diapsalma* at the same time they reveal the *diapsalmic* poetics that shapes the psalm.

One more crucial point. St. Gregory holds that "the final section [of the Psalter, i.e., Pss 108–150] alone has the song of praise continuous and unbroken from beginning to end in each psalm, nowhere being interrupted by *diapsalma*" (Heine, 159). Instead, says St. Gregory, the Psalter's final section carries the titles "Alleluia" or "An Ode of the Ascents" and so does not have *diapsalma* in the poems; for such psalms, he says, have "arrived at the peak of things" and are complete in themselves "through total perfection in the good" (ibid.).

Here, then, is my thesis about the nine words for the law in Psalm 118: Each acts in the poem the way *diapsalma* acts in the psalms: first to interrupt, then to deepen, and then to renew the song, all three in a single psalmic moment. Now, that St. Gregory's assertion needs to be qualified—as Heine tactfully puts it, "This statement is not quite accurate, for the fifth division of the Psalms (106–50) has *diapsalma* in psalms 139 and 142" (ibid., fn. 171)—does not, in my view, unmake St. Gregory's crucial understanding of psalmic poetics. Indeed, when one considers the apparent exception in psalms 139 and 142, one can in a certain sense validate St. Gregory's insightful interpretation of *diapsalma.* For, most assuredly, his reading can help illumine the action of the nine words in Psalm 118.

And it is in this light that we can turn to the first issue mentioned above: the absorption in Psalm 118 of the Hebrew word *mitzvot* ("precepts") into the two Greek words *entolai* ("commandments") and *dikaiomata* ("statutes"). This absorption can be best understood as an *incarnation*: the precepts become incarnate as the commandments and statutes. In their incarnation, we approach another of St. Gregory's central assertions—indeed, the very heart of all his discussions of the psalms: that the progress of the Psalter, from Psalm 1 to Psalm 150, is what he calls "the way to blessedness," a way wherein "one [can] attain to that measure of beatitude of which thought cannot calculate what lies beyond it by guessing and conjecturing, nor reason discover analogically what follows it" (Heine, 121–22).

In this psalmic blessedness, Gregory holds, "the whole creation, consisting of all things superior and all things inferior, has been united in one choir" and "our humanity unites with the angels" (ibid.). And this blessedness abounds, he says, "through increase, to perpetuity" (ibid.): abounds, that is, in that *unceasing aliveness* known as eternal life. The nine LXX words are best seen, then, as ways *into* that eternally unceasing aliveness, in which, St. Isaac the Syrian will say (three centuries after St. Gregory), one "even now breathes the air of the Resurrection" (*Homilies*, 46:224).

■　■　■

Since September 8, 1984, when I was received into the Orthodox Church, I have prayed the Psalms daily in my morning and evening private prayer; and since May 1988, when I was ordained to the subdiaconate, I have prayed through the entire Psalter every week of my life. Somewhere in the late eighties, I ran across this passage in *The Philokalia* and copied it out in my journal:

> The same brother also asked: "Why, father, do you find more joy
> in the psalms than in any other part of divine Scripture? And why,
> when quietly chanting them, do you say the words as though you
> were speaking with someone?" And Abba Philemon replied: "My
> son, God has impressed the power of the psalms on my poor soul as
> He did on the soul of the prophet David. I cannot be separated from
> the sweetness of the visions about which they speak: they embrace
> all Scripture." (II:347)

Sometime in April 1990, I wrote in my journal this single sentence: "The Psalms are, literally, life: *dynamis*" (Journal 1, p. 89)—a sentence that (I think entirely unconsciously) echoes Abba Philemon's phrasing about "the power of the psalms on my poor soul"; a sentence that expresses weakly what Abba Philemon is saying so movingly and what St. Gregory is saying so beautifully: *the Psalms are an entire way of life in prayer.*

I mention my experience in the Psalms in order to help articulate the final part of my thesis here about the nine words of Psalm 118. The nine words are *diapsalma* in their power to shape an entire earthly life of prayer because each of the nine (and two or more, or all of them together) act both *locally* (to fashion each specific line and each eight-line stanza of the psalm) and *globally* (to fulfill the Psalm's total spiritual and artistic plan). The way wherein global and local effects act upon each other at every moment of the poem helps explain something of Abba Philemon's experience of sweetness in psalmic prayer, a sweetness of vision about which every line and every stanza of Psalm 118 speaks so movingly and beautifully, and a sweetness focused by the nine words.

One other part of my experience in psalmic prayer is also, I think, worth mentioning here. To pray the Psalms regularly is to be attacked unceasingly. And the effects of ceaseless demonic attack are flatness of speech and restlessness of mind and a consequent vanishing of any sweetness of vision and the disappearance of any or all *dynamis* (power) arising from the nine words. If I try to battle directly the attack, then I immediately open the door to mental restlessness; if I try simply to lie low, then spiritual flatness instantly ensues. The only hope I have in such moments (and they are very frequent indeed) is to stay as attentive as I can to the psalm's actual words as they are actually occurring before me. For psalmic *dynamis*—the power of Psalms—is coming not at all from me but solely from the poems themselves. In other words, I have to forego both the arrogant hunger for success in direct battle and the suicidal delusion that I can stay under the demonic radar. I must, instead, at every moment let God (as Abba Philemon says) impress "the power of the psalms on my poor soul." I can manage to do this—rarely—for the very briefest of moments, perhaps three or four consecutive seconds some five or six times a week, mostly at night prayer but occasionally in the day. The effect on me of those few seconds is, however, always the same: something newly fresh yet delightfully familiar has just come into my heart.

In this way, then, my experience in psalmic prayer—superficial and self-absorbed as it is— nevertheless reflects some thin sliver of the great light that Abba Philemon movingly beholds, and the still deeper illumination that St. Gregory of Nyssa beautifully registers in his interpretation of *diapsalma*. For *diapsalma*, Gregory says, "occurs in a mysterious manner in the soul" (Heine, 158). The true mystery of Psalms is an experience of prayer that at once simultaneously interrupts and continues the psalmic music.

■ ■ ■

In this context, then, let us reflect for a moment upon the *sacred essence* of psalmic poetry. In the fourth century, when the Nicene Creed was composed by two separate councils some sixty years apart, the Greek word employed by both councils to describe God the Father was *poietes*, "poet," usually rendered in English as "Maker." Despite the rock-solid foundation in both Greek and English for "Maker" as the proper rendition, the Greek word *poietes* carries primary meanings sometimes blurred by that rendition. To repeatedly profess our firm belief in "one God, Father all-mighty, Poet of heaven and earth, of all things visible and invisible," is, I think, to disclose how very weakly and narrowly we usually conceive the essence of poetry. And in the light of the Creed, to conceive in weakness the essence of poetry is simultaneously to conceive in weakness the essence of God. Let us, then, explore the credal significance of *poietes* for a moment.

The key to the credal comprehension of the Father lies in the assertion of God's oneness of power to create distinct worlds, heaven and earth, each of which possesses both visible and invisible dimensions. Note very carefully: the invisible world of heaven *also* possesses a visible dimension while the visible world of earth also possesses an invisible dimension. The essence of the Father's creativity may thus be seen as residing in His power to hold open four dimensions in two realms—and in doing so in such a way that the Son of the Father becomes the fashioner of all things. The Father's essence is thus at once exceedingly complex and divinely simple: complex, in the sense that the Father is steering four dimensions in two worlds at the same instant He is giving to His Son the power to create all things; simple, in the sense that the essence of such complexity is the action of loving.

Now, when we turn to the sacred essence of psalmic poetry, we can see how the complex simplicity—and the simple complexity—of the Father's essence is perfectly expressed in the way wherein the *diapsalmic* intensities of the nine words are giving shape, in each of the twenty-two stanzas of Psalm 118, to two distinct worlds in four dimensions. That is, in Psalm 118, the nine words connect at every moment the heavenly "thou" of the Father with the earthly "I" of the psalmist; and this connection is, at every moment, being initiated and sustained by the Father's divine invisibility unceasingly giving itself in love to the psalmist's earthly visibility—and this action of the Father's love becomes at every moment incarnate as the psalmist's song. "Thy statutes have been my song," says the psalmist (Ps 118:54)—that is, the Father's acts of self-emptying love have, *in their essence,* become incarnated in and as the actual shape of the psalmist's poem—and they have done so (the psalmist continues in the same vein) "[i]n the house of my pilgrimage" (ibid.)—that is, in the actual dwelling place of the psalmist. To have such incarnation occur is (in the language of Ps 118) to be *taught* God's statutes (*didasko*); ten times in the psalm we have a form of "Teach me thy statutes"—surely emphatic in its steady repetition.

To pray the entire Psalter through each week is to engage the Psalms in such a way that, over a period of years, the nine words of Psalm 118—each and all *diapsalmic* in their cumulative intensities—begin to become actual *experience*: nine sharply distinct and uniquely patterned *experiences*, each as distinct from the others as the fingers on one's hands. This experiential basis of the nine words is what every single line of Psalm 118 focuses (better, *incarnates*) as the interaction between the divine "thou" and the psalmic "I": every line, that is, once we reach line 4 (which introduces the divine "thou") and then line 5 (which introduces the earthly "I"). Such experiential interaction *in* the poem produces, in anyone praying the poem, the experience Abba Philemon speaks of: "God has impressed the power of the psalms on my poor soul." The psalms possess this power because (as we have seen) God the Father is the *Poet* of Heaven and Earth, the One whose shaping presence is always and everywhere simultaneously visible and invisible. And the nine unique experiences triggered in us by the nine words become, both singly and collectively, a kind of lexicon in which one's own works and days grow always more deeply *defined*—defined not in any sense of becoming *delimited*, but, instead, defined in the sense of becoming increasingly *spacious*. As the psalmist of Psalm 118 says:

> I kept on walking in spaciousness,
> For I sought always thy commandments. (Ps 118:45)

Platysmos in LXX Greek, this word "spaciousness" occurs only here (and as an adjective, "spacious," in line 96) in Psalm 118 (and only twice more in the entire Psalter, in Psalms 17:19 and 117:5); hence, it is a word of unique power.

For each of the nine words in Psalm 118 possesses its own unique spaciousness—a definition, that is, which distinguishes that word from the other eight while simultaneously connecting it to them; a definition, therefore, at once visible and invisible. Thus, in praying Psalm 118, we can see (better: *behold*) the way wherein (for example) "commandment" differs from "statute" at the same time we can *experience* their substantial oneness in essence. The nine words may thus be said to be *homoousion* with respect to each other and yet each absolutely unique each in itself. This definitional reality of Psalm 118 accounts for why, in praying this psalm, one's experience in prayer is never merely a "feeling" but can instead be more accurately understood as an *ontological action*: as, that is, a sudden *diapsalmic* interruption of one's being that is nevertheless a deeper continuation of one's being. St. Gregory of Nyssa makes an astonishing and beautiful contribution to our understanding of this ontological action when he says that *diapsalma* is an "additional grace of knowledge for the benefit of those receiving the prophecy"—that is, for those praying the psalms (Heine, 157).

We can thus see why commandments (*entolai*) and statutes (*dikaiomata*)— the two most frequently used of the nine words (accounting for some 36 percent of all occurrences)—are so sharply distinguished. *Commandments* are the Father's actions of self-emptying love, first to the Son and then, through Him, to all of us. The commandments are the "additional grace of knowledge" given freely to us; hence, our truest response is to *keep* the commandments, to make ourselves into a "keep" that holds these actions in, *and as*, our hearts. The *statutes*, on the other hand, are these same acts of the Father and the Son *in* the whole of creation; hence, to be *taught* the statutes is to see the roots of our visible world as actually *implanted in* the invisible presence of the Father's deep love for the Son—and therefore, for all of us who (in Gregory's phrase) "receive the prophecy," take the divine into our hearts. To be taught the statutes is thus to fall always more deeply in love with God and the Creation. The two words are in this way sharply distinguished.

Yet they are also substantially connected: that is, they share the same substance and so may be said to be *homoousion* in the sense with which we say, "In the name of the Father, the Son, and the Holy Spirit"—and do *not* say, "In the *names* . . .": one Name and three Persons. In steadfastly refusing to give disproportionate weight either to the oneness of the divine Name or to the threeness of the divine Persons, Orthodox theology beautifully avoids both monarchianism and tritheism: avoids, that is, the heretical subordination of one or two of the Persons to a third as well as the heretical separation of the three into disconnected "gods."

Just so, Psalm 118's commandments and statutes (indeed, all nine LXX words) are sharply distinct yet one in essence. Such definitional oneness therefore requires of us in our psalmic prayer that we, at every moment, trust in a coherence higher than any of our own intellectual conceptions of it. For only such faith can keep at bay the twin darknesses of mental restlessness and spiritual flatness—and thereby become open to the light of psalmic prayer. And at the heart of this light in Psalm 118 is the action of loving, an action that creates and sustains the movement of all nine words throughout the entire poem, a movement everywhere and always at once both definitional and *diapsalmic*, a movement sometimes terrifying, sometimes exultant, and always logical.

I stand before my icons in prayer. It is nearly midnight. I feel flat and restless, and I want to rush through prayer and get to bed. Exhausted, I begin, and soon I hear:

> Thou art my God, I shall give thanks to thee; thou art my
> God, I shall exalt thee, I shall give thanks to thee, for thou hast
> heard me and hast become my salvation. (Ps 117:28)

A delight fresh yet familiar comes into my heart.

III

The Actions of Love
A Lexicon of the Nine Words for God's Divine Law

T he actions of love are, in LXX Psalm 118, focused in and by the nine words for God's divine law: *commandments* (37 usages), *statutes* (28), *law* (25), *word* (23), *testimonies* (23), *judgments* (20), *teaching* (19), *way* (17), and *path* (2). The nine words thus appear 194 times in the poem's 176 lines.

As anyone who does so will immediately confirm, to pray the Psalms regularly is to be ceaselessly attacked by demons. And to pray Psalm 118 regularly is to call forth a ninefold attack. For each of the nine words incarnates an action of God's love, an action that is therefore (as one psalm puts it) "working salvation in the midst of the earth" (Ps 73:12). Each of the 194 appearances of the nine can therefore be seen as the tip of a spiritual spear, a focal point toward which the demons are swarming while the angels are gathering. The demons are attempting to disfigure every appearance of the nine words; while the angels are sustaining the "figure" of Christ in each of the nine. For the nine words are each a verbal "icon" of Christ's actions of love, actions that are "working salvation in the midst of the earth." The person who regularly prays Psalm 118, therefore, soon discovers that not only do we have spiritually lethal enemies of prayer here on earth but we have also, in Jesus Christ, a God who overcomes all our enemies. Our death-dealing enemies are defeated triumphantly by our life-giving God.

Our psalmic studies must begin with this reality of psalmic prayer. Any lexicon of the nine words is therefore, to some degree, a *description* of the spiritual warfare occurring in—and at—each occurrence of the nine within the psalm. Such a description must reveal the unique demonic disfiguration of the particular word as well as disclose the triumph of "figuration" being brought about by Christ's loving action occurring in that same word. These two actions—disfiguration and transfiguration—occur almost (but not quite) simultaneously in Psalm 118. The former always occurs just *very* slightly before the latter; hence, the latter (the iconic figuration) is always *just* triumphing over the former: *just*, but decisively, triumphing. The *closeness* of these two actions helps drive the psalm's ceaseless movement into blessedness; for the poem's dynamic aliveness flows from this spiritual warfare. If our studies in psalms begin in the practice of psalmic prayer, then they also—if faithfully done—return to our prayer in psalms.

One further note. The nine words, being (of course) grammatical nouns, require in all 176 verses uniquely *definitive verbs*: ones that, at every moment, reveal the demonic disfiguration being actively overcome by the divine figuration. Each of the nine words thus is enacting the reality of spiritual obedience, the reality wherein the soul of the psalmist is discovering, at every moment, that obedience is life. In the words of Elder Ephraim of Katounakia (Mt. Athos), obedience is life because "obedience will bring about all things," for, "without obedience nothing will happen, whatever else we might do."[80]

Every genuine *action* on earth is therefore triggered by the obedience that, as Christ's love, is defeating every demonic disfiguration; and outside this action of obedience, there is—quite literally—nothing. Again, Elder Ephraim: "Obedience is humility . . . Through obedience Christ bestows prayer . . . Prayer is the result of obedience. When you have obedience, you will also find prayer . . . When you don't have obedience, you don't find anything else either. And even if you do have something, you will lose it" (ibid.).

Without obedience, you have nothing at all, the Elder is saying; without obedience you are unable to *act* in any sense. Conversely, every verb in Psalm 118's 176 lines is *making active* one of the nine words, making happen over and over (194 times) that salvific figuration of Christ's love: a figuration wherein Christ is trampling down death by His death and resurrection.

The LXX Greek verb in Psalm 118 signifying "to love"—*agapan*—occurs thirteen times in the psalm, ten times having "I" as the subject, three times with the third person ("those" or "servant"): that is, all the images have the psalmist (or his fellow believer) as the agent of the action. The object of the action changes: five times it is "commandments"; four times it is "law"; twice it is "testimonies"; once it is "teaching"; and once it is the divine "Name" (not one of the nine words). Here are the first two occurrences of the verb *agapan*, in two successive lines:

> I kept on meditating in thy commandments
> For I have deeply loved them.
> With upraised hands, I loved thy commandments,
> And I kept on pondering thy statutes. (Ps 118:47–48)

The *commandments* are best defined this way: they are God's acts of self-emptying love for His creation (and everything within it, including ourselves); hence, to love these commandments is to actualize them in—*and as*—one's own behavior. And as these two lines make very plain, such actualization of God's commandments can occur only when the agent of it sustains an inward assent. Here, the LXX Greek verb reflects accurately the Hebrew; for as does the imperfective mode of the Hebrew verb, the Greek imperfect tense signals an action that has begun at some point in the past, that is now being sustained in the present, and that shows no sign of ever ceasing ("kept on meditating"; "kept on pondering").

The variety of verbs used in Psalm 118 to signify this sustained inner assent helps give the poem its vivid richness of texture. Here are the first ten such verbs in Psalm 118: "searching" and "seek" (l. 2); "praise" and "learn" (l. 7); "I have hidden" (l. 12); "delight" (l. 19); "ponder" and "comprehend" (l. 15); "meditate" and "never forget" (l. 16). That *agapan* (to love) does not occur until line 47 (nearly one-third of the way through) is significant, for the progress of the poem is precisely the *creation* of this capacity in the psalmist.

One measure of the *success* of this progression can be noted in the fact that six of the thirteen cases of *agapan* occur after line 131; and three of the six occur in successive lines 165 to 167—and a fourth occurs just before, in line 163. The sequence of verbs in Psalm 118 is ordered to this end: the deepening of the psalmist's every inward impulse (hence, of ours also) into the action of loving, a deepening everywhere occurring through the practice of obedience, a practice discernible in every verb of Psalm 118.

What unmakes the commandments is therefore clearly that disobedience known in the psalms as "contempt." Psalm 88 concludes this way:

> Remember the contempt, O Lord, I suffered in my heart,
> contempt all thy servants suffer from all the nations,
> Contempt, O Lord, thine enemies have used to darken that
> reconciling exchange given by thy Christ. (Ps 88:50–51)

Contempt for another person is also contempt for human personhood in itself; hence, it is contempt for God Himself in that action of love whereby He reconciles—in His self-emptying love for us—all earthly creatures with their divine Creator. Our contempt therefore disorders every commandment of God's by asserting that we are ourselves our own makers, not God. As Psalm 99 puts it: "Know that the Lord, he is God, that he has made us, and not we ourselves . . ." (Ps 99:3). And in what may be the most terrifying line in the entire Psalter, Psalm 108:25 has: "I have become their contempt." Here is the demonic goal of all human contempt, and it is the destruction of all the commandments of God—the destruction, that is, of all loving obedience.

One further note. LXX Greek *entolai* (commandments) translates Hebrew *mitzvot* thirty-one times and *piggudim* six times. While a *mitzvah* is an action of self-emptying love for another, a *piggudah* is something left in trust, as in grain stored against a famine (BDB 824a and b). Thus, the loving action that is a commandment becomes saving nourishment for the agent as well as for the recipient of that act of love.

The second most frequently used of the nine words in Psalm 118 is "statutes." With the LXX Greek word *dikaiomata* translating twenty-three times the Hebrew plural *chuggim* and five times the plural *piggudim*, we may note that the Hebrew noun *chuggim* arises from the verb meaning "to cut into," "to inscribe deeply" (BDB). A *chuggah*, then, is an action performed by God in creating the world and everything in it, an action that sustains in the earthly creation the generative power of the divine Creator. Combined with *piggudim* (see above), the LXX *dikaiomata* can be defined as follows: *statutes* are the divine "cuttings-into" (or inscriptions) made by God in the creation and left there by Him to be the nourishment that fuels our own true creativity.

At one point in his account of his experience with the Jesus Prayer, the anonymous nineteenth-century Pilgrim says this:

> The prayer of my heart gave me such consolation that I felt there
> was no happier person on earth than I, and I doubted if there could
> be greater and fuller happiness in the kingdom of heaven. Not only
> did I feel this in my own soul, but the whole outside world seemed
> to me full of charm and delight. Everything drew me to love and
> thank God: people, trees, plants, and animals. I saw them all as my
> kinsfolk; in all I found the image of the name of Jesus Christ.[81]

The Pilgrim's experience helps define Psalm 118's statutes. The Pilgrim can discover the image of Christ everywhere in the world precisely because that image has been *cut into* the world by Jesus Christ in His actions as the One (in the words of the Creed) "through Whom all things were made" (*di' ou ta panta egeneto*). These acts of inscription *are* the statutes of Psalm 118, and the overall progression of Psalm 118 is, in part, governed by the teaching of these statutes to those who are praying the great psalm.

The third of the nine words, *law*, occurs twenty-five times in Psalm 118, while the fourth, *word*, occurs twenty-three times. Interestingly, the two LXX Greek words—*nomos* (law) and *logos* (word)—rhyme with one another in a way similar to the way the two Hebrew words rhyme: *torah* (law) and *dabar* (word). Both sets are made up of two-syllable words; both sets employ either consonantal or vocalic echoings. What interests us in these sonic patterns is the connection they have to the semantic meanings of the two words.

For—succinctly put—*law* is the direct manifestation of God in the present instant of human history while *word* is the direct articulation of that instant of manifestation. We may thus see law and word as the direct incarnations in human history of the commandments and the statutes, possessing the same eternal roots and therefore exhibiting the same salvific flowering. *Nomos* (law), for example, is what the Apostles behold at the Transfiguration—Christ "was transfigured before them" and "His face shone like the sun and His clothes became as white as the light" (Matt 17:2); while *logos* (word) is the voice of the Father saying, "This is My beloved Son, in whom I am well pleased. Hear Him!" (Matt 17:5).

In this way, then, *nomos* and *logos* can be said to be, for us, the experience wherein we can directly see what is being actively spoken to us by God. Like the Apostles, we *see* the divine light; and like them, we *hear* the divine voice; as in the Transfiguration, the two phenomena become one experience. Thus, the root of this experience may be best understood as the experience of Wisdom—as Psalm 103 puts it:

> O Lord, how manifold are thy works, in wisdom thou hast made them all. The earth is filled with thy creations. (Ps 103:24)

The multiplicity of God's works of wisdom is like the Apostles' experience of transfigurative light—it fills all things; the unity of God's wisdom is like the single voice of the Father proclaiming, "This is My beloved Son . . . Hear Him!" (Matt 17:5). This combination of the law's multiplicity of light with the word's oneness of sound is vividly emphasized in LXX Greek phrasing in this line from Psalm 103: *panta en Sophia*, "all things in Wisdom." It is also like the Pilgrim's discovery of the kinship of all things in his experience of prayer, in which he beholds and hears the statutes of God inscribed in all things of creation (in "people, trees, plants, and animals").

What unmakes this illumined experience of salvific kinship in *nomos* (law) and *logos* (word) is what the Psalms depict as the assault of enemies. Who are these enemies, we may ask, and what do they seek to do? I shall begin to approach this subject so crucial to all psalmic study by telling of a nightmare I had some thirty or so years ago: a one-time occurrence that has nevertheless sustained its vividness for me to this day. In the dream I am in an open field at dusk, some ten yards from the fence. About thirty yards away from me is a herd of twenty or so bulls, each massively powerful as it begins to paw the ground. Suddenly, they all lift their heads and open wide their huge mouths and begin roaring at me, and then they all—in one ferocious pack—rush hurtling toward me. Terrorized, I turn and begin to run—and all at once I am awake, fully awake, my ears ringing with the dreadful sound of their roaring. Yet I am safe.

The waking effect of this dream has remained unaltered these three decades or more: There exist those whose whole will is entirely focused on my violent destruction. Nevertheless, they cannot reach me—*ever*.

Some ten years after this dream and after I had become Orthodox and had begun to pray the Psalms, my attention was riveted by this passage from LXX Psalm 21, the psalm whose opening line is spoken by Christ on the cross: "Why hast thou forsaken me?"

> Many young bulls have surrounded me, fat bulls have encircled me.
> They open wide their mouths against me, like a raging and
> roaring lion. (Ps 21:12–13)

Here was my dream, fully articulated; and so also was the impact I felt:

> I am poured out like water, my bones are all scattered,
> my heart is like wax melting into my stomach. (Ps 21:14)

The burning question of the psalm is drastically plain: Where *are* you, O God, in my agony? The psalm responds with even more drastic clarity:

> For he has not despised nor scorned the beggar's plea, nor has he
> hid his face from me, and when I cried to him, he heard. (Ps 21:24)

The psalm is therefore saying that, when all your words have become upraised into and as "the beggar's plea," then you will experience that transfiguration of all your words into the praise of God. The psalm continues:

> The poor shall eat and be satisfied, those who seek him will praise
> the Lord, their hearts will live forever. (Ps 21:26)

"Forever": the LXX Greek is "unto ages of ages" (*eis aiona aionos*); and as the psalmist says three lines further: "My soul lives on in him" (Ps 21:29). When (as we said) all of our words have become all of God's praise, then the actions of all our enemies will become still more circumstances for still greater praise of Him.

And in this praising of God, there is discovered that experience of kinship living at the heart of God's law (*nomos*) and His word (*logos*): the experience of Christ's divine figuration in and as the created world. The old woman whom the Pilgrim meets in his travels tells him of the time when she was "a young and pretty girl" about to be married, and her bridegroom suddenly died the day before their wedding. "This frightened me," she says, "so that I utterly refused to marry at all . . . I made up my mind to live unmarried, to go on a pilgrimage to the shrines and pray at them." She continues:

> However, I was afraid to travel all by myself, young as I was; I feared evil people might molest me. But an old woman-pilgrim whom I knew taught me wherever my road took me always to say the Jesus prayer without stopping, and told me for certain that if I did, no misfortune of any sort could happen to me on my way. I proved the truth of this, for I walked even to far-off shrines and never came to any harm. My parents gave me the money for my journeys. (Way, 99)

This beautiful account illumines the first line of Psalm 118: "Blessed are the blameless in the way, / Who walk in the law of the Lord." As she walks the lands of Holy Russia, she is kept safe in and by her love of God's law and word. "I have sought thee with my whole heart," says the psalmist of Psalm 118 in line 10, in full awareness that in such seeking and loving lies all salvation. The Pilgrim asks her, "Have you made a habit of this prayer for long?" and she answers, "Since I was quite young, yes, and I couldn't live without it, for the Jesus prayer [has] saved me from ruin and death" (ibid.).

Ruin and death—spiritual, physical, and psychological—are precisely what all psalmic enemies seek for all those who pray the Psalms. And the kinship experienced by the Pilgrim and the old woman is the sure sign that both together "walk in the law [nomos] of the Lord" (Ps 118:1), being quickened into life in Christ "according to thy word" (Ps 118:25).

It should also be noted that the old woman describes her teacher-pilgrim from years ago as telling her "always to say the Jesus prayer without stopping" (ibid.). This teaching—so central to all experience of Orthodox prayer—can be seen as having interesting reflections in the Psalms. In Psalm 71, for example, a Davidic psalm to his son Solomon, we find this line spoken by David about Solomon: "He shall live, and Arabian gold shall be given to him; they shall pray to him without ceasing, all the day long shall they bless him" (Ps 71:15). The LXX Greek phrasing for "pray . . . without ceasing" is *proseuxontai . . . dia pantos;* literally, "pray . . . throughout everything"—that is, prayer that crosses great spiritual distances (the Greek *dia* is always fairly emphatic). King Solomon, as a Scriptural icon of Wisdom's dominion, thus becomes the "figure" who best expresses the old woman's—and the Pilgrim's—experience of walking "in the law of the Lord" (Ps 118:1).

One final note about law (*nomos*). The central experience of law in Psalm 118 is the miracle of light:

> Take away the veil from my eyes
> That I may see the wonders in thy law. (Ps 118:18)

"Take away the veil" translates the single LXX Greek verb literally construed as "apocalypsize" my eyes. To see fully the law is thus to have one's eyes become apocalyptic as they behold the actions of divine light occurring in the world of actual human history: actions that are *thaumasia* (wonders). To *hear* of these wonders is to experience them as *logoi* (words); and, as the Pilgrim says of his hearing the old woman's account, "I was overjoyed to hear this, and knew not how to thank God for this day, in which I had been taught so much by examples of spiritual life" (*Way*, 99). *Nomos* (law) and *logos* (word) are the grounds of our joy.

The fifth word for divine law in Psalm 118—*testimonies*—also occurs twenty-three times. The LXX Greek word for *testimonies* discloses much of its primary significance: *martyriai*. Always in the plural, the *martyriai* (testimonies) may be defined as follows: *testimonies* are the witnesses in present human activity of past divine actions. For Orthodox Christendom, *testimonies* include such things as clerical vestments, liturgical music, service texts, incense, chalice, altar cloths, and prosphora: that is, everything of worship that can be seen, heard, touched, smelled, and tasted. The *testimonies* also include the lives of the saints, the accounts of the martyrs, and the writings of the Church Fathers. Taken together, then, the sensory evidences of all the testimonies constitute what Psalm 118 describes as wealth (*ploutos*).

> I delight in the way of thy testimonies
> As much as in every kind of wealth. (Ps 118:14)

And those who search (*exereunao*) God's testimonies—who actively dig down into the depths of this long-accumulated Orthodox sensory wealth—do so, says the psalmist, in the fullest love for God:

> Blessed be those searching his testimonies,
> Who seek him with the whole heart. (Ps 118:2)

And just as the actions of law (*nomos*) are described as "wonders" (*thaumasia*), so, too, the testimonies are characterized as "wondrous" (*thaumasta*):

> Wondrous are thy testimonies,
> My soul therefore deeply searched them. (Ps 118:129)

"Deeply"—*dia touto*, says the LXX Greek phrasing: searching that acts ceaselessly, that prays without ceasing.

The sixth word—*judgments*—occurs twenty times in Psalm 118, four times in the singular (LXX *krima*), sixteen times in the plural (*krimata*). The *judgments* can be defined as the revelations of God in *judicial* terms, that is, as specific applications of God's words in situations of human dispute or conflict, applications that divinely resolve human conflict. The *judgments* differ from, say, the *law* (*nomos*) in their immediate specificity to the issues of conflicts as well as in their immediate impact on our lives. We can, if we choose, ignore both the divine light of the Transfiguration (*nomos*) (Matt 17:1–2) and its divine articulation (*logos*)—doing so, of course, at our own great spiritual peril, as the next passage in Matthew's Gospel reveals. But we can no more ignore the actions of God's judgments than can the father of the afflicted son ignore his son's agonies: "he often falls into the fire," the father tells Jesus, "and often into the water" (Matt 17:15). For this demonic disfiguration of a human son fully reveals the consequence of ignoring the heavenly transfiguration of the divine son. And, in this sense, the disfiguration can be said to constitute a *judgment*: not at all as divine punishment or retribution, but rather as divine revelation—as, that is, the revelation of the God we must ourselves *choose* to follow, and can never be *compelled* to follow. The psalmist says in Psalm 118:

> I have chosen the way of truth.
> I have never forgotten thy judgments. (Ps 118:30)

Always to remember the divine *judgments*, then, is to enter into that paradisical consciousness known by Eastern Orthodox Christendom as Memory Eternal, that consciousness wherein we remember God ceaselessly—and are remembered by Him unendingly.

In this light, it is worth noting that one area of human conflict can be seen in the text itself of the psalms: that is, whether we are to give more weight to the Masoretic Hebrew or to the LXX Greek. Yet, if we approach the matter as a place where God's judgment is occurring, then we can see that there exists a point where Masoretic Hebrew and LXX Greek are *together* pointing toward the vanished Ur-Hebrew text. This point is irrevocably lost to Hebrew *except* insofar as it gives itself, in kenotic love, to LXX Greek; and it is comparably lost to the Greek except insofar as it gives itself in love to the Hebrew. For in this reciprocal action of kenotic loving, the two (conflicting) texts together point to the vanished—but still active—Ur-Hebrew prototype, and therefore God's judgment is enacted.

Note, too, that the judgments are, in Psalm 118, described as *gracious*:

> Take away my scorn, which I dread,
> For thy judgments are gracious. (Ps 118:39)

As we earlier saw, scorn or contempt (same word in LXX Greek, *oneidismos*) un-makes every divine action of love on earth. The judgments, on the other hand, are "gracious" (*chresta* in LXX Greek).

The seventh word—"teaching" (LXX *logion*)—is related in the Greek to *logos*, and it can be defined in this way: *teaching* is the expressed voice of God, the divine word become incarnate as a reality fully audible to human comprehension; hence, *teaching* is Scripture experienced as the living voice of Christ. Occurring nineteen times in LXX Psalm 118, *logion* reveals a beautiful dimension of its meaning in the first usage:

> In my heart I have hidden thy teachings,
> That I might not sin against thee. (Ps 118:11)

To hide God's teachings in one's heart is—in our phrasing—to know them "by heart": that is, to have them as part of one's deepest personhood. And it is in this light that we can best understand the LXX "rhyme" between *logion* and *logeion*, a word signifying the priest's oracular *breastplate* in Exodus (see Exod 28:15). To have God's *logia* (plural of *logion*) by heart thus means to be divinely armored against the violent assaults of sin.

The eighth and ninth words—"way" (LXX *hodos*) and "path" (LXX *tribos*)—are closely related in meaning, and they can be defined in this fashion: *way* and *path* are the actual human practice of moving toward God. The two words emphasize the *actual practice* of this movement; hence, their most immediate psalmic significance is the practice of prayer. In the second of the seventeen LXX occurrences of *way*, we see this:

> For the workers of iniquity
> Have never walked in his ways. (Ps 118:3)

Those who are "blameless in the way" (line 1) are, says the psalmist, those who sustain the practice of prayer even—and perhaps *especially*—in the midst of great social evil: evil so widespread and endemic as to have become systemically established in the very culture itself.

I talked today (July 4, 2006), at some length, with an American Orthodox acquaintance who has spent the past three years in China, directing the national office of his international electronics company. Under Communist Party authority, Chinese politico-economic culture has become so corrupt that he must include in his company's annual budget a line-item expense for the bribery of Party officials (it is called "entertainment," he told me). I listened—ever sicker at heart—to his descriptions of these countless "workers of iniquity" and the culture that creates and rewards them: and finally becomes nothing other than those works of iniquity.

He paused, his intelligent eyes heavy with the weight of something that was very like—well, actually *was*—despair. I said to him, "There's a psalm that describes the 'injustice [that] lies even to itself' [Ps 26:12]. The next line," I added, "says 'I believe I shall see the Lord's goodness in the land of the living' [Ps 26:13]. The psalmist knows he can't fix the evil himself; but he also deeply believes that *God's* goodness—not his own—will be seen in the land." My friend's eyes became suddenly very still. I went on. "You now, it'd be good for you to pray the psalms every morning and evening. The psalms formed the very mind of Christ Himself." His eyes filled with tears. "Thank you," he said. "Really, really thank you."

"Path" is used twice in Psalm 118 (ll. 35 and 105) and, like its synonym "way," signifies the active discipline of psalmic prayer. Here are the two occurrences:

> Guide me on the path of thy commandments,
> For I have desired this. (Ps 118:35)

> Thy word is a lamp to my feet
> And a light to my paths. (Ps 118:105)

The LXX Greek for "path" (*tribos*) differs from "way" (*hodos*) in being a slightly more archaic word; hence, it carries a sense of high antiquity, even something of the air of nobility now entirely vanished but still distinctly remembered. In this way, then, *tribos* reveals the glory of God working salvation here and now:

> Make known thy ways to me, O Lord,
> And teach me thy paths. (Ps 24:4)

And this illumined psalmic path of prayer is, I am certain, what my friend glimpsed in our conversation this week: a path regnant with divine glory—and therefore filled with the fullest strength of God's presence.

This path of fullest presence includes the reality of divine wrath. The psalmic account of the Exodus from Egypt contains this vivid moment:

> He cast on them his anger's rage, anger and rage and affliction,
> as angels of destruction among them.
> He made a path for his anger, not sparing their souls from death,
> and giving into death their cattle. (Ps 77:49–50)

If God works our salvation here and now in our actual lives (and He does), then He bestows His "angels of destruction" upon us so as to guide us "like a flock out into the wilderness" (Ps 77:52). The path of this death-dealing anger becomes, for us, the way into the *eremos* of psalmic prayer: unto, that is, the place where our iniquitous world has fallen completely away from us and has become—for the first time—the real world of God's direct creation.

Each of the nine words, then, as we said at the start, is a focal point for spiritual warfare, a point where demons are swarming and angels are gathering. Thus, the nine words share a common substance—they are, as I have suggested, *homoousios* with respect to each other, always convergent yet always distinct. This consubstantiality of the nine is what sustains their distinction while emphasizing their convergence. Sometimes one of the nine words seizes all our attention and dominates us; at another time, yet another of the nine does so. All nine, though, are revelatory actions of God's salvific love.

IV
The Procession of Holy Wisdom
The Movement of LXX Psalm 118

On August 26, 1988, I was in Kiev as a member of a small group of American Orthodox pilgrims come to celebrate one thousand years of Orthodoxy in Russia. That August afternoon in Kiev, we were taken to the Church of St. Sophia, an eleventh-century church wrecked by the Tatars in the fourteenth century, looted by the Nazis in 1942, closed by the Soviets in 1946, and, in 1988, in use only as an ecclesiastical museum. As we entered, I looked up into the two soaring domes, and in the bright August sunlight I beheld two large and extremely beautiful eleventh-century mosaics, one of Christ Pantocrator, the other the Theotokos—and I drew in my breath. The downward gaze of the Theotokos literally took my breath away. I was stunned by Her beauty, and Psalm 118 bespoke my state: "My soul lies prostrate on the earth, / Quicken me according to thy word" (Ps 118:25). My long journey of 4,200 miles was met by Her gaze down all the way into me. Inscribed on the inner surfaces of the two Kievan domes were the statutes of God's life-creating energies. I met Her gaze—and my whole life swerved into depths I could not begin even to negotiate, let alone command. In other words, I fell in love: "quickened," as the psalmist says. And each morning and evening of my life, I fall still deeper in love. As best I can.

This gaze of the Mother of God—dynamic in its stillness, unendingly perceptive, deeply humble—draws ever closer to us yet remains in a self-poised peacefulness. It is present in every truly Orthodox icon. It is the gaze of Holy Wisdom—the love of and for the Son of God whom the Holy Mother bears—the very gaze of heavenly beauty incarnate on earth, at once perfect in itself and perfective in its effects. This gaze of the Holy Mother holds the Wisdom that guides the movement of LXX Psalm 118, shaping in us the ongoing liturgy of our hearts: that is, the liturgy of our very being, our *ontos*.

■ ■ ■

Two brief texts can help us better to understand. Consider, first, this verse from the eighth chapter of Proverbs. Wisdom is speaking:

> Hearken to me, I shall speak sacred things,
> My lips shall yield straight things. (Prov 8:6)

Mary, the Theotokos, Oranta,
Cathedral of St. Sophia, Kiev. Photo: Natalia Bratslavsky.

"Sacred things" is, in LXX Greek, *semna*, while "straight things" is *ortha*. Clearly synonyms, *semna* and *ortha* are both the consequences of an inward action of comprehension, an action wherein the listeners' attentiveness is moving into an engagement with the speaker's voice as the voice is moving toward the listeners. That is, God's Wisdom is here becoming incarnate as we, the earthly listeners, are being made holy, divinized.

Consider now this verse from LXX Psalm 118:

> My lips shall overflow in song
> When thou teachest me thy statutes. (Ps 118:171)

The LXX Greek prefix to "overflow" is *ek*, a preposition that carries in Greek the primary meaning of "proceeding outward from." The "statutes"—which are the divine "cuttings-into" (or inscriptions) made by God in the creation and left there by Him to be the nourishment that feeds our own true creativity (see Chapter III)—*proceed from* the Father, *through* the creation, *to* the psalmist in the divine act of teaching. And this divine procession is met by the movement of song that proceeds from the psalmist to the Father: a reciprocal procession. Thus, the song's patterning—that is, the poetics of the psalm—constitutes a movement that follows perfectly the action of being taught what the Father has inscribed (has *deeply cut*) into the creation—that is, His statutes. And the psalmist's very being, his *ontos*, is augmented as it becomes capable of fully carrying this procession, a procession of Holy Wisdom.

Thus we can see that the psalmic "I" of the LXX Psalm 118 is steadily undergoing the impact of the divine "thou," steadily increasing in Holy Wisdom—and this steadiness of impact constitutes the poem's ongoing movement. In a sense, nothing ever "happens" in Psalm 118—precisely because of this steadiness. That is, at every moment in the 176 lines, the poem exhibits the full impact of God upon the psalmist; hence, at every moment, the poem is being completely fulfilled. This completeness is best comprehended as the action of love: the steady falling deeply in love with the God who creates heaven and earth and everything in them.

Each year in Kiev, on every September 8, the day of the Nativity of the Theotokos, Hagia Sophia is also celebrated. As we follow the movement of Psalm 118, we are in the procession of Holy Wisdom as it ascends up into the Holy Temple. In fact, in Kathisma 18 (Pss 119–133)—immediately following Kathisma 17 (the whole of Ps 118)—all fourteen psalms of the Kathisma bear the same title: "An Ode of the Ascents." These psalms were sung, in Hebrew practice, during the processional through the streets of Jerusalem up the Temple Mount and into the Holy Temple, with Psalm 133 beginning this way: "Behold, bless the Lord, all you servants of the Lord, you who stand in the Lord's house, in the courts of the house of our God." Psalm 118, then, is the way wherein one initiates and sustains this processional movement of—and into—"the courts of the house of our God," the temple of Holy Wisdom, a procession begun, in Kiev, in and as the birth of the Theotokos. The Kievan concelebration of Holy Wisdom with the birth of the Mother of God beautifully illumines the processional movement of Psalm 118.

The fifth or *He* stanza of Psalm 118 perfectly illustrates this movement of the whole poem. Here, in both Masoretic Hebrew and LXX Greek, the first word in each verse, a verb, is the ignition key to the line's movement:

33 Give me as law, O Lord, the way of thy statutes,
    And I shall seek it out always.
34 Give me wisdom to search deeply thy law,
    I shall keep it with my whole heart.
35 Guide me on the path of thy commandments
    For I have desired this.

36 Incline my heart to thy testimonies
    And not to endless desirings.
37 Turn away my eyes from empty things,
    Quicken me to live in thy way.
38 Establish thy teaching in thy servant
    That I may be rooted in fear of thee.
39 Take away my scorn, which I dread,
    For thy judgments are gracious.
40 Behold, I have longed for thy commandments,
    Quicken me in thy righteousness. (Ps 118:33–40)

Significantly, only one of the nine LXX words for God's divine law is omitted in this stanza (word, *logos*); the other eight are all employed. (Of the remaining twenty-one stanzas of Psalm 118, eight of them omit two words, seven omit three, and six omit four.) The eight words, in order of use in the *He* stanza, are *law; way* (twice used); *statutes; path* (one of two uses in all of Ps 118); *commandments* (twice used); *testimonies; teaching;* and *judgments.*

In both Masoretic Hebrew and LXX Greek, the first word in each line is a verb that acts as the "ignition key" to the line's movement. The *He* stanza's first verb is *nomotheteson,* an imperative construable as "law-implant [in me]." To have God implant His statutes is to initiate a double action: the spiritual movement of God to the psalmist and the rhythmic movement of the line to the concluding pronoun, *sou* (thou). That is, the psalmist's rhythmic movement in this line is matching God's spiritual movement to him. And this doubleness of movement characterizes, in fact, the action occurring in every line of Psalm 118: as God moves (spiritually) toward the psalmist, the psalm rhythmically moves toward God—and the two movements meet and interlock in the nine words. Here is the law of movement in LXX Psalm 118: the procession of Holy Wisdom.

▪ ▪ ▪

There is a passage in LXX Psalm 44 that beautifully illumines Psalm 118's processional movement:

11 For the king shall greatly desire thy beauty, for he is himself
    thy Lord.
12 And the daughters of Tyre shall worship him with gifts,
    the rich among the people shall entreat thy countenance.
13 The king's daughter is all glorious within, her clothing is
    woven with gold.

14 The virgins who follow after her shall be brought to the
king, those near her shall be brought to thee.

15 They shall be brought with gladness and rejoicing, they
shall enter into the king's palace. (Ps 44:1–15)

Gregory of Nyssa identifies the "King's daughter" of line 13 as the Church
Herself, and adds that Her inward glory is in fact psalmic meditation.[82] The
virgins' processional movement in lines 14 and 15 may thus be understood
as *responsive* to the King's movement toward the Church: a response at once
spiritually contemplative and poetically rhythmic. And *both* movements—
the King's toward the earthly Church and the ecclesiastical virgins' toward
the divine King—are initiated, sustained, and fulfilled by *desire*: God's for the
Church, ours (*in our virginity*) for Him.

And in many senses, *desire* is the central subject of the *He* stanza—indeed, of
the whole psalm:

> Incline my heart to thy testimonies
> And not to endless desirings. (Ps 118:36)

Pleonexia ("endless desirings") occurs only here in Psalm 118: occurs, so as to find
its true bearings and right movement. Desire that never ceases is the experience
of demonic reality; for *pleonexia* consumes everything and everyone until, in the
end, it consumes itself. To "incline [one's] heart" to the historically grounded
testimonies (*martyria*) of the Holy Church, on the other hand, is to enter the
very heart of the Holy Mother's desire: and there to become ontologically
augmented. That is, to enter into Her heart is to transfigure all earthly *pleonexia*
into the heart's deepest and truest desiring: into, that is, the desire that is
bounded (and not infinite) by its fulfillment in Christ. This inclining of the
heart, transfiguring *pleonexia* into finite longing, is the movement of Holy
Wisdom throughout LXX Psalm 118.

As Holy Wisdom gazes into the eyes of my prayer icon of the Holy Mother,
a movement of transfigured desire begins: that of Holy Wisdom toward Her,
Hers toward us, and ours toward Christ Himself. And this is the desire everywhere present in Psalm 118. Each morning, as I stand before my icons, my heart
is awake as I pray:

> O most Holy Mother, because I love You so much, I also love the
> Holy Prophet David of these psalms, who loves Christ our King and
> our God—in the very way Christ is loving David because, in writing
> these holy psalms, David is loving the Holy Mother.

Here is what I mean by the movement of Holy Wisdom in the Psalms: our love for the Holy Mother is flowing through the love of Christ for David who is loving both Christ and His Holy Mother. It is the heartfelt—indeed heart-filled—joy of this loving that, I believe, is what the psalmist is praying for in the fifth or *He* stanza of Psalm 118: "Incline my heart to thy testimonies / And not to endless desirings" (Ps 118:36). This inclining of the heart is the movement of Holy Wisdom throughout the psalm, and all the movement of Holy Wisdom in the psalm culminates in Her who is bearing the One who is our Lord and our Strength.

■ ■ ■

Line 37 of the *He* stanza adds another dimension to our understanding of the Psalm's movement:

> Turn away my eyes from empty things,
> Quicken me to live in thy way. (Ps 118:37)

The verbs act as the ignition to the half-lines. Note the *sequential* significance of these two verbs in line 37: to turn one's eyes from emptiness is to become quickened into a divinely given aliveness of movement; that is, the turning *causes* the quickening. Both the Masoretic Hebrew and the LXX Greek verbs for "becoming alive" are rooted in the sound of breathing in and breathing out, and both verbs therefore carry the significance of inward (or psychic) aliveness. To breathe the way of God is to become inwardly quickened in His eyes, and the soul awakens more fully and deeply with each and every breath as the heart follows the rhythmic movement of the psalmic lines.

The most perfect of all psalms in Scripture, known as the Magnificat, expresses this inward quickening this way: "My soul magnifies the Lord, and my spirit has rejoiced in God my Savior" (Lk 1:46), where "soul" is *psyche* in New Testament Greek, and spirit is *pneuma*: that is, both words signify the act of breathing. And the connection between Mary's song and Hannah's helps also to connect the Davidic narratives directly to the Psalms—and all of them to Christ. The movement of Holy Wisdom thus sustains heavenly aliveness across centuries of divine quickenings—these breathings in and out that *are* the poem.

The Magnificat's conclusion also sheds light on LXX Psalm 118's movement:

> He has helped His servant Israel
> In remembrance of His mercy,
> As He spoke to our Fathers,
> To Abraham and to his seed forever. (Lk 1:54–55)

This movement of living divine speech through holy persons and across the centuries can be rightly understood as the movement of Holy Wisdom, for the prophetic voice is at once unique to each prophet and consubstantial with all other prophetic voices; and this perfect combination of uniqueness and consubstantiality is a dynamic (not a static) combination, at once fully achieved and always striving toward this achieved fullness. In other words, Abraham is simultaneously the highest pinnacle and the way up into that dizzying height. As a result, movement is simultaneously an achieved stillness and a ceaseless striving, always completed and always seeking completion. What distinguishes such movement from the deadly whirlpools of *pleonexia* is the unending love of God—Psalm 118's "thou"—for the psalmist; for whereas *pleonexia* can never experience fulfillment in its prison of ceaseless desirings, the movement of Wisdom never ceases giving knowledge of the fullness of the divine Presence.

▪　▪　▪

Each stanza of LXX Psalm 118 further exhibits a 3-2-3 pattern of movement: the first three lines connect to the final three, while the middle pair acts as a pivot between the two triplets. In the *He* stanza, this pattern of movement is best seen in the way that line 35b—"For I have desired this"—prompts line 36 to raise the subject of "endless desirings" (*pleonexia*); which, in turn, prompts the subject of "empty things" in line 37, thereby pivoting the stanza toward and into transfigured "longing" for God's commandments (line 40b).

This 3-2-3 pattern of the stanzas in Psalm 118 is also *chiastic*: that is, the closing triplet speaks back to the opening triplet in such a way that the pivoting couplet may be said to be carrying forward the opening triplet into the closing one. Thus, in the *He* stanza, the pivot verb in line 37b—"Quicken me" (*zeson me*)—is repeated and fulfilled in line 40b—"Quicken me in thy righteousness"— while at the same moment, line 33 ("Give me as law, O Lord, the way of thy statutes, / And I shall seek it out always.") is being fulfilled by line 40 ("Behold, I have longed for thy commandments, / Quicken me in thy righteousness."). The 3-2-3 stanzaic pattern of movement is therefore at once linear and circular: linear, in that the movement always *gains* in significance as the stanza progresses; yet it is circular in that the movement's progress is always referring back to earlier lines as it completes their meanings.

Like the iconic gaze of the Holy Mother, the sacred voice of Wisdom progresses outward to transfigure its listeners through the action of loving and being loved. As the voice of Wisdom says in Proverbs: "I love those who love me: and they that seek me shall find me" (8:17); just so, the closing triplet of every stanza in Psalm 118 is transfigured, through the pivot-couplet, by the action of loving that streams forth from the opening triplet.

In the *He* stanza, this movement begins in the psalmist's cry for God's law to become *in him* the way of an unceasing search; then, in the pivot, the false unceasingness of *pleonexia* is thoroughly defeated; and this defeat opens the way for God's teaching (*logion*) to become deeply rooted in the psalmist— and, by the stanza's final line, the transfiguration of human desire into divine longing is accomplished.

The Talmud notes about the shape of the Hebrew letter *He* that guides this stanza that it "demonstrates how God fashioned the world to afford mankind an opportunity to exercise free will," continuing in this way:

> Above the left leg of the *He* [ה] is a small opening which symbolizes the passageway to Heaven. This passageway is narrow because the way to Heaven is not an easy one. At the bottom of the *He* is a wide opening which represents the lower passageway to Hell. The opening is wide to remind us that it is easy for man to fall if he does not make an effort to choose the path upward to God."
> (*Tehillim* V, 1431)

The point is interestingly reinforced when the LXX translators approach the Hebrew for line 33b. The Masoretic Text (MT) Hebrew reads: "I will cherish [the way of thy statutes] step by step," where "step by step" literally means "heel by toe"—that is, says the Talmud, the word is alluding "to a very small step, because those who walk [gingerly and cautiously, taking small steps] keep the toes of the back foot close to the heel of the front foot" (ibid.). Now, the Greek for this Hebrew phrase is *dia pantos*, literally "throughout everything," where the Greek preposition (*dia*) signifies movement through space, a movement first beginning, then traversing, and finally concluding in a spatial continuum. What is being "sought out" in line 33, then, is the way of God's divine statutes inscribed—cut into—the earthly landscape, a way at once very tiny yet plainly distinct at every moment: a way, that is, very much like the tiny opening in the Hebrew letter that guides the movement of the fifth stanza.

Two further points of interest: First, the Hebrew letter that guides the sixth stanza (ll. 41–48) is *waw*, a letter the *Kabbalah* calls "*the letter of truth*, because it stands perfectly straight; it is unbent and unadorned" (*Tehillim*, V, 1435). In line 43 of the sixth stanza, the MT Hebrew has *dabar emeth aid me'od*, while LXX Greek reads *logon aletheias heos sphodra*. This intensely (*sphodra*) true word is actually "in the mouth" of the psalmist—like a hook in a fish's mouth: "For I have hoped in thy judgments" (Ps 118:43). Thus, we may see that the tiny opening in the fifth stanza has been perfectly negotiated by the upstream movement of the psalmist;

and this movement is above all *redemptive,* for the mercy of God (MT *hesed;* LXX *eleos*) has landed (we may say) the psalmist, and thus messianic salvation has fully occurred; and this salvation fulfills every prophetic utterance (*Tehillim,* V, 1435), a processional fulfillment of every historical movement on earth. Here is the movement of Psalm 118.

The second point of interest is best approached through a beautiful text from *The Homilies of St. Isaac the Syrian.* St. Isaac begins Homily 26 this way:

> Every thing that is above another is concealed from what is beneath it. This is not, however, because it possesses by nature a sort of veil composed of some other body; therefore [when it wishes] it is able to uncover its hiddenness. No noetic essence acquires from outside of itself the distinction of its own rank, but these distinctions are confined within its motions. That is, to put the matter more plainly, it can without mediation more easily enter in to receive the primal light than a lower order [from] which, evidently, it does not differ in locality, but according to the high degree and capacity of its purity, or according to the measure of the noetic beings [therein] as regards their capacity to receive signs and powers from above. Every noetic essence is hidden from the essences that are below it; yet they are not concealed from them by nature, but by the excellence of their motions.[83]

To start from the end of this very beautiful passage: every line in every psalm possesses an "excellence of motion," a way of moving that perfectly fits the words and meanings of the line. And so *unique* is this movement that we may say (with Abba Isaac) that its excellence is *concealed* from all other lines by the unique "capacity of its purity." Purity of psalmic movement is therefore *at once* a matter of artistic shape and ascetic discipline. And this capacity for purity of movement arises from each line's *receptivity* "to receive signs and power from above." That is, each line's movement is steered solely by the way it can "without mediation . . . enter in to receive the primal light."

Two powerful consequences emerge for us. First, each psalmic line can be said to possess a noetic essence that *is* its perfect movement; that is, *its way of being is its way of moving.* Second, each line's movement enters directly (i.e., without mediation) into the primal light that is flowing from God. Taken together, these powerful consequences compel two questions of signal importance: What precisely is the "noetic essence [that is] . . . confined within [the] motions" of each line of psalmic poetry, and what exactly is this motion's definitive "capacity to receive signs and powers from above"? How may we, in both instances, *define* the terms St. Isaac is using?

We can begin to shape these definitions by, first, seeing more fully what St. Isaac is discussing here. His next sentence reads: "This I say concerning the orders of the holy powers, the orders of souls, and the orders of demons," and he continues: "The first are concealed from the second and the second from the third, by nature, place, and by respective movements" (26:129). With respect to knowledge, he says, these orders are hidden from one another, but "their ability to see one another is said to come from within their motions" (26:130). In other words, just as the angels can see both the human and the demonic orders, because of that angelic "excellence of motion [arising from] their capacity to receive signs and powers from above" (ibid.), so, too, the ontological fullness of every line of psalmic poetry—that is, every line's *stillness of being*—resides entirely in that line's unique "excellence of motion." We may thus say that the whole noetic essence of every psalmic line *is* its rhythmic cadence; hence, the noetic stillness is artistically dynamic, for the stillness is ceaselessly moving. And this dynamic stillness of each psalmic line exerts a powerful effect upon all the other lines in that psalm, an effect we can describe as entering into the state of *heightened attentiveness*. This is the state we enter when we find ourselves walking very slowly through a rich, natural landscape such as a New England forest, walking tiny step by tiny step, our eyes and ears and mind and whole heart and soul and spirit completely alert to any and every least natural stirring. What we very soon become aware of in such a state is expressed in LXX Psalm 103 this way:

> 24 O Lord, how manifold are thy works, in wisdom thou hast made them all. The earth is filled with thy creations,
> 25 As is this great and spacious sea that teems with countless things, living things both small and great.
> 26 There the ships ply their way, there is that Leviathan that thou madest to play there.

To see our earthly landscapes with such spiritual alertness is (says the psalmist in Psalm 103) to "sing to the Lord all my life" (l. 33): it is, in other words, to move in and with Holy Wisdom; it is to move *psalmically*, seeing simultaneously every tiny detail and the immense Presence; it is to see both creation and Creator.

"The demons," St. Isaac says, "are not concealed from one another in their own orders; howbeit they do not see the two orders that are above them," and he continues: "For spiritual sight is the light of motion, and these very [motions] are their [i.e., noetic nature's] mirror and their eyes; but when the motions are darkened, they cannot see the orders above them."[84] The enemies in the psalms are then best understood as those who (like the demons) have so corrupted their excellence of motion as to be blinded to any higher orders. "So much for the demons," St. Isaac concludes (26:130).

But earthly souls, Abba continues, can "cleanse themselves and make their way back to their ancient created state "so that they will clearly see these three orders, that is, the order below them, the one above them, and one another [in their own order]." For us to return to our "ancient created state" is, Abba says, to purify our souls so that we see "in a spiritual manner with a natural eye, that is, the clairvoyant eye of insight" (ibid.). This clairvoyance permits the purified earthly soul to see—better: *to behold*—both the orders of angels above and the swarms of demons below. In other words, we can begin to see—*and to move in and by that seeing*—precisely in the way every psalmic line sees and moves and is: in the way of Holy Wisdom.

Such movement is also, the *He* stanza tells us, "the way of [God's] statutes"— once again, here is the stanza's opening line:

> Give me as law, O Lord, the way of thy statutes,
> And I shall seek it out always. (Ps 118:33)

The statutes are a *way* precisely because they are God's inscribings ("cuttings-into") of Himself in the creation, inscribings at once manifold in their countless myriads of living detail and unified in the directionality of all their motions toward (and finally *into*) God Himself. Thus, this way of the divine statutes is at once something we must *acquire* from God ("Teach me thy statutes," Ps 118 *passim*) and something we ontologically *become*:

> My lips shall overflow in song
> When thou teachest me thy statutes. (Ps 118:171)

Psalm 103 expresses this simultaneity of "being taught" and "having become" in this way:

> He gazes on the earth and it trembles, he touches mountains and
> they smoke.
> I will sing to the Lord all my life, I will sing psalms to my God
> for as long as I have being. (Ps 103:32–33)

The divine statutes—which are not only the earth and mountains of God's creation but are also the earthquakes and eruptions—these statutes, cut into the creation by God and acquired by us from Him, transfigure us in the Psalms to "sing to the Lord all my life" and with all my *being*. The LXX Greek verb used in the final phrase of line 33 is *hyparcho*, a verb (Lampe tells us) meaning "to exist in the beginning" (1435b); and in LXX Psalm 54, the participial form of the verb is used to describe an attribute of God Himself: *ho hyparchon pro ton aionon*, literally: "the Existing One before the ages." To have being is (in psalmic language) "to sing to the Lord"; and to have such being is to have entered fully into the state of heightened attentiveness that St. Isaac describes as acquiring "the clairvoyant eye of insight": the state, in other words, of having been taught God's statutes. And entering this state is the movement of Holy Wisdom, the way of Psalm 118.

V

Aspects of Beauty in LXX Psalm 118

A s he ends his Homily 26, St. Isaac the Syrian discusses the names of the nine angelic orders, having open before him a text attributed to St. Dionysius the Areopagite. St. Isaac translates from St. Dionysius' Greek into his own Syriac this extraordinary sentence:

> The beings of this first order are called beholders, not because they are beholders of noetic things as it were by sensible symbols, or because they are led up to the Deity by the diversity of the *theoria* of sacred Scripture, but because they are filled with light which is more sublime than all immaterial knowledge, and are brimming (as far as possible) with the divine vision of that supraessential and threefold Beauty Who is the Origin and Maker of beauty.[85]

"The first [order]," St. Isaac writes, "is composed of the great, sublime, and most holy Thrones, the many-eyed Cherubim, and the six-winged Seraphim." He notes that the "names of the orders are . . . interpreted from the Hebrew tongue: the Seraphim means those who are fervent and burning; the Cherubim, those who are great in knowledge and wisdom; the Thrones, the receptacles of God and rest" (26:131). Then St. Isaac translates the Greek of St. Dionysius, after which he continues: "These orders are given these names because of their operations. The Thrones are so-called as ones truly learned . . . ; the Seraphim, as those who make holy; the Cherubim, as those who carry . . ." (26:131–32). In this way, St. Isaac constructs very powerful clusters of significances for the Dionysian categories. The threefold order of Thrones, Seraphim, and Cherubim together behold the "threefold Beauty Who is the Origin and Maker of beauty" and are therefore themselves filled with this threefold beauty.

At the Anaphora of the Orthodox Liturgy of St. John Chrysostom (fourth century AD), the priest says a prayer of thanksgiving to God the Father, a prayer beginning: "It is meet and right" (*axion kai dikaion*).[86] It continues by describing the Father as "ineffable, inconceivable, indivisible, incomprehensible, ever-existing and eternally the same" (also attributing these attributes to the Son and to the Holy Spirit). The prayer goes on to conclude in this way: "We thank You also for this Liturgy which You graciously accept from our hands—even though

You are surrounded by thousands of archangels and tens of thousands of angels, by the Cherubim and the Seraphim, six-winged, many-eyed, soaring aloft on their wings, singing the triumphant hymn, shouting, proclaiming and saying . . ." The choir then completes the priest's prayer by singing: "Holy, holy, holy, Lord of Sabaoth, heaven and earth are full of Your glory; blessed is He who comes in the name of the Lord. Hosanna in the highest."

A few moments further on, the Liturgy then transforms the consecrated bread and wine into the Body and Blood of Christ, using the Greek aorist imperative verb to register the actuality of this change: "make this bread the precious Body of Your Christ, and that which is in this chalice the Precious Blood of Your Christ, making the change by the Holy Spirit." Crucial to this moment in the Liturgy is the grammar of the change. The aorist of the imperative verb "make" carries here not a temporal but an *aspectual* significance. That is, the command "make" is occurring not in the past but in a present that has gained the intensified actuality of the immediate past. The present participle of "making the change" is (besides being temporally present) also aspectually colored by the main verb to which it is subordinate. As a result, the grammar is saying, this transformation is occurring not merely in the present moment of time (though it *is happening* there, too) but, rather, in a *state* of heightened being, a state in which the present moment is raised up to meet the downpouring of tens of thousands of angels, including the Cherubim and the Seraphim, all of whom (in St. Dionysius' language) "are brimming . . . with the divine vision of that supraessential and threefold Beauty Who is the Origin and Maker of beauty." So essential is this aspectual significance, in fact, that some Orthodox priests will actually use in English the phrase "having made the change"—doing so, of course, to register the *factuality of the state* (as opposed to the mere temporal "moment") of this transformation. Only so, these priests plainly feel, can the consecration become *simultaneously* a present liturgical moment and an angelic state of beauty. In this way, then, the Liturgy is affirming *both* the actions of human hands *and* the cherubic-seraphic presences: that is, both present moment *and* heightened state: and in this way, the moment is *aspectualized*.

One further detail. The Liturgy refers to the Cherubim and Seraphim as "six-winged, many-eyed" (*hexapteryga, polyommata*)—adjectives drawn from the Hebrew prophetic tradition (see Isa 6:2). Their use here, in the Liturgy, helps us to further understand the state of heightened beauty occurring at—*and through*—this moment of angelic arrival on earth. Just as the six angelic wings intensify their flight, so their many eyes heighten their angelic perception: and we, too, can begin to enter with them into their state of heightened attentiveness. And what we see can help us begin to become (again using St. Dionysius' language) "brimming (as far as possible) with the divine vision of that supraessential and threefold Beauty Who is the Origin and Maker of beauty."

■   ■   ■

In Psalm 118 beauty arises from the movement of the poem. The best sense of this beauty is expressed by understanding *cadential shape* in the psalm—and throughout the Psalter. St. Gregory of Nyssa comments on the penultimate line of Psalm 150—"Praise him with resounding cymbals, praise him with triumphant cymbals" (Ps 150:5)—in this fashion:

> I take this [clashing of two cymbals] to mean the union of our nature with the angels . . . For such a combination, I mean of the angelic with the human, when human nature is again exalted to its original condition, will produce that sweet sound of thanksgiving through their meeting with one another. And through one another and with one another they [—this] combination of the angelic with the human nature [—] will sing a hymn of thanksgiving to God for His love for humanity which will be heard throughout the universe. For the coming together of *cymbal* with *cymbal* shows this . . . Whenever, then, the mercy of God again unites the two with one another, then what comes about from the two with one another will cause that praise to resound. (Heine, 121)

St. Gregory's insight is astonishing. The musical *connectedness* within the whole Psalter brings about *in us* a re-musicalization wherein our nature *combines in sound* with angelic nature. A key formulation of this harmony occurs in the phrase "through one another and with one another"—where St. Gregory's Greek reads: *di'allelon kai met'allelon*. The two Greek prepositions here used (*dia* and *meta*) emphasize, first (in *dia*), the crossing of space from one point to another, and, second (in *meta*), a joining together that creates union while sustaining distinction. That is, the Seraphim and Cherubim traverse the space between heaven and earth, in which our nature sustains its humanity while entering into angelic praise of God. The two are thus "fit together" in and as the harmony of both natures.

Every stanza of Psalm 118 possesses both a fixed and a "flowing" shape: a shape fixed by an eight-step alphabetic lineation and a shape flowing with a unique cadential experience. This second, or flowing, shape changes in every stanza to fit the encounter occurring in and between the angelic and the human natures; the first, or fixed, shape is therefore in every instance being "colored"—

more exactly: it is being "aspectualized"—by the unique cadential experience occurring in this encounter. For every stanza of Psalm 118 can be seen as taking place on that boundary between the angelic and the earthly realms, that boundary where the "tens of thousands of angels" are divinely encountering (as in the Divine Liturgy) the actual hands of human nature, as in the Liturgy. As a result, every fixed stanzaic shape is being "aspectualized" by every flowing shape in such a way that the poem's unceasing repetitions become intensification.

The key to this depth of intensification in Psalm 118 is in the significance the poem gives to the two most frequently used of the nine words for Law: "statutes" (*dikaiomata*; 30 usages in Psalm 118, all plural) and "commandments" (*entolai*; 30 plural, 1 singular). As we defined it earlier, the statutes are "the divine 'cuttings-into' (or inscriptions) made by God in the creation and left there by Him to be the nourishment that feeds our own true creativity" (see Chapter III). The statutes can therefore be said to be the fixed cadences in the creation, cadences discoverable only through psalmic song:

> Thy statutes have become my songs
> In the house of my pilgrimage. (Ps 118:54)

The Greek word here for "songs" is, in fact, a neologism coined by the LXX translators: *psalta* (for Hebrew *zemirot*). This coinage—unique in all Scripture—connects God's shaping of His creation to the psalmist's shaping of his song, a connection that sheds an interesting light upon the name given in the opening words of the Creed to God the Father: "I believe in one God, Father All-Mighty, *Poet* of heaven and earth . . ." Usually rendered "Maker," *Poet* is literally the Greek word used here: *Poietes*. The source of all human poetic energy on earth thus resides in God's "cuttings-into" the creation—resides, that is, in His statutes. And the way wherein the psalmist, in every stanza of Psalm 118, shapes the flowing cadence to the fixed alphabetic pattern reveals the fresh significances being developed and deepened in every stanza: "My lips shall overflow in song / When thou teachest me thy statutes" (Ps 118:174).

The commandments (*entolai*) emphasize this depth of intensification wherein fixed stanzaic shape becomes flowing stanzaic cadence. The commandments, as we saw, are "God's acts of self-emptying love for His creation" (see Chapter III). As such, then, the commandments can be understood to be the divine content of the action of creation: that is, as the content of God's heart. If the statutes are the fixed cadences cut into the creation, then the commandments are the outpourings from the creation flowing into our cadential praises of Him in our own acts of self-emptying love.

In 2 Kings (2 Samuel), chapter 23, we read the poem called "The Last Words of David" (l. 1). It begins this way:

> Faithful is Jesse's son, David,
> Faithful the man resurrected by the Lord,
> Faithful the one christened by Jacob's God,
> And beautiful are Israel's psalms.

The LXX word for "beautiful" used here is *euprepes* (translating Hebrew *na'him*; BDB 653b). Interestingly, St. Dionysius uses this same Greek word as a verb to describe the way wherein the fixed and the wandering stars together work in the heavens: "God [causes] the circular movements of the vast heavens, [both] the fixed orders of starry lights beautifying [*euprepon*] the sky and those special wandering stars, particularly those two rotating sources of light described as 'beautiful' [*kalos*] by Scripture [Gen 1:4] . . . and [together they are] enabling us to reckon our days and our nights, our months and our years."[87]

In construe, *eu-prepes* means "well-fitting" in the sense of fitting perfectly; and St. Dionysius' uses here permit us to understand the "fit" between the fixed and the wandering patterns of movement in the heavens as akin to the way the two cadential shapes move in the psalms. And just as God's actions of self-emptying love flow into the creation and, as statutes, become inserted there, so, too, the psalmist in Psalm 118 fits perfectly his loving experience of God into the loving creativity flowing from God. The commandments and the statutes thus meet, engage, and perfectly fit into one another. And, working together, they act in Psalm 118 to deepen the fixed patterns of every stanza at the same moment they are shaping every unique cadence.

▪ ▪ ▪

The experience expressed in every stanza—indeed, in every line—of Psalm 118 is best understood as the experience of intimacy: the intimacy occurring between the psalmic "I" and the divine "thou." The emergence of this primary experience occurs in stanza 1 of the poem. In line 1 of the psalm, both persons—the human "I" and the divine "thou"—are in the third person:

> Blessed are the blameless in the way,
> Who walk in the law of the Lord. (Ps 118:1)

The human person begins the poem in the plural, while the divine person begins as the singular modifier of "the law"—that is, "of the Lord." Line 2 sustains this distinction but adds a key singular modifier to the still plural human:

> Blessed be those searching his testimonies.
> Who seek him with the whole heart. (Ps 118:2)

The final phrase in the singular—"with the whole heart"—begins the poem's depiction of the singular psalmic human person. And, when taken with line 1's participial verb form ("those walking ones"; *hoi poreuomenoi*), "the whole heart" indicates the vast meaning of the human experience. These "searching ones" (*hoi exereunontes*), using their "whole heart," will experience the words of God in the way described by the rabbinic text entitled *Pesikta Rabbate*: "As the roots of a tree spread in all directions, so words of Torah enter and spread through the whole body of a man."[88] That is, this experience of intimacy will be, for us, something far greater than merely mental nourishment (though it will be that, too, of course); the human person will literally *walk* in the law, using the entire physical body and whole inward soul to do so. Such is the meaning of "the whole heart."

The *Philokalia* gives us the Patristic definition of this singularly important word, *kardia*, saying that it indicates, "not simply the physical organ but the spiritual centre of man's being, man made in the image of God, his deepest and truest self, or the inner shrine, to be entered only through sacrifice and death, in which the mystery of the union between the divine and human is consummated" (I:361). Then, line 3 opens a window on another human possibility, still remaining in the plural:

> For the workers of iniquity
> Have never walked in his ways. (Ps 118:3)

The LXX word "iniquity" (*anomia*) is plainly cognate with the "law" (*nomos*) of line 1, with alpha-privative having a strong significance: the total absence of all divine *nomos* produces the toxicity of *a-nomia* in the human person. This toxic condition is here understood as rendering the human person absolutely incapable of walking—an incapacity intensified by the plurality of "workers" (for no intimacy can occur when one of the intimates cannot—or, better, *refuses to*—become singular). And just as the human singular "I" requires a divine singular "Thou," so the plurality of workers in line 3 serves to close the window—even though the toxicity of *anomia* will continue to be engaged throughout the poem.

Then, in line 4, the divine second-person singular fully appears:

> Thou hast charged that thy commandments
> Be kept most diligently. (Ps 118:4)

The line emphatically (in Greek) begins with "Thou" (*su*), an emphasis not at all required by the grammar of Greek but, rather, by the poem's central drama of intimacy—an emphasis then intensified by the LXX text's final word of the half-line, "thy" (*sou*). Intensity, in fact, is the line's whole significance, intensity achieved by the highly emphatic adverb *sphodra* (here, "most diligently"), used as line 1's final word in Greek. Note, too, that this emergence of the divine second-person singular has the effect of relegating the human presence to a wholly secondary status; that is, to the status of an implied subject of the middle aorist infinitive *phylaxasthai* ("to be kept"). It is as if the banishing of the plurality of iniquitous workers had led to such an effect. Yet, line 4 also opens the window of intimacy; for *sphodra* (used in this line for the first of ten times in Psalm 118—with twelve usages in LXX texts other than Rahlfs') is indeed the Greek adverb of maximum intensity. In our keeping of God's commandments, then, lies the way of intimacy.

The fifth line of the stanza then establishes the singular human presence as fully capable of entering into intimacy with God, an establishment that is a prayer and *not* an assertion.

> O that my ways be all directed
> To the keeping of thy statutes. (Ps 118:5)

This distinction between prayer and assertion accounts for the beautiful *way* in which the human presence occurs: as a divine modification of human "ways." The possessive pronoun "my," in Greek, is the word *mou*; in Hebrew it is simply a single-letter suffix added to the Hebrew word for "ways" (*derek*). These tiny strokes in the fifth line of both Hebrew and Greek serve the same immense end in the psalm: the human entry into the divine intimacy.

In the closing hours of the year 2003, on December 31, I was in Vatopaidi Monastery on Mount Athos, having arrived as a pilgrim the previous afternoon. An American-born monk, Father Matthew, showed the three of us (my son Benedict, our friend Mark, and myself) the monastery's reliquary. Among other blessed treasures at Vatopaidi, he showed us a belt woven by the Mother of God and worn by Her. As I bent to kiss the glass case where the belt lay, I sensed all at once a strong clearing in my heart: the weariness and anxieties of long travel suddenly lifted for a moment, and it was as if I could directly see Her beautiful hands weaving this sash at that very moment. Awestruck, I turned to Father Matthew; but he was already showing us another treasured relic, his plain Wisconsin voice flowing on with warm explanation. The moment was quickly gone—but the experience is endless for me. For I have seen with my whole heart the grace of Her hands.

And this endlessness of experience is what defines the intimacy of line 5: "the keeping of thy statutes." To keep the divine inscriptions (or "cuttings-into") that are God's statutes is to sustain relation—for all eternity—to the actual work of God's hands in shaping the creation: to sustain the intimacy. Such sustaining is not at all a consequence of an action of one's personal will; it is, instead, the result of letting one's ways be directed by God. The LXX verb used here for "directed" (*kateuthuno*) is made up of the Greek word for "straight" (*euthus*) combined with the Greek preposition meaning to "go down into" (*kata*). Hence, the verb can be rightly understood to signify the incarnate reality of actually moving through the creation in the ways inscribed by God—and thus (say LXX lexicographers) the verb also means "to flourish" (Lust II:249b). Such flourishing is the direct consequence of intimacy with God.

Thus, in line 6, the first and immediate result happens to the psalmist:

> Then I shall not be ashamed
> When I behold all thy commandments. (Ps 118:6)

This first consequence of intimacy is twofold: the condition of not being ashamed and the beholding of God's commandments. Both verbs are first-person singular: the human partner has now emerged in the poem, never to leave the experience of intimacy. "To be ashamed" is, in LXX Greek, *epaischunomai*—a verb used in the whole of the Psalter only in this line of Psalm 118: hence, its significance is essential to our understanding.

Psalmic shame is the absence of all psalmic beauty, the collapse of all psalmic shape into the isolative toxicity of *anomia* (iniquity). It is therefore the complete obliteration of what Psalm 88 powerfully calls the "reconciling exchange / Given by . . . Christ":

> Remember the contempt, O Lord, I suffered in my heart,
> contempt all thy servants suffer from all the nations,
> Contempt, O Lord, thine enemies have used to darken that
> reconciling exchange given by thy Christ. (Ps 88:50–51)

The aim of all psalmic enemies is to produce exactly this darkening; for such a condition—far more than merely bodily death—is primarily *ontological* in its consequences: "I have become their contempt" (Ps 108:25). And to have *become* the contempt of the enemies is to have unmade every experience of intimacy: the reconciling exchange has become the darkness of total isolation. Personhood is thereby wrecked, and the psalmist thus descends into the pit of autonomous selfhood.

I am counted among those who go down into the pit, like a man
no one would help, like a man free among the dead,
Like mangled men lying in graves whom thou rememberest no
more, like those snatched from thy hand.
They have laid me in the lowest pit, in dark places, in death's
shadow. (Ps 87:4–6)

And, as this passage from Psalm 87 reminds us, to suffer such ontological wreckage is to follow Christ Himself through the crucifixion and down into the tomb, where—through the presence of Psalm 118 in Holy Saturday Matins—death is in fact overthrown:[89] "Then I shall not be ashamed [i.e., I shall not remain ontologically beyond the "reconciling exchange"] / When I behold thy commandments" (Ps 118:6). In their enacting of the content of God's heart, the commandments serve to rescue the psalmist from the toxicity of spiritual *anomia*; for as he beholds—as he fully and deeply sees all the way into the commandments, he enters into the depths of God's heart: into, that is, the reconciling exchange given by Christ.

But the stanza is not over—nor, of course, the whole poem. For the futurity of the final three verbs serves to sustain the stanza's (and whole poem's) central drama of seeking God:

6 Then I shall not be ashamed
   When I behold all thy commandments.
7 I shall praise thee with upright heart
   As I learn thy righteous judgments.
8 I shall keep thy statutes,
   Do not utterly forsake me. (Ps 118:6–8)

The psalmist seeks, and finds, and then seeks still further, always risking the loss of the saving exchange as he unceasingly—line by line, stanza after stanza—deepens his experience of intimacy with God. This risking of everything creates, in line 7, the psalmically defining experience of praise-giving: "I shall praise thee" (*exomologesomai soi*). The Hebrew verb translated here is *yadah* (BDB 392a), a verb exhibiting the striking semantic property of meaning (in different grammatical forms) both "to throw" and "to give praise"—"perhaps," say the lexicographers, "from gestures accompanying the act" (ibid.). A further Hebrew meaning is "to confess" (BDB 392b) in the sense of both confessing God as one's savior and confessing one's sins to God. All three Hebrew significances are gathered in and fully expressed by the LXX verb, with the additional emphasis given by the preposition *ex-*, meaning "[move] out from." Giving of psalmic praise therefore becomes, in line 7 of the stanza, the way of sustaining the experience of intimacy.

A line from an earlier psalm can help deepen our understanding of line 7:

> The Lord is my helper and my defender, in him my heart hopes
> and I am helped, and my whole flesh flourishes; with my whole
> will I shall confess him. (Ps 27:7)

This flourishing is the result of the psalmist's heart—and "whole will"—throwing itself into the action of confessing God (*exomologesomai*: the very same verb form occurs here), a confessing that is also the act of praising. Similarly, a line later in Psalm 118 speaks further to line 7:

> At midnight I rose to give thee thanks
> For the righteousness of thy judgments. (Ps 118:62)

"To give thee thanks" is, in LXX Greek, this same verb: *exomologeisthai soi*, and the LXX phrasing of line 62 exactly matches the phrasing of line 7: *ta krimata tes dikaiosynes sou*, "the judgments of thy righteousness." One of the nine words for law in Psalm 118 (see Chapter III), "judgments" occurs sixteen times in the plural and four times in the singular, and they are best defined as "specific applications of God's words in situations of human dispute or conflict, applications that divinely resolve human conflict" (see Chapter III). The immediacy of this application connects the judgments to the flowing cadences of the psalm in the sense that their *specificity* partakes of the incarnation: just as God really became human flesh and blood in Christ, so, too, the judgments of God really incarnated divine righteousness on earth.

Hence, with line 7 of the poem, the crucial psalmic subject of *righteousness* emerges in Psalm 118. The Hebrew word is defined in the masculine form as "what is right, just, normal" and in the feminine as "God's attribute as sovereign" (BDB 841b, 842a. Fabre d'Olivet comments beautifully on each of the three consonants of *sadek* this way:

> s: scisson, term, solution, goal, and when it begins a word, the
> consonant signifies movement toward the word's final sign;
> d: the abundance that occurs in and through division; and
> k: astringency and trenchancy in, and as, actual materials.[90]

That is, *sadek* is the impulsion to divide actuality with sharpness, the actualized movement sharply cutting the material world. Like the "judgments," then, *sadek* is the incarnate "cutting-into" the world, the sword that gives shape, the ax that clears and clarifies the land. In translating *sadek*, the LXX *dikaiosyne* is (says Lampe, 369b) a divine attribute that finds its likeness in human persons. *Dikaiosyne* is thus the quickening of the human into movement toward—*and into*—God, a movement that is the spiritual sword of divine clarification, a shaping of the human that is simultaneously the giving birth of the divine. To learn the judgments of divine *sadek* is therefore to be *cut into* by God's clarifying sword and thus to experience life-giving intimacy with Him; in d'Olivet's terms it is to become abundant through division.

VI
The Drama of Intimacy

I

O n August 23, 1988, I was in the Russian town of Sergiev Posad (then called Zagorsk), at the church, founded by St. Sergius of Radonezh, called Holy Trinity. Part of a small group of American Orthodox believers come to Russia to recognize the millennium of Orthodoxy in Russia, I and my fellow pilgrims entered to join the hundreds of other hushed pilgrims crowding the church that hot summer afternoon. I identified the faint voices from the front of the church as the voices of Orthodox monks softly chanting psalms. People were exiting in twos and threes along the walls, and we began to inch slowly forward toward where the monks—two of them I now could see—were chanting in turns as they faced one another over the head and foot of a coffin, and over the entire coffin was placed a glass dome maybe ten inches high. Here was what we had traveled over two hundred miles to behold: the incorrupt body of St. Sergius. One by one, the pilgrims were going up three steps to the area on the *amvon* where St. Sergius lay, kissing the dome above the saint, and then saying a brief prayer or petition. After half a minute or so, another monk—not one of the chanters—would lightly touch the pilgrim's shoulder or arm, then help him or her to another set of three steps leading back down to the church floor. Already another pilgrim would be at the saint's tomb.

As I bent to kiss St. Sergius' folded hands, I found myself saying softly: "Holy and blessed Saint Sergius, guide me in my life, lead me on thy path, and pray to God for me." Since that long-ago summer moment, I have said this brief prayer each morning and evening to the blessed Saint, always with the sharpest memory of what I wrote in my journal that August night in 1988: "I will remember all my life the depth of the *presence* of Saint Sergius: some dozen yards all round the casket there was a field of humming energy that was almost perceptible light." Intimacy of spiritual contact participates in the incorruptibility of God.

The drama of Psalm 118 takes place at just this point of contact. In its love for the boundary between the psalmic "I" and the divine "thou," it reveals at every moment that only in loving the boundary can there arise the intimacy that saves the human and reveals the divine. We can say of such intimacy precisely what Psalm 118 emphasizes in Orthodox patterns of psalmic prayer:

Holy Trinity–St. Sergius Lavra,
Sergiev Posad, Russia. Photo: Shutterstock.

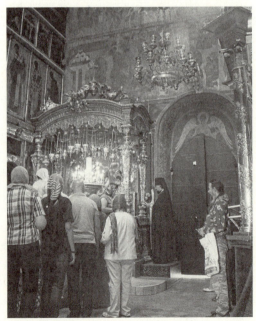

Pilgrims visiting St. Sergius' relics.
Photo: Arthur Lookyanov.

"I shall never forget thy statutes, / In them thou hast quickened me to life" (to a life that will never die), and "I opened my mouth, I drew in my breath, / I longed for thy commandments" (Ps 118: 93, 131). To be quickened into undying life is to touch, and to be touched by, God's life; and to open one's mouth and draw in one's breath is to begin to sing the psalms of unceasing praise.

These two lines, widely separated in Psalm 118, are given a unique emphasis by the Orthodox monastic practice (accepted by all of Orthodoxy) of dividing the Psalter into twenty sections, called *kathismata*, and then subdividing each *kathisma* into three *stases* or subsections. This practice arose plainly for liturgical reasons; and by the twelfth century AD the practice had been everywhere accepted in Orthodoxy.

The first of the two lines is marked as the *mese*, or midpoint, of the entire poem and is a line emphasized in its liturgical presentation:

> I shall never forget thy statutes,
> In them thou hast quickened me to life. (Ps 118:93)

What is striking is that this line occurs five lines *after* the poem's numerical mid-point at line 88, and it is the fifth line of its stanza; hence, the emphasis is dramatic.

The second of the two lines concludes the second stasis of the seventeenth kathisma (the whole of the kathisma is the entirety of Psalm 118):

> I opened my mouth, I drew in my breath,
> I longed for thy commandments. (Ps 118:131)

What is unusual—and therefore emphatic—about having line 131 *conclude* the second stasis of this kathisma is that such a conclusion interrupts the fixed eight-line stanzaic pattern sustained in the poem's other twenty-one stanzas: thus, the kathisma division cuts across the stanzaic division.

Both lines (93 and 131), then, achieve dramatic emphasis by overriding their stanzaic patterns, one (93) five lines into its stanza, the other (131) three lines in. So important are these two lines, then, that we may rightly say that they together contain the key to all monastic—hence, all Orthodox—comprehension of the psalm's drama of divine and human intimacy.

■　■　■

On August 30, 1988, on the penultimate afternoon of our pilgrimage to Russia, I had grown tired from the whirlwind schedules of the Soviet In-tourist Bureau and I chose to stay in my hotel room, where I fell deeply asleep and experienced this long dream:

I am in a Soviet city where Orthodox Christendom—and all other religion—is illegal. I meet in a courtyard a fellow believer about my age—someone with whom years ago I had been part of a small but very devout group of secretly practicing Jews. We clasp hands and embrace joyfully in wonderful sunlight. The courtyard is surrounded by high white walls on every side and is packed with (I now see) scores of other believers. Suddenly I see a low, squat truck whisk into the courtyard and begin to crush and kill the other devout believers. Then, the truck swings toward me (my now-terrified friend flees, screaming), and at the instant it is about to crush me I hold up a single large folio page of psalmic Hebrew: and, unswerving, the truck simply passes through me, and the three people driving it become illusions that vanish in the sunlight now streaming from the page of psalmic Hebrew. And I awaken.

Shocked but somehow refreshed, I pick up my journal and write down this dream, ending the account this way: "strong sense that at the moment the vehicle was to make contact I *passed on into* another realm wherein I am to carry on the devout life."

My dream, then, can be said to have taken place at the boundary where two worlds touch—the same boundary where, at the end of every autumn, the chill death of earthly winter can begin its slow, painful journey into the Paschal joy of earthly resurrection: and, thus, the same boundary where, in Psalm 118, the drama of intimacy is occurring at every moment in the poem.

■   ■   ■

On October 7, 1337, the novice-monk Bartholomew was blessed by his abbot to enter fully into monastic vows. The abbot named him Sergius, and at Holy Communion, the chronicler tells, "the air of the church was heavily scented" with a sweetly angelic odor.[91] Retiring to a tiny cell in the forest of Radonezh, the monk Sergius began a life of solitary prayer. One night, we are told, Sergius entered the church to sing Matins; the chronicler continues:

> When he began to sing, the wall of the Church suddenly opened and the Devil entered, accompanied by a multitude of his servants. They attacked the blessed one, gnashing their teeth and taunting him, "Flee from this place or we will destroy you and you will die at our hands." Armed with prayer, the saint said in a loud voice, "Let God arise, let His enemies be scattered" (Ps 67:1).[92]

Sung at every Pascha, Psalm 67 proclaims the Resurrection of Christ, going on to shout this wondrous line: "Our God is the God of salvation, and to the Lord, to the Lord are the paths out from death" (Ps 67:20). The "paths out from death" are, in LXX Greek, *diexodoi*, literally the "paths" (*hodoi*) all the way through (*dia*) and out (*ex-*) from death: from, that is, the death-dealing isolation of earthly existence out into life-giving intimacy. Note, too, that this line from Psalm 67 immediately follows a *diapsalmic* moment, that pause wherein the Holy Spirit interrupts the ongoing music of the psalm in order to deepen the psalm's spiritual content (see Chapter II). The *diapsalma*, we now may say, is a boundary moment in a psalm, a moment where the intimacy between psalmist and God is interrupted so as to flow deeper and still deeper.

Such is also the way the newly blessed monk Sergius began his works and days in psalmic prayer: at the boundary where—in the fashion of a *diapsalma*—two worlds touch in deepest intimacy.

A text much loved by the monk Sergius in his lifetime of prayer comes down to us (as it had to Sergius) in St. Luke's Gospel. Spoken by the Theotokos, it can, in St. Luke's beautiful Greek, be rightly understood as the most perfect of all psalms:

1   My soul magnifies the Lord,
     My spirit has rejoiced in God my savior

2   For He has beheld His handmaiden's humility,
     All generations shall henceforth call me blessed.

3   For He who is powerful
     Has done great things to me,
     And holy is His name,

4   And His mercy is upon those who fear Him
     From generation to generation.

5   He has shown strength with His arm,
     He has scattered the arrogant
     In the discourses of their hearts.

6   He has cast the powerful
     Down from their thrones
     And has exalted the humble.

7   He has filled the hungry with good things,
     The rich He has sent empty away.

8   He has helped His servant Israel
     In remembrance of His mercy,

> 9 As He spoke to our fathers,
> To Abraham and his seed forever. (Lk 1:46–55)

The first line describes perfectly the process occurring in Psalm 118 as the drama of intimacy. As the psalmist's soul at every moment touches the divine presence, it is experiencing two distinct worlds at once: the vast world of human spiritual intensity and the unendingly greater world of divine loving. The experience is therefore one wherein the human soul is itself divinely magnified as it engages in the magnification of the divine (a point beautifully echoed in Lucan Greek: *megalynei* and *megaleia*).

Midpoint in the poem is a crucial line:

> He has shown strength with His arm,
> He has scattered the arrogant
> In the discourses of their hearts. (l. 5)

The "arrogant" (*hyperephanoi*), says Lampe (1439b), exhibit the "sin which destroys the soul," the sin that, "coupled with *hubris*," is the first sin. "We will magnify our own tongues, our lips are our own; who is Lord over us?" says Psalm 11:4 (and here is the first use of *megalynei* in the LXX Psalter). What unmakes the soul, then, is the arrogance of self-praise of one's inward discourse, that self-praise wherein one's heart loses all capacity for intimacy with the divine. As Christ becomes incarnate within Mary, He scatters in us every self-praising arrogance.

The Lucan Greek for line 5's word "discourse" is *dianoia*, a word used extensively in *The Philokalia* to signify that mental function whereby one formulates concepts *about* the divine, but never *directly experiences* the divine. St. Isaac the Syrian characterizes the *dianoia* as "that swift-winged and most shameless bird," darting here and everywhere in its disruption of prayer. *Dianoia* in us, then, needs to be scattered by God in order that we may enter into intimacy with Him.

A passage from Ilias the Presbyter in *The Philokalia* helps us better to comprehend this scattering: "When through continuous prayer the words of the psalms are brought down into the heart, then the heart like good soil begins to produce by itself various flowers: roses, the vision of incorporeal realities; lilies, the luminosity of corporeal realities; and violets, the many judgments of God, hard to understand" (III:59).

Planted by psalmic prayer, these flowers replace the heart's discourses with the fragrance of the divine made incarnate on earth. "Prayer unites with the Bridegroom," says Ilias, "a soul wounded by nuptial love" (III:43); and every intimacy is fully consummated, every hunger fulfilled. What makes the

Magnificat the most perfect psalm is its luminously clear comprehension of what is hardest to understand: that reality of intimacy where two worlds touch and are quickened into life.

■   ■   ■

In early June 1989, as spring warmth came finally to the White Mountains of northern New Hampshire where we then lived, I received a brief note and a small package from Evgeny Tislenko, a seminarian at St. Sergius Academy whom I had met the previous August on my pilgrimage there. His English was excellent, and the two of us had talked that day at some length about the icons the monastery displayed in its tiny archeological museum. Among other things, he said that the iconic face seems at first glance to be severe and heavy, but "behind the holy face is light coming toward you"; and he went on, "the face is at every instant in the process of becoming pure light." Evgeny's eyes were filled with this blessed light as he spoke.

Some ten months later, his note to me—mailed a few days earlier from California by another American Orthodox pilgrim to whom he had recently entrusted the task—spoke with joy of our meeting, and sent prayers that this prosphora bread will reach me safely. I opened the package, and in my hand I held a small but beautiful prosphora loaf depicting St. Sergius praying before the Theotokos. I carried the bread to my icon shelf, where that evening I offered my prayer in psalms to the Saint and also for his servant Evgeny. Since June 1989, I have remembered in prayer St. Sergius and Evgeny Tislenko each morning and evening. The bread has remained as beautifully fresh as the day I received it, a tiny icon of the incorrupt; and once at prayer, my gaze was drawn down to see it, briefly, glowing with light.

Prosphora loaf from
Holy Trinity–St. Sergius Lavra.

The words of the psalms—"brought down into the heart," Ilias says—become the roses of heavenly incorruption, the lilies of earthly luminosity, and the violets of divine judgments "hard to understand" in their intricate patterns. In becoming so, the words of psalms can be seen to exhibit what St. Isaac the Syrian terms "a noetic ray": "Those who in their way of life are led by divine grace to be enlightened are always aware of something like a noetic ray running between the written lines which enables the mind to distinguish words spoken simply from those spoken with great meaning for the soul's enlightenment" (1, p. 6).

Note carefully: the noetic ray is not *in* the written lines but, rather, runs *between* them. For—when the psalmic words are carried down into the heart of the one praying them, the noetic ray acts so as to become the roots that enter into the soil. And once they take root in that soil, the words can become for us the various flowers of incorruption: and thereby can scatter in us that inner discourse our arrogant hearts otherwise sustain. And we then can enter the drama of intimacy wherein we open our mouth and draw in our breath, longing for God's commandments: a drama that is (in St. Isaac's words) an entire way of life.

The whole of Psalm 118 is, at every moment, teaching this drama to those praying the psalm: How best to enter into the drama, how to sustain it truly, and how to conclude it rightly? The psalm's final line is:

> I have gone astray like a lost sheep,
> Seek out thy servant,
> I have never forgotten thy commandments. (Ps 118:176)

To realize fully and finally that one has "gone astray" is to scatter every last and least vestige of one's inner discursive arrogance (i.e., one's *dianoia*), and thereby to have begun the work of noetic flowering. To be one who is "lost" (*apololos*) is, the Greek lexicographers tell us, to be one who is wrecked, destroyed, and utterly devastated (LSJ 207b; Lampe, 200b), a LXX sense that retains perfectly the sense of the Hebrew word used here in line 176: *abad*, meaning "to perish, to be exterminated" (BDB 1a). This final wreckage of one's *dianoia* opens the way into Memory Eternal: "I have never forgotten thy commandments" (Ps 118:176).

And when all *dianoia* in us is scattered, we can begin to escape the dreadful spiritual affliction described in Psalm 12:

> When can I put an end to my soul's endless plans, having terror in
> my heart every day? How long will my enemy be exalted over me?
> (Ps 12:2)

The soul's "endless plans" (*boulai en psyche mou*) are the fevered spinnings of *dianoia*, and as such, they are the inward death of a capacity for true intimacy. This inward death then spreads to infect the whole of outward creation, an infection that kills every lily of earthly luminosity: that is, it kills all of God's statutes on and in the earth, all the divine "cuttings-into" (or inscriptions) made by God in the creation and left there by Him to be the nourishment that feeds our own true creativity (see Chapters II and III). And then terror descends upon us.

Conversely, when all our *dianoia* is scattered, we can begin to experience the earth as filled with luminosity—as, here, in Psalm 148:

> 7 Praise the Lord from under the earth, you serpents and all
>   the deeps,
> 8 Fire and hail, snow and ice, stormy wind fulfilling His word,
> 9 Mountains and all the hills, fruitful trees and all cedars,
> 10 Wild beasts and all cattle, creeping things and wild birds,
> 11 Kings of the earth and all peoples, princes and all judges of
>   the earth,
> 12 Both young men and maidens, elders together with children:
> 13 Let them praise the Lord's name, for his name alone is exalted,
>   his splendor is over earth and heaven. (Ps 148:7–13)

Each (indeed every) element in the creation could be—in the spins of *dianoia*—a cause for the soul's endless terror; instead, in this psalm, each is experienced by the psalmist as participant in the joyful praise of God's intimate loving. The result is "splendor" (*exomologesis*). The word *exomologesis* is used in Patristic literature primarily to mean (Lampe tells us, 499b) *confession*, and it thereby can come to signify the voluntary cessation of one's isolation from God and the choosing instead of intimacy with Him. In Psalm 148, such choosing is exhibited by every created thing, even including the mountains (see l. 9 above). The Hebrew word for "mountain" is *har* (BDB 249a), and Rashi explains "the root of *har* is *harah, pregnant*, because the mountains which bridge from the earth's surface resemble the contour of a pregnant woman, and they are full of [priceless] minerals and metals" (*Tehillim*, V, 1724).

To choose praise of God over one's own fevered, isolative discourses is to magnify the Lord—and thereby to enter into that drama of intimacy with Him in which all things are participating—and all things are fruitful.

The range in these seven lines from Psalm 148 is thus, as we see, complete: beginning under the earth and going up into the realms of earthly weather, and the mountains and all the vegetative kingdoms ("Fruitful trees and all cedars"), and thus through the animal worlds of wild and domesticated beasts, all the way up into the peopled realms where kings and judges, old and young "praise the Lord's name" (l. 13): all and everything participates in this intimacy with God, an intimacy concluding most joyfully in the drama of the whole Psalter. The result indeed is *confession* as a splendor (*exomologesis*) that "is over earth and heaven" (l.13), the splendor of intimacy with God that arises from psalmic words having been taken down into the "good soil" of a heart become thoroughly cleansed of all its isolative *dianoia*.

Every line of Psalm 118 is charged with this splendor: with, that is, this scattering of *dianoia* and this fulfilling of the hunger for luminosity. As such, every line magnifies the Lord. A good light is found in Psalm 32:

> The Lord scatters the counsels of nations, he makes men's
> thoughts become as nothing, he makes as nothing the counsels
> of kings. (Ps 32:10)

Though the LXX verb used here slightly differs from the one used in Lucan Greek (*diaskedazo* here; *diaskorpizo* in Luke), the lexicographers concur that their meanings are convergent to the point of being nearly identical. Both verbs also occur in Psalms to signify the same complex phenomenon: the action of God scattering human *dianoia* so as to permit the flowers of divine illumination to take root in the good soil of our souls—or else (reversely) the action of human violence against the divine so as to bring about the cold triumph of human isolation and the consequent death of all intimacy.

In Psalm 118, we find this darker use of *diaskedazo*:

> It is time for the Lord to act,
> They have shattered thy law. (Ps 118:126)

When "men's thoughts" become increasingly *something*, then God's law (*nomos*; *torah*) is shattered (*diaskedazo*); and the two words rhyme similarly in Hebrew, Greek, and English (scatter/shatter). Equally, the rhyming of the first syllables in the English pair of verbs (*sk-/sh-*) nicely matches the prepositional prefix repeated in both Greek verbs (*dia*). The point is thus made vividly clear in LXX Greek and English: the psalmic process of creating earthly luminosity constitutes the drama of psalmic intimacy; and this is also the process of psalmic prayer—of being taught God's statutes: "Blessed art thou, O Lord, / Teach me thy statutes" (Ps 118:12).

▪ ▪ ▪

In the autumn of 1983, I was teaching first-year Latin at Plymouth State College in Plymouth, New Hampshire. Mid-October was in the high beauty of splendid colors found in northern New England, and I was in my office-hours when a student who had missed several classes that week appeared at my door. Earlier that day I had gotten a note from the department secretary about a phone call from this student explaining that her aunt had died. Rising from my chair, I greeted her and said I was sorry to hear of her aunt's death. She burst into tears. I had her sit down, and, between sobs, she explained that her husband's mother had died last spring, and he hadn't been able to absorb it yet, and she couldn't turn to him for support now, and "death seems everywhere now, just everywhere." She sobbed deeply.

After a bit, I said: "You're a very good student, B., and you can do schoolwork when you're ready again. Right now you've got grieving to do—you and your husband—and your work is not to avoid or evade any of it."

She nodded. I asked her if she'd like to see the College counselor. She nodded again, saying she was so *very* tired, *so* tired.

I tried the counselor and found him in and willing to see her if she could come in fifteen minutes. I told her and she nodded once more.

Hanging up the phone, I turned again to B., and I told her about the night some ten years ago when I got the phone call telling me my father had died, and how I cried and cried—but then stopped; and I really didn't finish until years later. I told her that grief seems to take about eighteen months from start to finish, no matter when you start, even if it's years after the death.

She listened deeply, her tears stilled now. It was time for her to go. We stood up, and I lightly embraced her for a moment, saying, "You're not alone." And she left.

For the rest of the year's work in Latin, B. was steadily successful, and she never mentioned our conversation again. At year's end, she sent me a card and a letter after the final grades were in. In part she wrote: "The support and kindness you gave me last fall made it possible for me to have the strength to continue my studies, as well as the courage to look at each day with hope instead of sorrow. Even as I sit here writing this note I can feel the emotion welling up inside me, for I realize I couldn't have made it without your help. And it is very important to me that you realize how much you did for me."

Some nine months later, on August 2, 1984, I came upon this passage from Ladislaus Boros' book entitled *Hidden God*[93]:

> How does a man acquire the strength to open himself up to
> another's need and darkness, to rise above his own misery and burden
> himself with the burdens of another's life? How can a man who is

himself broken by life help another human being? How can he make another's life easier? The answer is quite simple—with words spoken into the darkness, to a stranger, and continually, faithfully repeated: "You are not alone."

That August evening of 1984, I wrote this passage of Boros' in my journal, adding: "I believe quite deeply that certain words—e.g., 'You are not alone'—are in themselves potent because Our Lord said or otherwise signified them, and that when we use them with one another, we are bringing Him closer to us, letting Him be in us, between us, around us."

A few weeks later, on September 8, 1984—the Feast of the Nativity of the Theotokos—I would be received into the Orthodox faith. On the eve of my reception, I wrote in my journal: "I feel already as though something very vast and venerable and warm and dark and exact is enfolding me, taking me in immense arms (soft dark wings?). It is the Church, it is the Bride of Christ Our Lord. And I too am to be wedded to Him" (30).

The drama of intimacy proclaimed in every line of Psalm 118 is the life of the Church. And you are never alone. Never.

II

In 2 Kings (2 Samuel), the chronicler describes the moment when King David gets up from his couch one afternoon and looks down from his palace roof to see Bathsheba, the wife of Uriah the Hittite, bathing, "and the woman was intensely [LXX *sphodra*] beautiful" (2 Kgs 11:2). Rabbinic tradition tells how, after David struck down Goliath, he sought to behead the giant but was unable to find the knot to untie the linked chain mail protecting the giant's neck and head. Uriah came up to David. "If you will give me an Israelite woman as wife, I will show you the knot to untie the chain mail." David consented, and Uriah showed David the knot hidden in the sole of the dead Goliath's foot. "God was angry with David," the rabbinic commentary continues, "for promising a daughter of Israel to a gentile. He desired that Bathsheba, the woman who had been preordained to be David's wife, should be Uriah's wife first. The Sages say, 'Bathsheba was designated as David's mate from the six days of Creation, but David took her before the proper time'" (*Tehillim*, II, 651). Thus the intimacy between David and Bathsheba, though ordained "from the six days of Creation," begins as the violence of adultery: a violence punishable in Jewish law by death (Lev 20:10). In other words, the intimacy between them begins in illicit darkness and proceeds to preordained splendor. How does this movement occur?

David sleeps with Bathsheba, and she conceives a child. So David arranges for her soldier husband, Uriah (who is fighting in the front lines of David's armies), to be sent back home on leave. David's plan to have Uriah sleep with Bathsheba (and thus be considered as father to the child she has already conceived by David) fails in the face of Uriah's loyalty to his comrades still at the battle lines. He says to David: "My comrades are encamped in the open fields, and shall I go into my house to eat and drink, and sleep with my wife? How could I do this?" (LXX 2 Kgs 11:11). Instead, Uriah sleeps in the palace hallway with David's servants, his civilian comrades from before the current wars.

It is a question of some moment to ask whether Uriah might not be entirely innocent in this exchange with the King. For the months of intimacy between David and Bathsheba could very easily have become palace gossip— and therefore just as easily been passed on to Uriah the moment he arrived in Jerusalem; certainly (as Moshe Garseil has proposed) he could have been told the first night he bunks down in the palace hallway with his old friends (Alter, 253). The narrative gives no hint to confirm this supposition; but neither does it at all preclude it. Assuming for the moment its truth, Uriah becomes a potentially very dangerous enemy to David (one can easily imagine the possibilities for blackmail)—as well as a rival for Bathsheba. In any event, David immediately arranges for Uriah to be sent back to the battlefield the next day— carrying with him a letter to the field commander Joab saying, "Station Uriah in the severest of the front lines, retreat from behind him, so he will be wounded and killed" (2 Kgs 11:14). It happens exactly as David plans, and Uriah is slain.

The biblical account continues: "When the wife of Uriah heard that Uriah her husband was dead, she mourned for her husband. And when the time of mourning ended, David sent for her and took her into his house, and she became his wife and bore him a son. But [the chapter concludes] the thing David had done was evil in the Lord's eyes. And the Lord [the next chapter begins] sent Nathan to David" (2 Kgs 11:26–12:1).

How, we must again ask, given such a beginning, can the intimacy between David and Bathsheba ever possibly enter into the psalmic realm of earthly splendor? The answer lies in Psalm 50, entitled "A Psalm of David, When Nathan the Prophet came to him, after he had gone into Bathsheba, the wife of Uriah." For this psalm perfectly enacts the process of repentance and thus discloses some of the deepest significances in the psalmic drama of intimacy; and thereby Psalm 50 sheds great light on the primary meaning of Psalm 118.

In this light the possibility that Uriah may be (or may easily become) a particularly dangerous blackmailer of the king assumes its greatest urgency. For if David is simply exterminating dangerous vermin in his household, it is one thing. But if he is cold-bloodedly murdering the lawful husband of Bathsheba so as to cover up adultery, it is quite another. In other words, is David simply sinning against Uriah—or has he become entirely iniquitous? Or (using the terms of Psalm 50) is David merely superficially wounded or is he—as is a leper—systemically infected? For if it is the prior condition (i.e., sin), he is fairly easily cured. But if it is the latter, then he—like the leper—needs the deepest cleansing. Truly genuine intimacy of the kind that David desires with Bathsheba requires clarity on this question.

From this perspective, then, we can see why the biblical narrative is so thoroughly silent on the question of Uriah as potential vermin. The narrative is silent about Uriah—and here is the crucial point—because *it makes no difference.* That is, Uriah's *potential* aggression cannot be preemptively struck down by David without David thereby becoming iniquitous (and not merely sinful) against Uriah. Psalm 50 begins by using three distinct words for David's actions against Uriah:

> Have mercy on me, O God, according to thy great mercy; according
> to the abundance of thy compassion blot out my transgression.
> Wash me thoroughly from my iniquity and cleanse me from my sin.
> (Ps 50:1–2)

The first word, *transgression* (LXX *anomema*), is an umbrella term that covers both *iniquity* (LXX *anomia*) and *sin* (LXX *hamartia*)—(see Lampe, 147b). *Sin*, says Lampe (81a), is mainly a nontheological word, and it means "a slip" or "a fall," as in a young child learning how to walk. *Iniquity*, on the other hand, is the systemic infection of a person's entire nature and is therefore equivalent to leprosy of the body.

The point is clear: at the very start of Psalm 50, David declares that his sin against Uriah *is also iniquity against him;* hence, as does the leper, David now needs to be *washed thoroughly* (LXX *epi pleion;* literally, "up to the greatest possible extent"), to be sprinkled with the very herb used by lepers (and those caring for them) for washing the sores of leprosy: *hyssop* (Ps 50:9). Thus begins, for David, the process of deep repentance (*katanyxis;* see above) that can transform even the darkest drama of violently fake intimacy into the true splendor of genuine intimacy. This process of repentance is the only way to restore splendor to the drama of intimacy; and in Psalms (and, indeed, in all Scripture), this is a difficult and harsh healing:

> Thou hast shown thy people harsh things, thou hast made us drink
> down the wine of deep repentance. (Ps 59:3)

Often translated "compunction," this "deep repentance" (LXX *katanyxis*) is beautifully glossed in *The Philokalia*: "The state of one . . . becoming conscious both of his own sinfulness [i.e., iniquity] and of the forgiveness being extended to him by God, a mingled feeling of sorrow, tenderness and joy" (I:428). St. Gregory Palamas explicitly connects the wine of deep repentance in Psalm 59 to the wine that gladdens the heart in Psalm 103:15, saying that the wine of deep repentance "crushes the passions . . . and fills [the soul] with blessed joy" (ibid., IV:314). Thus, even the "harsh things" (LXX *sclera*) are experienced as the direct gifts of God, as gifts that restore the deepest intimacy with Him. For as David says in Psalm 50, the violence of his intimacy with Bathsheba has been most deeply violence against intimacy with God Himself: "Against thee, thee alone, have I sinned" (Ps 50:4). In repentance, David is thus healing this deep violation.

And thereby, Psalm 50 reveals a central fact about the experience of genuine repentance: it is not primarily a psychological one, but is, rather, a theological-spiritual experience; it heals the spirit of David and thereby heals his soul. In other words, by cleansing him of the leprosy of iniquity, genuine repentance makes David "hear joy and gladness" (*agalliasin kai euphrosynen*; Ps 50:8).

In this light, then, one can best understand the meaning of sacrifice in Psalm 50: the scattering of one's *dianoia*, of one's endless hungering for self-exaltation. Now, the psalm expresses in two successive lines two distinct views of sacrifice:

16 For if thou hadst desired a sacrifice I would have given it;
    thou wilt not be pleased even with whole burnt sacrifices.
17 A sacrifice to God is a broken spirit, a broken and
    humbled heart God will not count as nothing.
18 Do good in thy good pleasure to Zion, and may
    Jerusalem's walls be built up.
19 Then thou shalt be pleased with a sacrifice of righteous-
    ness, with offering and whole burnt sacrifices; then shall
    they offer young bulls on thine altar. (Ps 50:16–19)

Yet the psalm's final line seems, on the face of it, to be supporting once more the sacrifice of animals.

Let us begin with the final line. Rabbinic commentary holds that only if our animalistic self-will (i.e., our *dianoia*) is extinguished shall our animal sacrifices be pleasing (*eudokia*). Radak paraphrases these three lines of Psalm 50 in this way: "You, O Lord, despise our animal sacrifices when *not* accompanied by our broken heart; but You do *not* despise, O Lord, our broken-heartedness even if not accompanied by animal sacrifice" (*Tehillim*, II, 662). Hence, there emerges from Psalm 50 this Rabbinic insight: "Young bulls symbolize deep repentance" (ibid.)—a repentance that restores intimacy through the action of surrendering (i.e., sacrificing) one's own mouth to the Lord: "O Lord, thou shalt open my lips and my mouth shall declare thy praise" (Ps 50:15).

It is this restoration of fullest intimacy with the divine that heals David's broken intimacy with Bathsheba—and also accounts for the entry of Psalm 50 into the Orthodox liturgy:

> Create in me a pure heart, O God, and renew a right Spirit
> within me.
> Do not cast me away from thy presence, do not take thy Holy
> Spirit from me. (Ps 50:10–11)

The moment in the Liturgy when (in Slavic practice) these two lines are spoken by the priest is the moment when the divine is arriving at the deepest contact with the human: the moment when the bread and wine will become the Body and Blood of Christ. This eucharistic significance given these central lines of Psalm 50 arises from the deepest intimacy imaginable on earth or in heaven: the entering into—and the being entered by—Christ Himself.

■   ■   ■

After Vespers on September 7, 1984, the eve of my entry into the Orthodox faith, Fr. Vladimir Sovyrda and I sat in the social room of the church reading together through the ceremony of my reception. I tried now and then to express to him something of my very immense joy. He would listen to a few words, smile kindly, and then continue going through the service with me. Later that night, at home, I wrote in my journal this passage:

> I think the joy of the convert is a strange thing, at once ephemeral
> and perfect. Ephemeral: for this blush of love can happen only once,
> before the full weight of the Church's immense life has filled every
> tiny corner and cell of my life—some slender quicklight of loving and
> not the full rich universal conflagration that is God's love in the Holy
> Church. Perfect: because all our lives we try to recapture—or grasp
> once—that bright first intensity when, for the tiniest second at that
> intensity's heart, the Kingdom of Heaven opens perfectly and fully.

And before this perfect transience, or ephemeral perfection, another person can only smile, and go on. Why? Wouldn't it be useful, even instructive, to sit together and simply look into this quicklight—and to see the Kingdom of the Heart? No, for such an exercise would (some 999 times out of 1,000) become something very like self-congratulation, even self-worship.

But what about that one chance in a thousand? Yes: and God will let you know unmistakably when that moment comes. It wasn't that night.

■   ■   ■

When David repents of his violent intimacy with Bathsheba—the murder of her husband—he opens the way into a genuine intimacy with her, a way that leads them first to the death of the son they had illicitly conceived. When the infant falls gravely ill, the biblical narrator tells us, "David implored God for the sake of the lad, and David fasted, and he came and spent the night lying on the ground."[94] He fasts for seven days, and "it happened on the seventh day that the child died." On hearing the news, David rose from the ground, bathed, "and came back to his house and asked that food be set out for him, and he ate." Shocked at David's behavior, his servants ask: "For the sake of the living child you fasted and wept, and when the child was dead, you arose and ate food?" David's response to the servants is one of the most moving and beautiful in all Scripture: "While the child was still alive I fasted and wept, for I thought, 'Who knows, the Lord may favor me and the child will live.' And now that he is dead, why should I fast? Can I bring him back again? I am going to him and he will not come back to me."

Alter says of this moment in the narratives of David: "In place of David the seeker and wielder of power, we now see a vulnerable David, and this is how he will chiefly appear through the last half of his story" (ibid.). In other words, David becomes at this point capable of the deepest and truest intimacy; and he thus transfigures the violently dark drama with Bathsheba into one of brightest splendor.

The next sentence in the narrative confirms fully this transfiguration: "And David consoled Bathsheba his wife, and he came near to her and lay with her [*ekoimethe met'autes*; 2 Kgs 12:24], and she bore a son and called his name Solomon, and the Lord loved him" (ibid.). David's lying down with her (*koimaomai*; Lampe, 761b) is now blessed by God with a son whose name will come to signify wisdom, Solomon, the son to whom David will address the magnificent Psalm 71, where he says: "He shall live, and Arabian gold shall be given to him; they shall pray to him without ceasing, all the day long shall they bless him" (Ps 71:15).

The Arabian gold flowing to Solomon represents the unceasing flow of prayer to him as the man who, like Christ, saves the helpless poor and the needy from the iron grip of oppression:

> For he rescued the needy from the oppressor's hand, the poor who had
> no helper.
> He shall spare the poor and needy, he shall save the souls of the
> needy. (Ps 71:12–13)

In this sense, then, Solomonic wisdom is the very heart of psalmic prayer, restoring and fully healing every broken intimacy. And such wisdom flows back to bless the splendor of his parents, David and Bathsheba, a splendor that has come forth from the wine of deep repentance. Thus, Psalm 50 informs the drama of intimacy in Psalm 118.

For Psalm 118's drama of intimacy arises anew in every line; that is, the intimacy between psalmist and God is, at every moment, opening fresh dimensions. In this light, then, the final line of Psalm 118 gains great significance:

> I have gone astray like a lost sheep,
> Seek out thy servant,
> I have never forgotten thy commandments. (Ps 118:176)

To be, at the close of the poem, the "lost sheep" is to realize fully the fundamental urgency driving the psalmist throughout the entire poem: the need to be found and to be cared for. In Psalm 141, David is pinned down by enemies and hiding in a cave: "I looked on my right, and I saw that no one had recognized me, that all flight had failed me, that no one saw deeply my soul" (Ps 141:4). Here is the perfect description of the "lost sheep": "no one saw deeply my soul." Such psychic invisibility occurs, in Psalm 141, early in David's life, when he is being sought by King Saul's death squad. Late in his life, David flees his palace as he is sought by his homicidal son Absalom; and the psalm of this moment exactly echoes the psalm of David hiding in the cave—and it is, in fact, the next psalm in the Psalter:

> For the enemy has tormented my soul, he has laid low my life to
> the earth, making me dwell in dark places like one who has been
> long dead,
> And my spirit has fallen into depression, my heart deeply troubled
> within me. (Ps 142:3–4)

The torment of spiritual depression (*akedia*) arises from the cessation of every intimacy—indeed, the cessation of every capacity for any intimacy. Such depression of spirit becomes, then, either a terminal psychic darkness ("like one who has been long dead") or (the steady psalmic decision) the cause of still deeper prayer: "Hear me speedily, O Lord, my spirit has forsaken me;

turn not thy face from me or I shall become like one who goes down into the pit" (Ps 142:7).

Here is the unceasing psalmic plea for intimacy with God. "Turn not thy face [*prosopon*] from me" can thus be paraphrased this way: "Sustain intimacy between thy personhood [*prosopon*] and mine," that intimacy wherein I become blessed with fully recognized personhood as gift from thee: "My whole being [*hypostasis*] is from thee" (Ps 38:7). Now, the process wherein the LXX word *prosopon* ("face") comes to include what the LXX word *hypostasis* signifies ("total being" or "personhood") is a complex, multi-layered—and decisive—process: for the conceptual experience (or experiential concept) of personhood defines both the hidden essence and the visible substance of every intimacy between human and divine. Indeed, personhood is what David and Bathsheba bestow upon one another in the wine of deep repentance; and psalmic personhood is the gift bestowed by God in the drama of intimacy.

■　■　■

I am a twin. My brother, David (as I wrote this on December 12, 2006), was sickened by multiple cancers of the lung, the liver, and the spine. His oncologist asked him very compassionately, "Are you depressed in spirit?" explaining that she had had patients like him who—simply by sustaining good spirits—had lived several years with afflictions such as his. "Don't keep it a secret," she counseled my brother. Her call to him was precisely the call to sustain the drama of intimacy by not becoming "like one long dead," one "who goes down into the pit" (Ps 142:7). It is the call, in other words, to become the "lost sheep" of Psalm 118's final line. For only in so doing can one enter into that drama wherein (as Psalm 38 beautifully expresses) one knows that one's "whole being [*hypostasis*] is nothing before thee" and, simultaneously, that "my whole being [*hypostasis*] is from thee" (Ps 38:5 and 38:7). This apparent paradox of our hypostasis—it is nothing compared to God; it is our fullness given us by God—finds its resolution in every line of Psalm 118. For such resolving is what moves the drama of intimacy that is Psalm 118.

VII

The Alphabetic Psalms
The Witness of the Other Seven

I n the Psalter, there are eight psalms written in the alphabetic pattern, with lines in psalmic sequence beginning with the letters of the alphabetic sequence. The greatest of these eight psalms is, clearly, Psalm 118. But what shall we say of the other seven? What witness do they bring to bear on Psalm 118? The other psalms (in LXX numbering) are Psalms 9, 24, 33, 36, 110, 111, and 144.

It is important to recall, at the outset, that the alphabetic sequences in all eight psalms occur solely in Hebrew. Neither the LXX translators, nor any subsequent translator into any other language, attempted to reflect anything whatsoever of the Hebrew alphabetic sequences—with the single (and crucial) exception of the LXX translators retaining the names of the twenty-two letters of the Hebrew alphabet as "titles" for the twenty-two Greek stanzas of Psalm 118. In other words, the eight psalms raise the issue of *untranslatability*. What, we must ask, is the spiritual significance of this untranslatable aspect of these eight psalms?

Now, the untranslatability *from* Hebrew possesses a strongly significant root *in* Hebrew itself. For the alphabetic sequence works this way in the Hebrew psalms: the twenty-two letters in the sequence are, at every moment in the eight psalms, giving themselves over and becoming the very words of the psalm. This action of alphabetic self-giving thus acts in Hebrew to create a unique psalmic metaphor: the sequence metaphorically acts to show how God the Father is giving Himself in love to the Incarnate Word, His Son, Who in turn is revealing Himself as God. "Whoever has seen Me has seen the Father," says Christ (John 14:9); just so: whoever has seen the words of the Psalms has seen the alphabetic sequence become fully incarnate. Christ adds: "Believe Me that I am in the Father and the Father in Me, or else believe Me for the sake of the works themselves" (John 14:11). The Hebrew alphabet is in the words of the Psalms in the same way the words, in the lines of these eight psalms, are in alphabetic sequence. At once exact metaphor—and vastly more than merely metaphor—the alphabetic sequences in the eight LXX psalms reveal the nature and action of God.

In this light, let us approach the final of the eight alphabetic psalms in the LXX Psalter:

1   I shall exalt thee, my God and my King, I shall bless thy name forever and unto ages of ages.

2   Every day I shall bless thee and sing praises to thy name forever and unto ages of ages.

3   Great is the Lord and greatly to be praised; his greatness exceeds every measure.

4   All generations shall praise thy works, they shall declare thy mighty power,

5   They shall speak of the great glory that is the majesty of thy holiness, they shall recount thy wondrous works.

6   They shall speak of the power of thy fearsome deeds, they shall recount thy great majesty.

7   From them shall pour forth the memory of thy rich goodness, they shall rejoice in thy righteousness.

8   The Lord is gracious and merciful, longsuffering and abundant in mercy.

9   The Lord is gracious to all, his mercies are on all his works.

10   Lord, let all thy works praise thee, and let all thy saints bless thee.

11   They shall tell of thy kingdom's glory and they shall speak of thy lordship,

12   So all the sons of men may know thy lordship and the glory of thy kingdom's magnificence.

13   Thy kingdom is a kingdom for all ages, thy dominion is unto ages of ages.

14   The Lord is faithful in his words and he is holy in all his works.

15   The Lord steadies all those who stumble, he lifts up all those struck down.

16   All eyes look to thee in hope, thou givest them their food in due season.

17   Thou openest thy hand and all living things are satisfied in thy good pleasure.

18   The Lord is righteous in all his ways and he is holy in all his works.

19 The Lord is near to all who call on him, to all who call
    upon him in truth.

20 He shall do the will of those fearing him, he shall hear
    their supplications, and he shall save them.

21 The Lord preserves all who love him, but all sinners he
    shall utterly destroy.

22 My mouth shall speak the Lord's praise; let all flesh bless
    his holy name from henceforth and forevermore.

There are several unique elements in the Hebrew and Greek texts of Psalm 144. First, the Hebrew Masoretic Text (MT) has exactly 150 words, one word (say the Rabbis) for each of the 150 psalms in the Psalter. Second, the Hebrew text of LXX Psalm 144 exhibits one missing letter of the alphabet—the fourteenth letter, *nun*, is omitted in the sequential arrangement of the initial Hebrew letters of the lines in this psalm. Third, the Greek text of Rahlfs' LXX prints *two* different versions of line 13, the second of which anticipates line 18. Here are the three lines in question, numbered according to Rahlfs' Greek text:

> Thy kingdom is a kingdom for all ages, thy dominion is unto
> ages of ages. (144:13)
> The Lord is faithful in his words and he is holy in all his works.
> (144:13a)
> The Lord is righteous in all his ways and he is holy in all his
> works (144:17)

Thus, a hypothesis emerges: the LXX line 13a translates the lost Hebrew line that begins with the letter *nun*. But several objections immediately arise. It is nearly impossible to construe any run of Hebrew psalmic words from this Greek line that could begin with an initial *nun*. Moreover, the LXX textual witness to line 13a is so uncertain as to the line's substantial presence as to cast doubt on its very existence (a doubt that Rahlfs registers by the hesitant numbering he employs for the line: 13a). But deeper than these textual matters is the significance that the Rabbinic tradition perceives in the missing letter *nun*: the Talmud (Berachos 4b) explains that David omitted this letter because it is the initial letter of the verse from Amos 5:2: "She has fallen [*nafelah*] and will not rise again, the maiden of Israel" (*Tehillim*, V, 1694). The LXX Greek readings for Amos 5:2 strengthen the case for deliberate omission: "There is none that shall raise her up" (*ouk estin ho anasteson auten*); for the phrase is asserting that no resurrection (*anastasis*) can ever occur. Thus, to say that "she has fallen" (*nafelah*) is to claim that, once she is wrecked, the maiden who is Israel is always wrecked. And all psalmic truth vigorously denies this claim.

Moreover, the Rabbis continue, the line that follows line 13 in Hebrew "provides the remedy for Israel's helplessness (using Rahlfs' LXX numbering, which matches the MT Hebrew):

> 13 Thy kingdom is a kingdom for all ages, thy dominion is
>   unto ages of ages.
> 14 The Lord is faithful in his words and he is holy in all his works.

"Without God," the Rabbis say, "*the maiden of Israel* must stumble but—upheld by God—she stands straight" (*Tehillim*, ibid.). Therefore, "*Maharal* concludes that the association of the letter *nun* with *nafelah* is not coincidental but essential, for *nun* stands alone, and therefore *must* fall, because it has nothing to support it in time of danger" (ibid.). Thus, the missing letter *nun* in alphabetic Psalm 144 is significantly deliberate.

Yet the LXX textual witness cannot be wholly ignored, for line 13a carries extraordinary meanings, both in itself and in the context. The first use of line 13a—"the Lord is faithful in His words" (*pistos kyrios en tois logois autou*)—asserts the ontological bond between the "Lord" and "His words"; that is, His words *are* the acts of His earthly creativity. To be faithful (*pistos*) in one's words, then, is to *essentialize* those words as one's acts; and such essentialization is best understood as the action of incarnation. "And God said, let there be light, and there was light" (Gen 1:3): here is the psalmic model of creativity, a model best seen as incarnational in its defining action, a model wherein the being (or *ontos*) of every created reality on earth *is* the word spoken by God. For this reason (as we discover in the second part of line 13a), God "is holy in all His works." His works, that is, ontologically *are* His holiness.

In context, too, line 13a provides a perfect bridge between lines 13 and 14, for line 13's assertion of God's eternal kingdom and dominion—"Thy kingdom is a kingdom for all ages, thy dominion is unto ages of ages" (144:13)—stands in sharp (indeed, *precipitous*) contrast to line 14's assertion of human stumbling. With the intervening line 13a, however, its model of incarnational creativity becomes the sure way wherein divine power can be seen as grounded in the human world, grounded in such a way that the *steadying* power of God (LXX *hyposterizo*) is experienced in the world as the ontological substance of that world. Contextually, then, LXX line 13a perfectly fits the key significances of the three lines. Hence, the LXX brings a special witness to Psalm 144.

One further Rabbinic note is worth our attention. In examining the "uniqueness of the letter *nun* . . . the Midrash (*Shemos Rabbah* 15:8) . . . notes that when Balaam unwittingly blessed the Jewish people, he said *hen 'am l'badad yishepon*,

Behold this people dwells alone (Numbers 23:9)" (*Tehillim*, V, 1694). The Hebrew word "behold" (*hen*) denotes uniqueness, the Rabbis believe, because its two Hebrew letters—*h* and *n*—"have the numerical values of five and fifty, respectively" (ibid.), numbers which "cannot combine with another number" to form ten or one hundred (ibid.). That is, five and fifty can only be doubled; hence—and this is the crucial insight—the letters *hn* "stand alone" and thus "constitute a fitting paean to Israel's solitude" (ibid.).

The LXX conclusion, then, is that line 13a is at once creatively present to the psalm and deliberately absent from it. The line is present in the sense that its textual presence provides an ontological connection between God's dominion and the earthly creation, a connection that steadies the earth while making it simultaneously capable of holiness. Yet the line is absent in the sense that the letter *nun* remains missing; and the resulting absence produces the Hebrew word count of 150 words uniquely for this psalm. Hence, the "Talmud (Berachos 4a) states that whoever recites this psalm three times every day is assuredly a *ben 'olam haba*, a person [worthy] of the World to Come" (ibid.). In other words, the absent presence (or present absence) of the missing line deepens every spiritual experience of praying this psalm.

Taking the LXX text as definitive for Psalm 144, then, let us again ask the question: What is the significance of the alphabetic sequence for comprehending the spiritual experience of the psalm (and, indeed, of the entire Psalter)? St. Gregory of Nyssa provides us a crucial starting point. In the opening of his eighth homily on *The Song of Songs*, Gregory refers to St. Paul's extraordinary account of being "raised up to the third heaven" (2 Cor 12:2) as the start of St. Paul's definitive spiritual experience of *epektasis*, of the infinite "reaching forward" toward unceasingly greater knowing of God (Phil 3:13–14). Gregory then cites three verses from the Psalter "to underscore [in Heine's words] God's infinity and the ceaseless ascent of the soul towards this infinite God" (Heine, 72). Gregory's first citation is Psalm 144:5: "They [i.e., all generations] shall speak of the great glory that is the majesty of thy holiness, they shall recount thy wondrous works" (my translation). Gregory's conclusion is powerful: since God is boundless, we shall continue *for all eternity* the process of comprehending Him.

Gregory's second citation is Psalm 83:7: "They shall go from strength to strength." He concludes that prayer in the Psalms shall continue in the next world—and will never cease. Finally, Gregory cites Psalm 91:8—"But thou, O Lord, art the Most High for ages"—and therefore those participating in God's good glory "will always have a greater participation in God throughout eternity,"[95] a participation *analogos auxanomenos*, "always unceasing."[96] Thus, even though God is "always higher and loftier than the capacity of those who are [unceasingly] rising" toward Him (Heine, 72), we unceasingly "go from strength to strength" (Ps 83:7) in our ascent.

One further point. We mentioned earlier that, in his extraordinary discussion of the LXX psalmic word *diapsalma* (MT Hebrew *selah*), St. Gregory of Nyssa defines the term as a momentary pause in psalmic song that deepens the direct spiritual content, after which the psalmist takes up the song anew, "again entwining the words with the melody" (Heine, 150). Now, the word used here by Gregory for "entwine" is *eneiro* (Lampe, 470a), a verb we may construe as "to graft all the way into," the way a tree branch is grafted onto a tree trunk—or the way (says Gregory elsewhere) wisdom can be grafted onto our teaching (see Lampe's definition, 470b). Such engrafting—or entwining— of psalmic melody with psalmic words can also be seen as describing the way the alphabetic sequence is joined to the sequence of psalmic lines: a joining that exhibits (as does *diapsalma* in Gregory's reading) two contrary motives at once. That is, Gregory explains, the Holy Spirit is, on the one hand, always speaking in the psalmist and, on the other hand, interrupts the psalmic song so as to introduce "something more divine" (Heine, 158). Gregory's point is both extremely subtle and deeply significant: *diapsalma* is an action of the Holy Spirit that impedes the continuity of the [psalmist's] song at the very moment the Spirit "was always speaking in him [i.e., the psalmist]" (ibid.).

Just so, the engrafting of the alphabetic sequence of letters with the psalmic sequence of lines both *interrupts* and *continues* the psalmic song: *interrupts*, in the sense of causing a pause to occur so that the next letter in the alphabet can initiate the next line; and yet this engrafting also *continues* the song as the psalm sustains an ongoing development of thought. In this sense, then, the alphabetic sequence, in all these eight psalms, becomes a crucial dimension of *psalmic poetics*: of, that is, the theory of poetic composition that underlies and nurtures the way psalms are composed.

As we noted above, Psalm 144 is the final alphabetic psalm in the LXX Psalter. One of its subjects is a reprise of a central psalmic concern: the presence of enemies. Now, enemies in the psalms, as John N. Day reminds us, continually provide the occasion—neither for retaliation, nor capitulation—but for prayer.[97] (Day quotes wonderfully a sentence from E. M. Bounds: "Prayer is not preparation for the battle, prayer *is* the battle" [Day, 34]). The battle against enemies is also—most profoundly—an inward battle. Hence, the struggle against enemies in Psalm 144 may be best understood as inward battle, one that

St. John Climacus vividly describes in his *Ladder of Divine Ascent* in his account of the novice monk Isidore:

> [The] most holy shepherd [i.e., the Abbot of the monastery], after accepting him [i.e., Isidore], found that he was full of mischief, very cruel, sly, fierce, and arrogant. But with human ingenuity, that most wise man contrived to outwit the cunning of the devils, and said to Isidore: "If you have decided to take upon yourself the yoke of Christ, then I want you first of all to learn obedience." Isidore replied: "As iron to the smith, so I surrender myself in submission to you, holy father." The great father, making use of this comparison, at once gave an exercise to the iron Isidore, and said: "I truly want you, brother, to stand at the gate of the monastery, and to make a prostration to everyone coming in or going out, and to say, 'Pray for me, father; I am an epileptic.'" And he obeyed as an angel obeys the Lord.
>
> When he had spent seven years there, he attained deep humility and compunction. (4:23)

This defeat of Isidore's arrogance and cruelty perfectly expresses the defeat of enemies described, for example, in LXX Psalm 82, where the enemies are characterized as "those that hate you, O Lord God." Isidore's years of prostrations signify that his sinful behaviors were, in fact, assaults against God Himself; as Day points out, "These are not fundamentally Israel's enemies—they are God's" (34). And the action of God against such enemies is, in Psalms, consistent and significant:

> So in thy storming shalt thou hunt them down, in thy rage
> shalt thou dismay them.
> Fill their faces with shame, O Lord, and they shall seek after
> thy name. (82:15–16)

Isidore's years of ascetic practice bring about his enemy's defeat through the action of compunction (LXX *katanyxis*), an action grounded *not* in our autonomous selves but, rather, in the relationship of God to us; for, as Psalms tell us, it is God—"and not we ourselves" (Ps 99:3)—who has "made us drink down the wine of deep repentance" (Ps 59:3; see Chapter VI). Our enemies are *first of all* God's enemies, and victory over them is entirely through God's action in us. Monk Isidore's experience is psalmic.

One further point from Psalm 82. The final three lines are:

> Fill their faces with shame, O Lord, and they shall seek
> after thy name.
> May they be disgraced and dismayed unto ages of ages,
> may they be confounded and destroyed,
> So that they may know that thy name is Lord, that thou
> alone art Most High over all the earth. (Ps 82:16–18)

Note carefully: the enemies are to be "confounded and destroyed" at the same time "that they may know" thy kingship in seeking "after thy name." Day astutely puts the issue this way:

> Most Christians find that both sides of this request for deliverance
> stretch them beyond their comfort level. We find it difficult to plead
> for the conversion of our oppressors, and for those who oppress our
> brothers and sisters in the faith. But we also have a natural aversion
> to praying for the destruction of our enemies, for we know we must
> love our enemies. Both stretch us; both are right; and the results in
> either direction are up to God. The prayer is ours; the response is
> his. (35)

Day has perfectly articulated the psalmic experience of the enemies: it is the experience of being stretched in two different directions at once, a stretching that at once reduces us to helpless impotence in the face of our sinfulness and uplifts us to great power because of God's love for us. Isidore's response to his abbot—"As iron to the smith, so I surrender myself in submission to you, holy father"—thus becomes the only saving response we can make to the reality of enemy violence; for such a response is the only way we could even begin to reach anything resembling Isidore's "deep humility and compunction."

The first line of Psalm 144 initiates the Hebrew alphabetic sequence:

> 1 I shall exalt thee, my God and my King, I shall bless
> thy name forever and unto ages of ages.

The best approach to this *aleph*-line of Psalm 144 is by seeing it in the light of the final line of Psalm 105: "Blessed be the Lord God of Israel from everlasting to everlasting, and all the peoples shall say: Amen and amen" (105:48). St. Gregory sees the final lines of each of the Psalter's five great divisions, or Books,[98] as summarizing both the Book it concludes and the Psalter's aim as a whole. Psalm 105 ends Book IV, in which, says Gregory, "the prophet [David] has lifted the understanding of those ascending with him, and placed it beyond the vanity which the majority ambitiously pursue in this life, by showing those who live vainly how the delusion of the material life, which is unsubstantial and like a spider's web, advances to no good goal" (Heine, 108).

This "lifting of the understanding" (*dianoia*) is accomplished, in Psalm 105:48, by *embedding* the human capacity to praise God entirely *within* divine eternality, where the human singing forever endures. Book III has ended in the same way— "Blessed be the Lord forever. Amen and amen" (88:52)—as well as Books I and II: endings (says Gregory) that are actions of "thanksgiving which [abide] forever" (Heine, 120). That is, Gregory continues, "in the twofold repetition of the statement in the thanksgiving he [God] ordains it forever" (ibid.). In line 1 of Psalm 144 the psalmic capacity to "bless thy name forever" is a capacity that lives and acts "unto ages of ages" (144:1). "I take this [perpetuity] to mean," Gregory concludes, "the union of our nature with the angels" (Heine, 121), where *synapheia* is the Greek used by Gregory for "union"—a word of immense resonance for all Patristic understanding. The first line of Psalm 144, then, establishes psalmic song for all eternity.

The second (or *beth*) line continues and develops the first:

> 2   Every day I shall bless thee and sing praises to thy name
>   forever and unto ages of ages.

The shock of this line arises from its explicit joining together (in an act of intense *synapheia*) of "every day" (*hekasten hemeran*) with "ages of ages." The LXX Greek for "forever" employs extreme emphases: *eis ton aiona kai eis ton aiona tou aionos* (literally: "into the age and into the age of the age"). If an age (*aion*) is five thousand years, then the resulting millions or billions of years signal time beyond time: they signal, that is, angelic temporality actively participating in divine eternality. The psalmic "I" that praises the divine "thee" thus participates in this angelic time, a participation that the LXX Greek registers by extreme juxtaposition: *eulogeso se* (bless-will-I thee), a juxtaposition that the Hebrew comparably shows by prefixing "I" to the verb while suffixing "thee." With line 2, then, the psalmist enters into the angelic participation.

The third line (*gimel*) then turns its gaze directly on God:

> 3   Great is the Lord and greatly to be praised; his greatness
>   exceeds every measure.

A useful approach to this important moment in Psalm 144 can be found in *The Way of a Pilgrim*. About a week after he begins his practice in saying the Jesus Prayer, the Pilgrim one day finds himself weighed down by a "great burden": "Laziness, boredom, drowsiness and a cloud of disturbing thoughts seemed to overwhelm me" (*Way*, 20). He hastens to his teacher, who tells him this:

> Dearly beloved brother, a war has been declared against you by
> the world of darkness—a world which finds nothing as terrifying as
> heartfelt prayer and therefore tries by all means possible to confuse
> you and distract you from your purpose in learning how to pray.
> However, even the action of the enemy is permitted by God's will
> to the extent that it is necessary for us. It seems that your humility
> needs to be tested. . . . (Ibid.)

The Pilgrim recovers and, through perseverance in the practice, finds his
way—not *through* the cloud but, rather, deepening the practice while staying *in* it.
Psalm 144:3 registers precisely this deepening of psalmic prayer. The deepening
takes place in this fashion. The exuberance of the first few lines opens the way for
the psalmist to become like the Pilgrim: the sudden, sharp descent into spiritual
depression (cf. LXX Psalm 87 for a full disclosure of this terrible affliction). But—
and here is the point in Psalm 144:3—the *humility* of line 3 completely precludes
such a possibility by *focusing attention entirely upon God Himself and entirely away from the
psalmist*: "His greatness exceeds every measure." In exceeding every measure—every
peras: "end; consummation; perfection" (Lampe, 1060b)—God reveals Himself as
wholly beyond us at the very moment He wills us wholly into Himself. And
the single—indeed, the one and only—capacity we possess to respond rightly
to God's infinity and calling-forth is our capacity for humility: our capacity, that
is, to be nothing before God and therefore deeply responsive to Him. And such
capacity is what the Pilgrim discovers—just as the psalmist does in line 3.

The next three lines continue to express this blessed gift of humility:

> 4 All generations shall praise thy works, they shall declare thy
>   mighty power,
> 5 They shall speak of the great glory that is the majesty of thy
>   holiness, they shall recount thy wondrous works.
> 6 They shall speak of the power of thy fearsome deeds, they
>   shall recount thy great majesty.

The focus throughout these three lines (*daleth*, l. 4; *he*, l. 5; *waw*, l. 6) remains *not*
on the psalmist but, instead, on the whole of humanity uplifted into psalmic
song. (NB: The consistent plurals occur solely in LXX Greek; MT Hebrew
shows first-person singular in line 5.)

The LXX psalmic verb "recount" links these lines to the crucial moment in
the Genesis account when Isaac is told by his servant of the woman Rebecca
who is to become his wife: "and the servant told [*diegesato*] Isaac all that he
[the servant] had done [in finding Rebecca]" (Gen 24:66). Once Isaac heard

the servant's words (the Genesis narrator continues), "she became his wife and he loved her" (Gen 24:67). Thus, the servant's "recounting" triggers in Isaac—and therefore in the whole divine plan for Israel—the incarnation of marital love, an incarnation that establishes the love between husband and wife as the model for the love between the divine and the human. To "recount thy wondrous works" (Ps 144:5) is therefore to incarnate a "marriage" between God and all His people, a marriage (the psalmist says) that is a "great glory," a "majesty of . . . holiness," and a "wondrous work" (*thaumasia*). Again, the psalm's focus in these lines is upon the whole of humanity as the bride of God.

The seventh line completes the opening movement of Psalm 144:

> 7 From them shall pour forth the memory of thy rich goodness,
>   they shall rejoice in thy righteousness.

The key word here is "memory" (LXX Greek *mneme*; MT *zakar*). In both Greek and Hebrew the noun is joined to a powerful verb signifying that (in Rabbinic terms) "the words will not merely be spoken, but they will flow constantly and effortlessly, as waters flow in a living spring" (*Tehillim*, V, 1690). In this way, verse 7 prefigures Christ's magnificent words to the Samaritan woman in the Gospel of John: "The water that I shall give him will become in him a fountain of water springing up unto everlasting life" (John 4:14). In verse 7, the memory of God's "rich goodness" (*chrestotetos*) pours forth from the Israelite people as "water springing up into everlasting life," an outflowing that gives perfect expression to the marriage of divine and human.

The next seven lines (8–14) should continue the movement begun in the previous seven.

> 8 The Lord is gracious and merciful, longsuffering and
>   abundant in mercy.
> 9 The Lord is gracious to all, his mercies are on all his works.
> 10 Lord, let all thy works praise thee, and let all thy saints
>   bless thee.
> 11 They shall tell of thy kingdom's glory and they shall speak
>   of thy lordship,
> 12 So all the sons of men may know thy lordship and the
>   glory of thy kingdom's magnificence.
> 13 Thy kingdom is a kingdom for all ages, thy dominion is
>   unto ages of ages.
> 14 The Lord is faithful in his words and he is holy in all his works.

Note, too, that the central line of this second movement also concludes the first half of the entire psalm: "They shall tell of thy kingdom's glory and they shall speak of thy lordship" (144:11).

Rabbinic tradition explains that *malkut*, "*kingdom*, refers to the laws of nature, which are a glorious testimony to God's complete and comprehensive control of all aspects of His creation" (*Tehillim*, V, 1692). In this sense, then, *kingdom*, as used here, perfectly expresses the meaning of *statutes* in Psalm 118 (*huqqim* in MT; *dikaiomata*, in LXX): just as the statutes incarnate on earth certain creative acts of God's infinite mind, just so, this "kingdom's glory" incarnates the words of humanity's psalmic praise of God.

The fact that line 11 is, simultaneously, the center of the second movement of Psalm 144 and the conclusion to the psalm's first half gives great emphasis to the word "lordship" in this line. That the LXX word *dynasteia* carries many dark significances in Patristic literature, ones with overtones of violent authority (see Lampe's discussion, 391b), gives added weight to the word's use here in Psalm 144. For the word "lordship" in line 11 is entirely glorious in all its meanings, a glory described in the next line as possessing *megaloprepeia* (144:12), "magnificence," a word with entirely positive significances in Patristic literature (see Lampe, 835b). Thus, the semantic tensions of the psalm's center act to deepen line 11's power by crossing it with opposed currents—yet then uplifting those crosscurrents into purest praise.

The third set of seven lines (15–21) develops a crucial theme begun in line 12: "sons of men" (144:12). For with this phrase in line 12, Psalm 144 begins to specify the human agency of psalmic song, an agency that will remain plural until the final line: "My mouth shall speak the Lord's praise; let all flesh bless his holy name from henceforth and forevermore" (144:22).

> 15 The Lord steadies all those who stumble, he lifts up all those struck down.
>
> 16 All eyes look to thee in hope, thou givest them their food in due season.
>
> 17 Thou openest thy hand and all living things are satisfied in thy good pleasure.
>
> 18 The Lord is righteous in all his ways and he is holy in all his works.
>
> 19 The Lord is near to all who call on him, to all who call upon him in truth.
>
> 20 He shall do the will of those fearing him, he shall hear their supplications, and he shall save them.

21 The Lord preserves all who love him, but all sinners he
    shall utterly destroy.
22 My mouth shall speak the Lord's praise; let all flesh bless
    his holy name from henceforth and forevermore.

Standing astride all three sets of seven lines, this final line concludes the
incarnational action of the entire psalm. That is, the psalmist's abundant *love*
for God—a love registered in the first two lines of the paslm as the psalmic "I"
exalting and blessing God—becomes, in the final line, once more incarnate as a
specific "I." But, too, the *content* of this "I" includes all the pluralities of the entire
nation formed in the action of psalmic praise; hence, the "I" of line 22 becomes
one with "all flesh" (*pasa sarx*). It is worth noting, too, the conjunction occurring
in both Hebrew and Greek in this final line—MT Hebrew *basar shem*; LXX *sarx
to onoma*—words parallel in their shock value: in both, the word "flesh" is placed
directly against the holy "name" of God. In this way, then, Psalm 144 prepares
for that stunning shock in the prologue to John's Gospel: "And the Word flesh
became" (John 1:14). That is, *kai ho logos sarx egeneto;* where the high, nearly
angelic term *logos* is set right up next to the earthly, rotting carrion of *sarx.* Such
is the incarnational action, in both Psalm 144 and John's Prologue; such is the
action of God's love for humanity and the earth.

We began by noting that the alphabetic sequence in all eight alphabetic
psalms incarnates itself in and as the actual words of the psalms, creating what we
termed a "unique psalmic metaphor": the alphabetic "sequence metaphorically
acts to show how God the Father is giving Himself in love to the Incarnate
Word" (see above). We may now say that the actual words of Psalm 144 (and
all the alphabetic psalms) accomplish this incarnation through the action of
praising. Psalm 144 is the only psalm in the entire Psalter to carry as its title
the word "praise" (LXX *ainesis;* MT *tehillah*). In Hebrew, of course, the plural
form (*tehillim*) becomes the title used for the entire book of Psalms. In other
words, Psalm 144 achieves the incarnation of the divine in the earthly *through*
the human acts of praising the divine. Hence, the words of the eight alphabetic
psalms can be rightly understood as incarnational. And this fact raises, in turn,
the central question: what is the *speed* at which incarnation is occurring in the
alphabetic psalms?

VIII
The Incarnation of Love in Psalm 118
The Struggle Against Depression (*Unfinished*)

T he fourth stanza of Psalm 118 discloses a key dimension to our question concerning the speed—better: the *pace*—at which the incarnation of love occurs in Psalm 118.

> 25 My soul lies prostrate on the earth,
>   Quicken me according to thy word.
> 26 I declared my ways, and thou didst hear me,
>   Teach me thy statutes.
> 27 Make me comprehend the way of thy statutes,
>   I shall ponder thy wondrous works.
> 28 My soul has fainted from depression,
>   Strengthen me with thy words.
> 29 Put the unjust way far from me,
>   With thy law have mercy on me.
> 30 I have chosen the way of truth,
>   I have never forgotten thy judgments.
> 31 I have clung to thy testimonies,
>   O Lord, put me not to shame.
> 32 I have run the way of thy commandments
>   When thou didst enlarge my heart.

Especially significant is the fourth line of the fourth stanza:

> My soul has fainted from depression,
> Strengthen me with thy words. (118:28)

Depression (LXX *akedia*) can be understood in the Psalms as that psychic condition wherein love becomes disincarnated.

> Create in me a pure heart, O God, and renew a right Spirit
> within me. (Ps 50:10)

Depression is "a-heartedness" (*a-kerios*) in the sense that it deadens the heart's capacity to respond to the creation and everything (and everyone) in it. And this deadening of the heart's responsive power drains the creation of all God's love that is *in* the creation, inscribed there as His statutes. Thus begins the central spiritual warfare of Psalm 118: the struggle to incarnate all God's love and thereby to defeat all our depression.

The fourth stanza opens with a vivid depiction of depression's triumph:

> My soul lies prostrate on the earth,
> Quicken me according to thy word. (118:25)

The LXX word here translated "earth" is *edaphos* (Lampe, 405B). It means, first of all, "foundation, pavement," and is used by St. Gregory of Nyssa to signify "sacred text" (ibid.). In depression, then, the soul falls upon sacred text, and rather than drawing nourishment and love, it lies prostrate as if indeed dead; the LXX verb "quicken" is the verb used to describe the fetus' movement in the womb. To be quickened "according to [God's] word" is to allow that word to become incarnate in the depressed soul.

■   ■   ■

I had written this far in this chapter some two years ago, and only tonight—Holy Thursday (April 16, 2009)—take up my pen once more: may Christ have mercy on me.

On March 17, 2007, my twin brother, David, died after several years of battling with cancer. Linda, my sister-in-law, said to me on the phone when she called that evening: "He was fine yesterday, eating ice cream and chatting with the nurses. Then when I got to his room this morning, he was very quiet. We sat for an hour, then he said: 'I think I'll take a nap,' and turned to face the wall. Ten minutes later, he was dead."

Tonight, Carol-Xenia, my wife, read me aloud Psalm 118.

In January 2008, I began treatment for Lyme disease. My symptions were—and are—extreme fatigue and mental haziness: that is, disincarnation. My condition these past two years is best described by the LXX word *akedia*. At the Panikhida for David served by Fr. Andrew [Tregubov], Father said to me: "You must now live for him." Carol said tonight to me: "His [David's] salvation may depend upon your prayer for him."

My own daily prayer in Psalms for some twenty-three years began to dwindle the evening of March 17, 2007, and had wholly ceased by that summer.

Carol asked tonight: "Do you *want* to be healed? Or do you want to follow your brother?"

I wrote in my journal on Friday, February 2, 2007, about David entering the hospital for surgery: "He is positive, upbeat even, filled with praise for the brilliant surgical team . . . This is far indeed, it seems, from the Slough of Despond.[99] Can I live in his light? Can I raise up my (bedraggled) self from the Slough's darknesses and lassitudes by and with his joyous light?"

On December 12, 2007, I wrote: "The year comes to an end: so does my life in active love. Grief overwhelms me."

On January 3, 2008, the final entry in my journal read: "It seems I have Lyme Disease—today at 3 p.m. (now 11:15 a.m) I have an appointment with Dr. Carr who says (yesterday) I have Lyme or Lyme-like disease, not just a depression thing! . . . I keep wanting to tell David things about myself. Can he hear me?"

After I wrote those last words, in January 2008, I stopped writing my daily journal. Silence has reigned. Until tonight.

From a Letter to My Brother[100]

I

1/27/07. David, all through our childhood and young-boyhood, you were my leader, my "point man," the one who blazed the trail. I always lagged behind you, struggling to at least keep you in sight as you seemed always to be picking up speed and grace and command, unfailingly strong to my decidedly second-fiddle weaknesses. I semi-existed in your strong light; and yet I never—not even for the tiniest fraction of a moment—resented or envied your command. I *loved* the second-place-ness of who I was in the light of your superior graces. For you—*and here's the big point*—you never once lorded your command over me, never even hinted at the least superiority of personhood. We were—deeply and irrevocably—*twins*.

II

3/22/07. David, the mystery of our being twins overwhelms me now—now that I've lost you. Years ago—thirty years ago—I wrote a long poem about our child-hood home: about a home savaged by Dad's alcoholic violence; and I had a line somewhere in it that went: "Twins? It seems we haven't lived / two seconds the same." I meant, then, to register the stunning fact of how very differently we've chosen to live our lives.

And yet, now, I feel deeply that all our choosings kept on echoing each other's; better, that all *my* choices were in the light—the strong, beautiful light—of your choices.

Day six of your departing this life. David, I miss you, miss you, miss you. Pray for me, David, and pray for all of us, especially dear Linda, your angel on earth.

The mystery of being a twin does not cease at death, but grows richer and deeper. I see now that the differences have always been simply accents—like the same notes in slightly differing scales. I wish I knew music. Are all our lives convergent?

III

3/23/07. David, today I was refilling a prescription on the phone, and after I'd finished giving her all the information, she said (to check), "Now, this is for David Sheehan"—and I stopped her. "No, *Donald Sheehan*, D-O-N-A-L-D" (spelling loudly). Countless, countless times I've been called by your name, my dear; and whenever we've talked about this you'd echo, "Yeah, I keep getting called 'Donald.'" The persistence of this is what struck me: you've been gone now seven days, and this happens still, this mystery of twinness!

IV

3/23/07. That I've been undiagnosably unwell for the past two years or so— the major symptoms being fatigue, anxiety, and quasi-depression, including a weakening of my voice—seems to me now, this day (March 23, 2007), clearly involved with your illness and dying, dear heart. But I'm not sure how, except that it's part of our being twins.

On Saturday, March 17, at 8:30 p.m., when Nora[101] told me on the telephone of your death some two hours earlier, I cried out and yelled in pain, fell to the floor and began to weep and weep. And all my illness of two or more years coalesced into this moment of your death: coalesced and *focused*, the way a knife is solid and sharp: *and somehow clearer.* And the days since that moment have made the clarity somehow (but how?) more bearable, more capable of being healed.

V

I think of you and Mama now, hands joined in loving peacefulness. Her final words to you—"Be nice to everyone, and be careful crossing the street"—have become a song you now both sing to all of us who grieve so deeply now for you.

Pray for me, dear David, my twin, my love.

■ ■ ■

The second line of Psalm 118's fourth stanza begins: "I have declared my ways . . ." (l. 26). When I visited Mount Athos in Greece at the end of 2003, I asked an American monk at Vatopaidi Monastery, "What should a pilgrim to Mount Athos take back to the world?" Fr. Matthew thought a long minute, then looked at me. "Take back the *tone* of Mount Athos, the *savor*," he said.

The whole of the fourth stanza is filled with this Athonite tone and savor; and the pace of the stanza—that is, the movement of love's incarnation—can best be described as Athonite. By this I mean that the movement from lying prostrate on the earth (l. 25) to running the way of God's commandments (l. 32) is the active incarnation of love, by means of God's enlargement of the heart:

> I have run the way of thy commandments
> When thou didst enlarge my heart. (Ps 118:32)

The 3-2-3 stanzaic pattern of Psalm 118 here exhibits what Fr. John Breck terms a "rhetorical helix": "a three-dimensional spiral that progresses with increasing intensity about a central axis or focus of meaning" (*Shape*, 58).

My experience of visiting Mount Athos was an experience of my heart being made larger.

[The manuscript ends here.]

Artist's proof of a portrait of Don Sheehan by Gary Grier, 2010.

Memory Eternal, Donatos!
by Lydia Carr

We have traveled many miles and seen many friends since we left Charleston three weeks ago, but Don's life and death have remained at the forefront of my mind during our journey. Our physical movement has, in a sense, been mirrored by a palpable spiritual movement, and I am sure that Don himself has been spurring us along. I would like to reflect—however fumblingly—on my experience of Don's life and passing, and to express in some small way how his last days and hours, his death and his funeral have begun to bear fruit in our own lives.

Don was a remarkable man. He was professor of English at Dartmouth and passionate about a wide array of literature—from Dante to Dostoevsky. He was also curator of The Frost Place [in Franconia, New Hampshire] for some years. He translated the Psalms from the Septuagint Greek and he taught poetry workshops. For many years he lived "off the grid" in Vermont, without an indoor toilet or any other amenities. When his daughter-in-law Talia visited him and his wife, Carol, for the first time, he read the *Lord of the Rings* aloud with a headlamp on his head, because there were no lights.

At our wedding, Don—to whom I had spoken only a handful of times—told me he loved me. I remember feeling slightly embarrassed by his openness. He was truly able to express a sincere love for someone he barely "knew" in one sense, and yet whom he Knew simply by loving in a Christ-like way.

Taylor and I did not know Don much better when Lucia was born the following year, and we chose him as her Godfather on what I might have described several years ago as a "whim." I now know that it was truly Divine Grace guiding us to the most loving and pious person we could have chosen for our daughter. I remember being overwhelmingly touched at Lucia's baptism when he was able to quiet her and hold her attention by slowly moving a lit candle within her vision. He held her gaze with his eyes at times too, and it strikes me now that his openness was mirrored in the tiny baby on whom he shed his love. Like the few monastics I have met, Don had a childlike approach to people that was pure, loving, and without judgment. Every time that Don—who was already sick then—held Lucia for Holy Communion, he was moved almost to tears and thanked us as though we had done something immeasurably precious for him by helping him to bring her to the body and blood of Christ.

Don sanctified others with his love. I remember one meal that he, Carol, and Rowan shared with us not long before their move to South Carolina, when he was quite sick. He had very little appetite, but he was able to eat that night and had a second portion of the poached pears I had made for dessert. He thanked me as though I had done something far greater than prepare a simple dinner for a few friends, and in that way his love was both generous and humbling. Humbling, because my own was so paltry.

In May 2009, we traveled to Charleston to visit the Sheehans for the first time since their move South. Don was at a low point in his illness and was very frail. He could barely speak, although he was still able to walk stiffly, often with the help of someone else's arm. The few things I heard him say were "She's so beautiful" (about Lucia), "I love you," and "Please pray for me." He desperately wanted to be healed.

We planned this year's southern roadtrip back in March or April, entirely apart from the state of Don's health, and I remain overawed by how clearly God was guiding us as we blindly settled on the days that we would spend in Charleston. Only a week before our departure, we received a note that Don was not expected to live out the month, and we were shocked. I suppose we had been living with the reality of his illness for so long, his upswings and downswings, that we had lost sight of the fact that it was inexorably leading to his death.

We arrived at the Sheehans' house late on Saturday, in the dark, and it was absolutely silent when we got out of the car. We first saw Don on Monday morning. His physical appearance was startling—he had grown so gaunt, and his skin hung on him—and I was half-afraid that Lucia would not want to approach him. On the contrary, she kissed his hand and forehead without coaxing, and visiting Godfather ("Fah-weh") became a ritual for her those next few days. I held Don's hand and tried to tell him that I was happy to see him, that I loved him. I don't know how much I actually said, I only know that it probably wasn't enough. It is surprisingly difficult to talk to someone who is still and who cannot show signs of understanding. Yet, in spite of his paralysis, Don would make the sign of the cross over us whenever we saw him during our visit. I was amazed by how calm his eyes were despite the pain he was in. The only medications that Don was taking were those to help relax him enough that he could breathe to some degree, rather than aspirate his saliva. He refused morphine after being given it at the hospital. I think this made his journey towards death all the more striking, because even though he was unable to speak, he was so clearly *there* and so clearly understood what was happening around him. One afternoon, Taylor offered to read to him, and as soon as he sat down by the bed, Don picked up the pencil and wrote "SLOW!" on the pad of paper by his hand.

On Tuesday, Don was very sleepy and did not seem to be aware of much. The hospice nurse who came that morning said he would probably not live out the day. Fr. John [of Holy Ascension Orthodox Church in Mt. Pleasant, near Charleston] came to read the prayers for the dying and anointed him with the final unction. Then, Don opened his eyes and became very alert. Charleston friends came and went that afternoon, bidding him farewell. Rowan, Carol, and Taylor read to him from Elder Ephraim's *Counsels from the Holy Mountain* and from the Psalms. Then Don wrote "SING!" on his pad of paper, and Rowan and Talia started singing the psalms, beginning with Psalm 103. "Bless the Lord, O my soul, blessed art thou, O Lord." Their voices echoed in the hallway, and I left cleaning the kitchen to join the small group in Don's room. Joy and sorrow were mingled into something painfully beautiful, and the love in the room was tangible.

The last night Don was alive, we all gathered for evening prayers in his room, and when Lucia kissed him goodnight, we had her say "God bless you." He wrote "Good!!" on the pad of paper by his right hand. Two exclamation points.

We all stayed in Don's room after evening prayers, continuing to pray. Rowan read the prayers for the departing soul and said a few words about how intensely difficult it is for the soul to leave the body. Yet we are not to fear death. Taylor and I were both downstairs when Don passed a little after 1:00 in the morning. When we returned to his room, Rowan was singing the prayers for the newly departed, and the space was crowded with the young people from Holy Ascension who had come to help the household and to keep vigil. Once he had finished the prayers, the room emptied out, and Taylor and I stayed to weep with Carol, Rowan, and Talia, to mourn the passing of a beautiful and loving soul. Carol was the first to dry her tears, and she began reading psalms from the book for the preparation of the dead. When she received a phone call, I took her place and was immediately confronted with Psalm 30. As I chanted, the fifth verse struck me like a blow: "Weeping shall endure for the night, but joy cometh in the morning." Although my eyes were brimming with tears, I felt a great joy fill my soul, and I was once more overcome by God's purpose—by us being placed there, then, to witness Don's beautiful death, and by the reading of that line moments after I had stopped weeping.

I continued to chant in turns with Taylor, until Fr. John and Deacon Mark arrived.[102] Then, as they began to prepare the body with the help of Carol and Rowan, I went downstairs to polish Don's cross until it shone. That small duty seems very significant to me now. A couple of young men gathered fresh basil from the garden to scatter over Don's body. When I returned, they were washing Don all over and rubbing his body with aromatic oils, which filled the room with their scent. Then they dressed him in a white robe and combed his long white beard and hair. We chanted more prayers, psalms, and Scripture readings as they continued to prepare Don's body. Eventually, I succumbed to exhaustion and retired to bed.

The morning was bright, but it felt strange and pale to me, and there was a hush about the house. The two days that preceded Don's funeral are hard to remember clearly. Friends came and went, friends with great love and generosity, and the Sheehans were provided with more food than they (and we) could possibly consume. One friend, Jessica, with her husband, Mike, and children, brought a huge spread for what she called a "sittin' up," the Southern term for a wake. We enjoyed comparing these words to the Orthodox term "vigil," realizing they all meant the same thing!

There were numerous phone calls made and received. We tried to seem busy. One afternoon, the Sheehans told some delightful stories about the funny and annoying things that Don used to say or do. As someone who did not know Don before his illness, it was wonderful to hear about his sense of humor and his loud laugh. On Thursday, our friends Fr. Caleb and Matushka Nicki Abetti [Godchildren of Don's] arrived from Vermont, with their baby, Antony. That afternoon we all took an hour to go to the beach, and after being inside for so long, everything seemed more real. The sun was brighter, the sand scratchier, the water *wetter* than I had remembered. Life seemed so tangible after having witnessed a death. And it didn't seem wrong to run around in the water and laugh.

The best parts of those days were the times we spent saying morning and evening prayers in Don's room, around his body. There was a peace in the room, and he radiated whiteness. We all continued to kiss his forehead and hands each time we finished praying. The first time I did this the morning after his death, I was shocked by how cold he was. We had been kissing him a couple of times each day since we arrived, and although he was almost motionless during those times, he was warm and he was *there*. Lucia continued to ask to see "Fah-weh" and always said that he was sleeping. We told her that he would always be sleeping now, and that we would always pray for him to be with God. Although she didn't fully understand, she did not seem disturbed. But on Thursday, when we watched the men load the coffin into the SUV, Lucia did get upset. Somehow she seemed to sense the finality, and she kept asking for Godfather and crying.

We all proceeded to Holy Ascension for a Panikhida that evening. Then we returned for the funeral Friday morning. Miriam, Don's oldest granddaughter (almost 9), came up to me afterwards and exclaimed, "There were more people here than on a Sunday!" Don touched many people in Charleston, in spite of his illness, and they all came to show their love for him, Orthodox and non-Orthodox alike. We all stood in line after the service, to kiss Don for the last time, and then to embrace his family afterwards. It was difficult to hold back our tears as Fr. John closed the coffin. Then we drove to North Carolina, to Don's final resting place.

At the monastery, I was first struck by what a beautiful place Don's body would rest in. He was buried in a hayfield, not far from a little plot where five or six miscarried babies had been put to rest. How beautiful that they will keep each other company and that the nuns will be praying for them all daily. The burial was striking in its *realness*. The earth was bright yellowish-red, the grass around was green, we were surrounded by haybales. Birds were chirping, and as the sun went down the light became more dramatic. The mystery of our faith confronted me as Fr. Nektarios said, "Ashes to ashes, dust to dust" and threw a handful of dirt onto the coffin. Then it was lowered into the grave, and we threw fistfuls of dirt and lovely flowers down onto it. A little later, as people continued to take turns shoveling dirt into the grave, Rowan and Talia sang their beautiful setting of Psalm 103, and they were once more expressing joy in the midst of sorrow. "Bless the Lord, oh my soul." It is a great mystery that we are able to feel joy from those words even as we are burying a loved one.

Last week, I reread Don's lecture on Dostoevsky and Memory Eternal, a remarkable experience after having witnessed his own death and funeral. Eternal memory, he says, is both the love for one's neighbor and the love for God, through which we come to also feel God's love for us. In his words, this is "'a victory over death,' not at all because we erase the dead in our mind's oblivion (what secular culture calls 'getting over it') but precisely because we keep them so strongly, indeed so brightly present in our love . . . By holding another in our love, we are becoming like God in that we are remembering the seed of God in ourselves at the very instant we are seeing the fully ripened fruitfulness of the other in God." Don did that. And in some sense, I can feel his own death bearing fruit in our lives, calling us to keep him ever-present in our own memories, and through him to keep others in our love and memory. "Thus," as Don himself wrote, "what begins in isolative grief concludes in relational joy."

Weeping shall endure for the night, but Joy cometh in the morning. As we all came together to mourn Don's passing, to remember his life, and to pray for his salvation, we were in right relation to each other and were thus able to give birth to a real joy. I will be ever grateful that I was able to be present for that "relational joy," and that Don's life and death so clearly revealed themselves to me as a witness to Christ. Again, in Don's words, "the person who has died continues to act back into the lives of those who continue to love him or her." And so he has and does. Memory eternal, Donatos!

Numbering of Septuagint (LXX) Psalms

Septuagint Psalm Numbers	Hebrew Psalm Numbers
1–8	1–8
9	9–10
10–112	11–113 *(add 1 to the number of each psalm)*
113	114–115
114	116:1–9
115	116:10–19
116–145	117–146 *(add 1 to the number of each psalm)*
146	147:1–11
147	147:12–20
148–150	148–150

The Greek Text of LXX Psalm 118

Ἀλληλούϊα.
α' αλφ.

1 Μακάριοι οἱ ἄμωμοι ἐν ὁδῷ
οἱ πορευόμενοι ἐν νόμῳ κυρίου.

2 μακάριοι οἱ ἐξερευνῶντες τὰ μαρτύρια αὐτοῦ·
ἐν ὅλῃ καρδίᾳ ἐκζητήσουσιν αὐτόν.

3 οὐ γὰρ οἱ ἐργαζόμενοι τὴν ἀνομίαν
ἐν ταῖς ὁδοῖς αὐτοῦ ἐπορεύθησαν.

4 σὺ ἐνετείλω τὰς ἐντολάς σου
φυλάξασθαι σφόδρα.

5 ὄφελον κατευθυνθείησαν αἱ ὁδοί μου
τοῦ φυλάξασθαι τὰ δικαιώματά σου.

6 τότε οὐ μὴ ἐπαισχυνθῶ
ἐν τῷ με ἐπιβλέπειν ἐπὶ πάσας τὰς ἐντολάς σου.

7 ἐξομολογήσομαί σοι, κύριε, ἐν εὐθύτητι καρδίας
ἐν τῷ μεμαθηκέναι με τὰ κρίματα τῆς δικαιοσύνης σου.

8 τὰ δικαιώματά σου φυλάξω·
μή με ἐγκαταλίπῃς ἕως σφόδρα.

β' βηθ.

9 Ἐν τίνι κατορθώσει ὁ νεώτερος τὴν ὁδὸν αὐτοῦ;
ἐν τῷ φυλάσσεσθαι τοὺς λόγους σου.

10 ἐν ὅλῃ καρδίᾳ μου ἐξεζήτησά σε·
μὴ ἀπώσῃ με ἀπὸ τῶν ἐντολῶν σου.

11 ἐν τῇ καρδίᾳ μου ἔκρυψα τὰ λόγιά σου,
ὅπως ἂν μὴ ἁμάρτω σοι.

12 εὐλογητὸς εἶ, κύριε·
δίδαξόν με τὰ δικαιώματά σου.

13 ἐν τοῖς χείλεσίν μου ἐξήγγειλα
πάντα τὰ κρίματα τοῦ στόματός σου.

14 ἐν τῇ ὁδῷ τῶν μαρτυρίων σου ἐτέρφθην
ὡς ἐπὶ παντὶ πλούτῳ.

15 ἐν ταῖς ἐντολαῖς σου ἀδολεσχήσω
καὶ κατανοήσω τὰς ὁδούς σου.

16 ἐν τοῖς δικαιώμασίν σου μελετήσω,
οὐκ ἐπιλήσομαι τῶν λόγων σου.

γ' γιμαλ.

17 Ἀνταπόδος τῷ δούλῳ σου·
ζήσομαι καὶ φυλάξω τοὺς λόγους σου.

18 ἀποκάλυψον τοὺς ὀφθαλμούς μου,
καὶ κατανοήσω τὰ θαυμάσιά σου ἐκ τοῦ νόμου σου.

19 πάροικος ἐγώ εἰμι ἐν τῇ γῇ·
μὴ ἀποκρύψῃς ἀπ' ἐμοῦ τὰς ἐντολάς σου.

20 ἐπεπόθησεν ἡ ψυχή μου τοῦ ἐπιθυμῆσαι
τὰ κρίματά σου ἐν παντὶ καιρῷ.

21 ἐπετίμησας ὑπερηφάνοις·
   ἐπικατάρατοι οἱ ἐκκλίνοντες ἀπὸ τῶν ἐντολῶν σου.

22 περίελε ἀπ᾽ ἐμοῦ ὄνειδος καὶ ἐξουδένωσιν,
   ὅτι τὰ μαρτύριά σου ἐξεζήτησα.

23 καὶ γὰρ ἐκάθισαν ἄρχοντες καὶ κατ᾽ ἐμοῦ κατελάλουν,
   ὁ δὲ δοῦλός σου ἠδολέσχει ἐν τοῖς δικαιώμασίν σου.

24 καὶ γὰρ τὰ μαρτύριά σου μελέτη μού ἐστιν,
   καὶ αἱ συμβουλίαι μου τὰ δικαιώματά σου.

δ᾽ δελθ.

25 Ἐκολλήθη τῷ ἐδάφει ἡ ψυχή μου
   ζῆσόν με κατὰ τὸν λόγον σου.

26 τὰς ὁδούς μου ἐξήγγειλα, καὶ ἐπήκουσάς μου·
   δίδαξόν με τὰ δικαιώματά σου.

27 ὁδὸν δικαιωμάτων σου συνέτισόν με,
   καὶ ἀδολεσχήσω ἐν τοῖς θαυμασίοις σου.

28 ἔσταξεν ἡ ψυχή μου ἀπὸ ἀκηδίας·
   βεβαίωσόν με ἐν τοῖς λόγοις σου.

29 ὁδὸν ἀδικίας ἀπόστησον ἀπ᾽ ἐμοῦ
   καὶ τῷ νόμῳ σου ἐλέησόν με.

30 ὁδὸν ἀληθείας ᾑρετισάμην,
   τὰ κρίματά σου οὐκ ἐπελαθόμην.

31 ἐκολλήθην τοῖς μαρτυρίοις σου·
   κύριε, μή με καταισχύνῃς.

32 ὁδὸν ἐντολῶν σου ἔδραμον,
   ὅταν ἐπλάτυνας τὴν καρδίαν μου.

ε᾽ η.

33 Νομοθέτησόν με, κύριε, τὴν ὁδὸν τῶν δικαιωμάτων σου,
   καὶ ἐκζητήσω αὐτὴν διὰ παντός.

34 συνέτισόν με, καὶ ἐξερευνήσω τὸν νόμον σου
   καὶ φυλάξω αὐτὸν ἐν ὅλῃ καρδίᾳ μου.

35 ὁδήγησόν με ἐν τρίβῳ τῶν ἐντολῶν σου,
   ὅτι αὐτὴν ἠθέλησα.

36 κλῖνον τὴν καρδίαν μου εἰς τὰ μαρτύριά σου
   καὶ μὴ εἰς πλεονεξίαν.

37 ἀπόστρεψον τοὺς ὀφθαλμούς μου τοῦ μὴ ἰδεῖν ματαιότητα,
   ἐν τῇ ὁδῷ σου ζῆσόν με.

38 στῆσον τῷ δούλῳ σου τὸ λόγιόν σου
   εἰς τὸν φόβον σου.

39 περίελε τὸν ὀνειδισμόν μου, ὃν ὑπώπτευσα·
   τὰ γὰρ κρίματά σου χρηστά.

40 ἰδοὺ ἐπεθύμησα τὰς ἐντολάς σου·
   ἐν τῇ δικαιοσύνῃ σου ζῆσόν με.

ς᾽ ουαυ.

41 Καὶ ἔλθοι ἐπ᾽ ἐμὲ τὸ ἔλεός σου, κύριε,
   τὸ σωτήριόν σου κατὰ τὸ λόγιόν σου.

42 καὶ ἀποκριθήσομαι τοῖς ὀνειδίζουσί με λόγον,
   ὅτι ἤλπισα ἐπὶ τοὺς λόγους σου.

43 καὶ μὴ περιέλῃς ἐκ τοῦ στόματός μου λόγον ἀληθείας ἕως σφόδρα,
   ὅτι ἐπὶ τὰ κρίματά σου ἐπήλπισα.

44 καὶ φυλάξω τὸν νόμον σου διὰ παντός,
εἰς τὸν αἰῶνα καὶ εἰς τὸν αἰῶνα τοῦ αἰῶνος.

45 καὶ ἐπορευόμην ἐν πλατυσμῷ,
ὅτι τὰς ἐντολάς σου ἐξεζήτησα.

46 καὶ ἐλάλουν ἐν τοῖς μαρτυρίοις σου
ἐναντίον βασιλέων καὶ οὐκ ἠσχυνόμην.

47 καὶ ἐμελέτων ἐν ταῖς ἐντολαῖς σου,
αἷς ἠγάπησα σφόδρα.

48 καὶ ἦρα τὰς χεῖράς μου πρὸς τὰς ἐντολάς σου, ἃς ἠγάπησα,
καὶ ἠδολέσχουν ἐν τοῖς δικαιώμασίν σου.

ζ´ ζαι.

49 Μνήσθητι τὸν λόγον σου τῷ δούλῳ σου,
ᾧ ἐπήλπισάς με.

50 αὕτη με παρεκάλεσεν ἐν τῇ ταπεινώσει μου,
ὅτι τὸ λόγιόν σου ἔζησέν με.

51 ὑπερήφανοι παρηνόμουν ἕως σφόδρα,
ἀπὸ δὲ τοῦ νόμου σου οὐκ ἐξέκλινα.

52 ἐμνήσθην τῶν κριμάτων σου ἀπ᾽ αἰῶνος, κύριε,
καὶ παρεκλήθην.

53 ἀθυμία κατέσχεν με ἀπὸ ἁμαρτωλῶν
τῶν ἐγκαταλιμπανόντων τὸν νόμον σου.

54 ψαλτὰ ἦσάν μοι τὰ δικαιώματά σου
ἐν τόπῳ παροικίας μου.

55 ἐμνήσθην ἐν νυκτὶ τοῦ ὀνόματός σου, κύριε,
καὶ ἐφύλαξα τὸν νόμον σου.

56 αὕτη ἐγενήθη μοι,
ὅτι τὰ δικαιώματά σου ἐξεζήτησα.

η´ ηθ.

57 Μερίς μου κύριε,
εἶπα φυλάξασθαι τὸν νόμον σου.

58 ἐδεήθην τοῦ προσώπου σου ἐν ὅλῃ καρδίᾳ μου·
ἐλέησόν με κατὰ τὸ λόγιόν σου.

59 διελογισάμην τὰς ὁδούς σου
καὶ ἐπέστρεψα τοὺς πόδας μου εἰς τὰ μαρτύριά σου.

60 ἡτοιμάσθην καὶ οὐκ ἐταράχθην
τοῦ φυλάξασθαι τὰς ἐντολάς σου.

61 σχοινία ἁμαρτωλῶν περιεπλάκησάν μοι,
καὶ τοῦ νόμου σου οὐκ ἐπελαθόμην.

62 μεσονύκτιον ἐξηγειρόμην τοῦ ἐξομολογεῖσθαί σοι
ἐπὶ τὰ κρίματα τῆς δικαιοσύνης σου.

63 μέτοχος ἐγώ εἰμι πάντων τῶν φοβουμένων σε
καὶ τῶν φυλασσόντων τὰς ἐντολάς σου.

64 τοῦ ἐλέους σου, κύριε, πλήρης ἡ γῆ·
τὰ δικαιώματά σου δίδαξόν με.

θ´ τηθ.

65 Χρηστότητα ἐποίησας μετὰ τοῦ δούλου σου,
κύριε, κατὰ τὸν λόγον σου.

66 χρηστότητα καὶ παιδείαν καὶ γνῶσιν δίδαξόν με,
ὅτι ταῖς ἐντολαῖς σου ἐπίστευσα.

67 πρὸ τοῦ με ταπεινωθῆναι ἐγὼ ἐπλημμέλησα,
διὰ τοῦτο τὸ λόγιόν σου ἐφύλαξα.
68 χρηστὸς εἶ σύ, κύριε, καὶ ἐν τῇ χρηστότητί σου
δίδαξόν με τὰ δικαιώματά σου.
69 ἐπληθύνθη ἐπ' ἐμὲ ἀδικία ὑπερηφάνων,
ἐγὼ δὲ ἐν ὅλῃ καρδίᾳ μου ἐξερευνήσω τὰς ἐντολάς σου.
70 ἐτυρώθη ὡς γάλα ἡ καρδία αὐτῶν,
ἐγὼ δὲ τὸν νόμον σου ἐμελέτησα.
71 ἀγαθόν μοι ὅτι ἐταπείνωσάς με,
ὅπως ἂν μάθω τὰ δικαιώματά σου.
72 ἀγαθόν μοι ὁ νόμος τοῦ στόματός σου
ὑπὲρ χιλιάδας χρυσίου καὶ ἀργυρίου.

ι' ιωθ.

73 Αἱ χεῖρές σου ἐποίησάν με καὶ ἔπλασάν με·
συνέτισόν με, καὶ μαθήσομαι τὰς ἐντολάς σου.
74 οἱ φοβούμενοί σε ὄψονταί με καὶ εὐφρανθήσονται,
ὅτι εἰς τοὺς λόγους σου ἐπήλπισα.
75 ἔγνων, κύριε, ὅτι δικαιοσύνη τὰ κρίματά σου,
καὶ ἀληθείᾳ ἐταπείνωσάς με.
76 γενηθήτω δὴ τὸ ἔλεός σου τοῦ παρακαλέσαι με
κατὰ τὸ λόγιόν σου τῷ δούλῳ σου.
77 ἐλθέτωσάν μοι οἱ οἰκτιρμοί σου, καὶ ζήσομαι,
ὅτι ὁ νόμος σου μελέτη μού ἐστιν.
78 αἰσχυνθήτωσαν ὑπερήφανοι, ὅτι ἀδίκως ἠνόμησαν εἰς ἐμέ·
ἐγὼ δὲ ἀδολεσχήσω ἐν ταῖς ἐντολαῖς σου.
79 ἐπιστρεψάτωσάν μοι οἱ φοβούμενοί σε
καὶ οἱ γινώσκοντες τὰ μαρτύριά σου.
80 γενηθήτω ἡ καρδία μου ἄμωμος ἐν τοῖς δικαιώμασίν σου,
ὅπως ἂν μὴ αἰσχυνθῶ.

ια' χαφ.

81 Ἐκλείπει εἰς τὸ σωτήριόν σου ἡ ψυχή μου,
καὶ εἰς τὸν λόγον σου ἐπήλπισα.
82 ἐξέλιπον οἱ ὀφθαλμοί μου εἰς τὸ λόγιόν σου
λέγοντες Πότε παρακαλέσεις με;
83 ὅτι ἐγενήθην ὡς ἀσκὸς ἐν πάχνῃ·
τὰ δικαιώματά σου οὐκ ἐπελαθόμην.
84 πόσαι εἰσὶν αἱ ἡμέραι τοῦ δούλου σου;
πότε ποιήσεις μοι ἐκ τῶν καταδιωκόντων με κρίσιν;
85 διηγήσαντό μοι παράνομοι ἀδολεσχίας,
ἀλλ' οὐχ ὡς ὁ νόμος σου, κύριε.
86 πᾶσαι αἱ ἐντολαί σου ἀλήθεια·
ἀδίκως κατεδίωξάν με, βοήθησόν μοι.
87 παρὰ βραχὺ συνετέλεσάν με ἐν τῇ γῇ,
ἐγὼ δὲ οὐκ ἐγκατέλιπον τὰς ἐντολάς σου.
88 κατὰ τὸ ἔλεός σου ζῆσόν με,
καὶ φυλάξω τὰ μαρτύρια τοῦ στόματός σου.

ιβ' λαβδ.

89 Εἰς τὸν αἰῶνα, κύριε,
ὁ λόγος σου διαμένει ἐν τῷ οὐρανῷ.

90 εἰς γενεὰν καὶ γενεὰν ἡ ἀλήθειά σου·
    ἐθεμελίωσας τὴν γῆν, καὶ διαμένει.

91 τῇ διατάξει σου διαμένει ἡ ἡμέρα,
    ὅτι τὰ σύμπαντα δοῦλα σά.

92 εἰ μὴ ὅτι ὁ νόμος σου μελέτη μού ἐστιν,
    τότε ἂν ἀπωλόμην ἐν τῇ ταπεινώσει μου.

93 εἰς τὸν αἰῶνα οὐ μὴ ἐπιλάθωμαι τῶν δικαιωμάτων σου
    ὅτι ἐν αὐτοῖς ἔζησάς με, κύριε.

94 σός εἰμι ἐγώ, σῶσόν με,
    ὅτι τὰ δικαιώματά σου ἐξεζήτησα.

95 ἐμὲ ὑπέμειναν ἁμαρτωλοὶ τοῦ ἀπολέσαι με·
    τὰ μαρτύριά σου υυνῆκα.

96 πάσης συντελείας εἶδον πέρας·
    πλατεῖα ἡ ἐντολή σου σφόδρα.

ιγ΄ μημ.

97 Ὡς ἠγάπησα τὸν νόμον σου, κύριε·
    ὅλην τὴν ἡμέραν μελέτη μού ἐστιν.

98 ὑπὲρ τοὺς ἐχθρούς μου ἐσόφισάς με τὴν ἐντολήν σου,
    ὅτι εἰς τὸν αἰῶνά μοί ἐστιν.

99 ὑπὲρ πάντας τοὺς διδάσκοντάς με συνῆκα,
    ὅτι τὰ μαρτύριά σου μελέτη μού ἐστιν.

100 ὑπὲρ πρεσβυτέρους συνῆκα,
    ὅτι τὰς ἐντολάς σου ἐξεζήτησα.

101 ἐκ πάσης ὁδοῦ πονηρᾶς ἐκώλυσα τοὺς πόδας μου,
    ὅπως ἂν φυλάξω τοὺς λόγους σου.

102 ἀπὸ τῶν κριμάτων σου οὐκ ἐξέκλινα,
    ὅτι σὺ ἐνομοθέτησάς μοι.

103 ὡς γλυκέα τῷ λάρυγγί μου τὰ λόγιά σου,
    ὑπὲρ μέλι καὶ κηρίον τῷ στόματί μου.

104 ἀπὸ τῶν ἐντολῶν σου συνῆκα·
    διὰ τοῦτο ἐμίσησα πᾶσαν ὁδὸν ἀδικίας.
    [ὅτι σὺ ἐνομοθέτησάς μοι.]

ιδ΄ νουν.

105 Λύχνος τοῖς ποσίν μου ὁ λόγος σου
    καὶ φῶς ταῖς τρίβοις μου.

106 ὀμώμοκα καὶ ἔστησα
    τοῦ φυλάξασθαι τὰ κρίματα τῆς δικαιοσύνης σου.

107 ἐταπεινώθην ἕως σφόδρα·
    κύριε, ζῆσόν με κατὰ τὸν λόγον σου.

108 τὰ ἑκούσια τοῦ στόματός μου εὐδόκησον δή, κύριε,
    καὶ τὰ κρίματά σου δίδαξόν με.

109 ἡ ψυχή μου ἐν ταῖς χερσίν μου διὰ παντός,
    καὶ τοῦ νόμου σου οὐκ ἐπελαθόμην

110 ἔθεντο ἁμαρτωλοὶ παγίδα μοι,
    καὶ ἐκ τῶν ἐντολῶν σου οὐκ ἐπλανήθην.

111 ἐκληρονόμησα τὰ μαρτύριά σου εἰς τὸν αἰῶνα,
    ὅτι ἀγαλλίαμα τῆς καρδίας μού εἰσιν.

112 ἔκλινα τὴν καρδίαν μου τοῦ ποιῆσαι τὰ δικαιώματά σου
    εἰς τὸν αἰῶνα δι' ἀντάμειψιν.

ιε' σαμχ.

113 Παρανόμους ἐμίσησα
καὶ τὸν νόμον σου ἠγάπησα.

114 βοηθός μου καὶ ἀντιλήμπτωρ μου εἶ σύ·
εἰς τὸν λόγον σου ἐπήλπισα.

115 ἐκκλίνατε ἀπ' ἐμοῦ, πονηρευόμενοι,
καὶ ἐξερευνήσω τὰς ἐντολὰς τοῦ θεοῦ μου.

116 ἀντιλαβοῦ μου κατὰ τὸ λόγιόν σου, καὶ ζήσομαι,
καὶ μὴ καταισχύνῃς με ἀπὸ τῆς προσδοκίας μου.

117 βοήθησόν μοι, καὶ σωθήσομαι
καὶ μελετήσω ἐν τοῖς δικαιώμασίν σου διὰ παντός.

118 ἐξουδένωσας πάντας τοὺς ἀποστατοῦντας ἀπὸ τῶν δικαιωμάτων σου,
ὅτι ἄδικον τὸ ἐνθύμημα αὐτῶν.

119 παραβαίνοντας ἐλογισάμην πάντας τοὺς ἁμαρτωλοὺς τῆς γῆς·
διὰ τοῦτο ἠγάπησα τὰ μαρτύριά σου διὰ παντός.

120 καθήλωσον ἐκ τοῦ φόβου σου τὰς σάρκας μου·
ἀπὸ γὰρ τῶν κριμάτων σου ἐφοβήθην.

ις' αιν.

121 Ἐποίησα κρίμα καὶ δικαιοσύνην·
μὴ παραδῷς με τοῖς ἀδικοῦσίν με.

122 ἔκδεξαι τὸν δοῦλόν σου εἰς ἀγαθόν·
μὴ συκοφαντησάτωσάν με ὑπερήφανοι.

123 οἱ ὀφθαλμοί μου ἐξέλιπον εἰς τὸ σωτήριόν σου
καὶ εἰς τὸ λόγιον τῆς δικαιοσύνης σου.

124 ποίησον μετὰ τοῦ δούλου σου κατὰ τὸ ἔλεός σου
καὶ τὰ δικαιώματά σου δίδαξόν με.

125 δοῦλός σού εἰμι ἐγώ· συνέτισόν με,
καὶ γνώσομαι τὰ μαρτύριά σου.

126 καιρὸς τοῦ ποιῆσαι τῷ κυρίῳ·
διεσκέδασαν τὸν νόμον σου.

127 διὰ τοῦτο ἠγάπησα τὰς ἐντολάς σου
ὑπὲρ χρυσίον καὶ τοπάζιον.

128 διὰ τοῦτο πρὸς πάσας τὰς ἐντολάς σου κατωρθούμην,
πᾶσαν ὁδὸν ἄδικον ἐμίσησα.

ιζ' φη.

129 Θαυμαστὰ τὰ μαρτύριά σου·
διὰ τοῦτο ἐξηρεύνησεν αὐτὰ ἡ ψυχή μου.

130 ἡ δήλωσις τῶν λόγων σου φωτιεῖ
καὶ συνετιεῖ νηπίους.

131 τὸ στόμα μου ἤνοιξα καὶ εἵλκυσα πνεῦμα,
ὅτι τὰς ἐντολάς σου ἐπεπόθουν.

132 ἐπίβλεψον ἐπ᾽ ἐμὲ καὶ ἐλέησόν με
κατὰ τὸ κρίμα τῶν ἀγαπώντων τὸ ὄνομά σου.

133 τὰ διαβήματά μου κατεύθυνον κατὰ τὸ λόγιόν σου,
καὶ μὴ κατακυριευσάτω μου πᾶσα ἀνομία.

134 λύτρωσαί με ἀπὸ συκοφαντίας ἀνθρώπων,
καὶ φυλάξω τὰς ἐντολάς σου.

135 τὸ πρόσωπόν σου ἐπίφανον ἐπὶ τὸν δοῦλόν σου
καὶ δίδαξόν με τὰ δικαιώματά σου.

136 διεξόδους ὑδάτων κατέβησαν οἱ ὀφθαλμοί μου,
    ἐπεὶ οὐκ ἐφύλαξαν τὸν νόμον σου.
                          ιη' σαδη.
137 Δίκαιος εἶ, κύριε,
    καὶ εὐθὴς ἡ κρίσις σου.
138 ἐνετείλω δικαιοσύνην τὰ μαρτύριά σου
    καὶ ἀλήθειαν σφόδρα.
139 ἐξέτηξέν με ὁ ζῆλος τοῦ οἴκου σου,
    ὅτι ἐπελάθοντο τῶν λόγων σου οἱ ἐχθροί μου.
140 πεπυρωμένον τὸ λόγιόν σου σφόδρα,
    καὶ ὁ δοῦλός σου ἠγάπησεν αὐτό.
141 νεώτερός εἰμι ἐγὼ καὶ ἐξουδενωμένος·
    τὰ δικαιώματά σου οὐκ ἐπελαθόμην.
142 ἡ δικαιοσύνη σου δικαιοσύνη εἰς τὸν αἰῶνα,
    καὶ ὁ νόμος σου ἀλήθεια.
143 θλῖψις καὶ ἀνάγκη εὕροσάν με·
    αἱ ἐντολαί σου μελέτη μου.
144 δικαιοσύνη τὰ μαρτύριά σου εἰς τὸν αἰῶνα·
    συνέτισόν με, καὶ ζήσομαι.
                          ιθ' κωφ.
145 Ἐκέκραξα ἐν ὅλῃ καρδίᾳ μου· ἐπάκουσόν μου, κύριε·
    τὰ δικαιώματά σου ἐκζητήσω.
146 ἐκέκραξά σε· σῶσόν με,
    καὶ φυλάξω τὰ μαρτύριά σου.
147 προέφθασα ἐν ἀωρίᾳ καὶ ἐκέκραξα,
    εἰς τοὺς λόγους σου ἐπήλπισα.
148 προέφθασαν οἱ ὀφθαλμοί μου πρὸς ὄρθρον
    τοῦ μελετᾶν τὰ λόγιά σου.
149 τῆς φωνῆς μου ἄκουσον, κύριε, κατὰ τὸ ἔλεός σου,
    κατὰ τὸ κρίμα σου ζῆσόν με.
150 προσήγγισαν οἱ καταδιώκοντές με ἀνομίᾳ,
    ἀπὸ δὲ τοῦ νόμου σου ἐμακρύνθησαν.
151 ἐγγὺς εἶ σύ, κύριε,
    καὶ πᾶσαι αἱ ἐντολαί σου ἀλήθεια.
152 κατ' ἀρχὰς ἔγνων ἐκ τῶν μαρτυρίων σου,
    ὅτι εἰς τὸν αἰῶνα ἐθεμελίωσας αὐτά.
                          κ' ρης.
153 Ἰδὲ τὴν ταπείνωσίν μου καὶ ἐξελοῦ με,
    ὅτι τὸν νόμον σου οὐκ ἐπελαθόμην.
154 κρῖνον τὴν κρίσιν μου καὶ λύτρωσαί με·
    διὰ τὸν λόγον σου ζῆσόν με.
155 μακρὰν ἀπὸ ἁμαρτωλῶν σωτηρία,
    ὅτι τὰ δικαιώματά σου οὐκ ἐξεζήτησαν.
156 οἱ οἰκτιρμοί σου πολλοί, κύριε·
    κατὰ τὸ κρίμα σου ζῆσόν με.
157 πολλοὶ οἱ ἐκδιώκοντές με καὶ ἐκθλίβοντές με·
    ἐκ τῶν μαρτυρίων σου οὐκ ἐξέκλινα.
158 εἶδον ἀσυνθετοῦντας καὶ ἐξετηκόμην,
    ὅτι τὰ λόγιά σου οὐκ ἐφυλάξαντο.

159 ἰδὲ ὅτι τὰς ἐντολάς σου ἠγάπησα·
κύριε, ἐν τῷ ἐλέει σου ζῆσόν με.

160 ἀρχὴ τῶν λόγων σου ἀλήθεια,
καὶ εἰς τὸν αἰῶνα πάντα τὰ κρίματα τῆς δικαιοσύνης σου.

κα' σεν.

161 Ἄρχοντες κατεδίωξάν με δωρεάν,
καὶ ἀπὸ τῶν λόγων σου ἐδειλίασεν ἡ καρδία μου.

162 ἀγαλλιάσομαι ἐγὼ ἐπὶ τὰ λόγιά σου
ὡς ὁ εὑρίσκων σκῦλα πολλά.

163 ἀδικίαν ἐμίσησα καὶ ἐβδελυξάμην,
τὸν δὲ νόμον σου ἠγάπησα.

164 ἑπτάκις τῆς ἡμέρας ᾔνεσά σοι
ἐπὶ τὰ κρίματα τῆς δικαιοσύνης σου.

165 εἰρήνη πολλὴ τοῖς ἀγαπῶσιν τὸν νόμον σου,
καὶ οὐκ ἔστιν αὐτοῖς σκάνδαλον.

166 προσεδόκων τὸ σωτήριόν σου, κύριε,
καὶ τὰς ἐντολάς σου ἠγάπησα.

167 ἐφύλαξεν ἡ ψυχή μου τὰ μαρτύριά σου
καὶ ἠγάπησεν αὐτὰ σφόδρα.

168 ἐφύλαξα τὰς ἐντολάς σου καὶ τὰ μαρτύριά σου,
ὅτι πᾶσαι αἱ ὁδοί μου ἐναντίον σου, κύριε.

κβ' θαυ.

169 Ἐγγισάτω ἡ δέησίς μου ἐνώπιόν σου, κύριε·
κατὰ τὸ λόγιόν σου συνέτισόν με.

170 εἰσέλθοι τὸ ἀξίωμά μου ἐνώπιόν σου·
κατὰ τὸ λόγιόν σου ῥῦσαί με.

171 ἐξερεύξαιντο τὰ χείλη μου ὕμνον,
ὅταν διδάξῃς με τὰ δικαιώματά σου.

172 φθέγξαιτο ἡ γλῶσσά μου τὸ λόγιόν σου,
ὅτι πᾶσαι αἱ ἐντολαί σου δικαιοσύνη.

173 γενέσθω ἡ χείρ σου τοῦ σῶσαί με,
ὅτι τὰς ἐντολάς σου ᾑρετισάμην.

174 ἐπεπόθησα τὸ σωτήριόν σου, κύριε,
καὶ ὁ νόμος σου μελέτη μού ἐστιν.

175 ζήσεται ἡ ψυχή μου καὶ αἰνέσει σε,
καὶ τὰ κρίματά σου βοηθήσει μοι.

176 ἐπλανήθην ὡς πρόβατον ἀπολωλός·
ζήτησον τὸν δοῦλόν σου, ὅτι τὰς ἐντολάς σου οὐκ ἐπελαθόμην.

NOTES

1 The following quotation was called to my attention by Dr. Mary Ford, Associate Professor of New Testament at St. Tikhon's Seminary. I cite it here for the endearing picture it offers of the author's forebears—his like-minded kin—whom Don and I have always felt to be calling the Irish home to their Orthodox roots through their prayers reaching across the centuries: "Irish monasticism, for all its leaning toward scholarship, was always conscious that the ultimate use of the Bible lay in its always being a guide, of universal import, for life and for law. In order to show its immediate relevance to given situations, and to the ascetic ideal that they sought to preach, the Irish permitted themselves some textual liberty . . ." (Raphael Loewe, "Medieval History of the Latin Vulgate," *Cambridge History of the Bible*, ed. G. W. H. Lampe [New York, NY: Cambridge University Press, 1969], 131). —*Ed.*

2 *The Way of a Pilgrim and The Pilgrim Continues His Way*, trans. R. M. French (San Francisco, CA: HarperCollins, 1965). Hereafter cited in the text as *Way*.

3 J. D. Salinger, *Franny and Zooey* (New York, NY: Little, Brown, 1961; 1991). Hereafter cited in the text as *Franny*.

4 Elmer O'Brien, S.J., *Varieties of Mystic Experience* (New York, NY: New American Library, 1965).

5 This lecture was first delivered at the Orthodox Monastery of the Transfiguration, Ellwood City, PA.

6 Ute Possekel, *Evidence of Greek Philosophical Concepts in the Writings of Ephrem the Syrian* (Walpole, MA: Peeters, 1999), 234.

7 Henry George Liddell, Robert Scott, Sir Henry Stuart Jones, et al., *A Greek-English Lexicon* (Oxford: Clarendon Press, 1968), 28a. Hereafter cited in text as LSJ.

8 *The Ascetical Homilies of St. Isaac the Syrian* (Brookline, MA: Holy Transfiguration Monastery, 1984), 42:210; hereafter cited as *Homilies* or simply with homily and page number. A revised edition of the *Homilies* was published in 2011. See also the Glossary entry for St. Isaac. —*Ed.*

9 Citations of Psalms herein are from Donald Sheehan, *The Psalms of David, Translated from the Septuagint Greek*, ed. Xenia Sheehan and Hierodeacon Herman Majkrzak (Eugene, OR: Wipf & Stock, 2013). Numbering is according to the Septuagint (LXX), for which see Appendix A and the Glossary. —*Ed.*

10 St. Ephrem the Syrian, *Hymns on Paradise* (Crestwood, NY: St. Vladimir's Seminary Press, 1997), 33.

11 Orthodox service for the departing soul, *Service Book of the Holy Orthodox-Catholic Apostolic Church*, trans. Isabel Florence Hapgood, 1922, p. 369. Later editions are available. —*Ed.*

12 Kathleen McVey and John Meyendorff, *Ephrem the Syrian: Hymns*, Classics of Western Spirituality (Mahwah, NJ: Paulist Press, 1989), 119. Cited in text hereafter as *Hymns*.

13 I am grateful to Mat. Ann Sovyrda and her family for giving their kind permission to publish this account of Fr. Vladimir's passing. —*Ed.*

14 Title quotation from Fyodor Dostoevsky, *The Brothers Karamazov*, trans. Richard Pevear and Laryssa Volokhonsky (San Francisco, CA: North Point Press, 1990; reprinted New York, NY: Vintage, 1991), 591. Hereafter cited as *Brothers*. The author recommended this translation as "getting the Orthodoxy right." This lecture was delivered at Marlboro College, Marlboro, Vermont; and at Dartmouth College, where it has been on the Dartmouth College website for a number of years under

the title "Dostoevsky and Memory Eternal: An Eastern Orthodox Approach to *The Brothers Karamazov*." —*Ed.*

15 John D. Zizioulas, "The Contribution of Cappadocia to Christian Thought," *Sinasos in Cappadocia*, ed. Frosso Pimenides and Stelios Roades (National Trust for Greece: Agra Publications, 1986), 34–35. Hereafter cited as "Cappadocia."

16 Victor Terras, quoted in Dostoevsky, *Brothers*, 788, fn. 10.

17 Carolyn Chute, *The Beans of Egypt, Maine* (New York, NY: Harcourt Brace, 1995). —*Ed.*

18 René Girard, philosopher, historian, literary critic, practicing Catholic, was born in France, educated in the United States, and ended his long academic career at Stanford University, retiring in 1995. He is best known for his controversial and radical theory of mimetic violence, developed after extensive research in a surprisingly wide variety of fields. Girard understands violence as beginning in the human inclination to imitate others, to desire what they desire, and ending in acts of sacrificial violence, as most fully revealed in the Christian Gospels. Bullying is a troubling contemporary example, or the violence that has erupted in recent years at certain athletic games; but Girard points to it at every level, from the nursery, to the family, to literature, to the advertising industry, to international warfare—political, economic, and religious. See, for example, his books *Violence and the Sacred* (Johns Hopkins, 1979); *Things Hidden Since the Foundation of the World* (Stanford, 1987); *I See Satan Fall Like Lightning* (Orbis, 2001).

The author studied, taught (most often in combination with the Gospel of Mark), and wrote about Girard for a number of years, on one occasion speaking at a West Coast gathering of Girardian scholars, and on another hosting Professor Girard as a speaker at Holy Resurrection Church in Claremont, New Hampshire. In the last decade or more of his life, however, he had come to find the Girardian explanation insufficient for a variety of reasons. I include this beautiful essay here because I believe it helps to reveal the trajectory along which he was moving—toward a fully Orthodox understanding of the issues Girard had so brilliantly understood and analyzed, and a profoundly Orthodox answer to the problem of envy and violence. —*Ed.*

19 René Girard, *The Girard Reader*, ed. James G. Williams (Chestnut Ridge, NY: Crossroad/Herder, 1996), 268. Hereafter cited as *Reader*.

20 Gil Bailie, *Violence Unveiled: Humanity at the Crossroads* (Chestnut Ridge, NY: Crossroad Publishing, 1996).

21 The Orthodox understanding of desire is that it is indeed natural to us, given to us by God to ignite the soul's intense longing for God in the mystery of deification (see Glossary). At the fall, when the human soul separated itself from God, this desiring nature became dislocated, corrupted, and animal-like, identifying itself no longer with God but with the things of the world. (For further discussion of desire, see the *Philokalia*, comp. St. Nikodimos of the Holy Mountain and St. Makarios of Corinth; trans. and ed. G. E. H. Palmer, Philip Sherrard, and Kallistos Ware [London, Boston: Faber and Faber, 1981], *passim*.) It is therefore on these earthly things that the fallen soul focuses, perceiving them, in its delusion, to be its "own," barely even distinguishable from *itself*. In reality, fallen humanity, sharing a common nature, is deeply responsive and attracted one member to another, but, without the deifying presence attainable through holy desire, the attraction turns to self-assertion and rivalry. Cf. sec. V, p.47. —*Ed.*

22 It is interesting to note here that the Orthodox understanding of marriage is that two people are joined and held in prayer within the believing community, to stand before God to be consecrated to serve Him together, as one. No vows are taken in the marriage service, which is rather a confession of mutual faith and love for God in which the bride and groom are "crowned" with the crown of the holy martyrs. Marriage is, in other words, a Cross, like monasticism, a place and a way to meet God and grow to be like Him in kenotic loving. —*Ed.*

23 John Milton, *Paradise Lost*, Book 1, l. 63.

24 Joseph the Hesychast of the Holy Mountain (1895–1950), quoted in St. Isaac, *Homilies*, ix.

25 In 2013, Hilary Mullins published a tribute to the author, "The Transfiguration of Don Sheehan," in the online magazine *Numerocinq*. In it she quotes him as saying, each year at The Frost Place Festival of Poetry he hosted: "Your work at this conference is to make the art of at least one other person better and stronger by giving—in love—all your art to them." It bore great fruit, year after year, in an environment (writers' workshops) generally known for envious competitiveness. —*Ed.*

26 In this single case, I have retained the author's earlier translation of the line rather than the one offered in Sheehan, *Psalms*—"Remember how I am created"—as the earlier version is a more word-for-word rendering that makes the use of the word "substance" or *hypostasis* explicit. —*Ed.*

27 Fyodor Dostoevsky, *Demons*, trans. Richard Pevear and Laryssa Volokhonsky (New York, NY: Knopf, 1994).

28 Title quotation is from Genesis 1:2. This lecture was first delivered at Holy Cross Greek Orthodox School of Theology, Brookline, Massachusetts, and later at Middlebury College in Middlebury, Vermont. A shorter version of it has been published in John Chryssavgis and Bruce V. Foltz, eds., *Toward an Ecology of Transfiguration: Orthodox Christian Perspectives on Environment, Nature, and Creation* (New York, NY: Fordham University Press, 2013). —*Ed.*

29 *Little Russian Philokalia. Vol. III. A Treasury of Saint Herman's Spirituality* (New Valaam Monastery, Ouzinkie, AK: St. Herman Press, 1989).

30 Panayiotis Nellas, *Deification in Christ: Orthodox Perspectives on the Nature of the Human Person*, trans. Norman Russell (Crestwood, NY: St. Vladimir's Seminary Press, 1987), 57.

31 At the Fourth Ecumenical Council (Chalcedon, 451) the word *prosopon*, "person," was elevated to doctrinal status by the Chalcedonian Definition, which included these words: ". . . One and the Same Christ, Son, Lord, Only-begotten; acknowledged in Two Natures unconfusedly, unchangeably, indivisibly, inseparably; the difference of the Natures being in no way removed because of the Union, but rather the properties of each Nature being preserved, and (both) concurring into One Person and One Hypostasis; not as though He were parted or divided into Two Persons, but One and the Self-same Son and Only-begotten God, Word, Lord, Jesus Christ . . ." —*Ed.*

32 Vladimir Lossky, *The Mystical Theology of the Eastern Church* (Crestwood, NY: St. Vladimir's Seminary Press, 1976), 172–73.

33 The reader may ask at this point, as I did: What of St. Herman's death and miracles? Why did his repose manifest at first as a withdrawal of grace? The record is clear that St. Herman knew this would happen and that his death itself was touched by considerable grace, as recorded in the *Little Russian Philokalia*, Vol. III:

He foresaw the time of his earthly departure, and when the time came [on the 25th of December 1837 (Old Calendar)] he was surrounded by his beloved orphans and spiritual children who were reading the Acts of the Apostles by his bedside. At that moment they recorded that his face suddenly began to shine and the cell was filled with a divine fragrance and they knew that their elder was dead. That same evening, others in the village of Katani on Afognak Island recorded that they saw an unusually bright column of light rising in the air above Spruce Island. The Creole Gerasim Vologdin said, "It looks as though Fr. Herman has left us" and they all began to pray to God.

The record is also clear that the saint had prophesied to his Aleut follower Ignatius that he would be forgotten: "Thirty years will pass after my death, and all those who live now on Spruce Island will be dead [many from an epidemic the saint had also predicted], but you alone will remain alive, and you will be old and poor when I will be remembered" (recounted on the OCA.org website under "Herman's Prophecies for the Future," and in many other places). All that he had prophesied took place, and in 1867, exactly thirty years after the saint's death, Bishop Peter of Alaska began a formal investigation into his life and, in 1894, Fr. Herman's story became known to the outside world. Seventy-six years were still to pass before, on August 9, 1970, Fr. Herman was glorified as a saint by the Orthodox Church in America.

And indeed, there was no absence of miracles and prophecies both before and after the saint's repose, especially among the native Alaskans whom he had served and loved so faithfully. These were and are a simple, quiet people, not given to public display. Having met and talked with some of them, I suspect there are countless intercessions that will never be publicly known because they regard him still as their Apa who always cares for them. Why tell his little secrets to the world?

One early miracle was noted publicly, however:

> In 1842, five years after the passing away of the Elder, Innocent, Archbishop of Kamchatka and the Aleutians, was near Kodiak on a sailing vessel which was in great distress. He looked to Spruce Island, and said to himself, "If you, Father Herman, have found favor in God's presence then may the wind change!" It seems as though not more than fifteen minutes had passed, said the Bishop, when the wind became favorable, and he successfully reached the shore. In thanksgiving for his salvation, Archbishop Innocent himself conducted a Memorial Service (Panikhida) over the grave of the Blessed Elder Herman. (See http://www.pravoslavie.ru/english/st-herman-alaska.htm.)

The conclusion I draw is that the very *withdrawal* of grace the author describes herein was itself a miracle, a witness in the negative to the reality of the saint's deifying effect on the small portion of the natural world he had been given to care for, and thus a confirmation of his humble sanctity. —*Ed.*

34 Reprinted herein by permission of the author.

35 His full name was Herman Squartsoff; he fell asleep in the Lord on December 6, 2013. Memory Eternal, Herman! —*Ed.*

36 For the text of the Orthodox Divine Liturgy, see *Service Books of the Orthodox Church: The Divine Liturgies*, 3rd ed. (South Canaan, PA: St. Tikhon's Press, 2013).

37 A version of this essay has been published in James Jordan and James Whitbourn, *The Musician's Trust* (Chicago, IL: GIA Publications, 2013), under the title "Shakespeare's *The Winter's Tale*: The Way of Beauty and Stillness." —*Ed.*

38 See *The Way of a Pilgrim and The Pilgrim Continues His Way*, trans. R. M. French (San Francisco, CA: HarperCollins, 1965).

39 Archimandrite Vasileios, *Beauty and Hesychia in Athonite Life*, published in Greek in 1994, translated into English in 1996 (Montreal: Alexander Press, 1996); hereafter cited in text as *Beauty*. "Hesychia" is usually translated "stillness." See Glossary. —*Ed.*

40 Shakespeare, *Winter's Tale*, I, ii:190–207. Act, scene, and line are hereafter given in the text. —*Ed.*

41 Title quotation is from Psalm 87:12 (LXX). This lecture was first delivered at The Robert Frost Farm in Derry, New Hampshire, probably in 2006. —*Ed.*

42 "An Old Man's Winter Night" from the book *The Poetry of Robert Frost*, edited by Edward Connery Lathem. Copyright © 1916, 1969 by Henry Holt and Company, copyright © 1944 by Robert Frost. Reprinted by permission of Henry Holt and Company, LLC. All rights reserved.

43 Randall Jarrell, *Poetry and the Age* (New York, NY: Knopf, 1953), 30. Hereafter cited in text as *Poetry*.

44 *The Mystical Theology*, in *Pseudo-Dionysius: The Complete Works*, trans. Colm Luibheid with Paul Rorem (Mahwah, NJ: Paulist Press, 1987).

45 Sydney Lea, *Ghost Pain* (Louisville, KY: Sarabande Books, 2008).

46 St. John Climacus, *The Ladder of Divine Ascent* (Boston, MA: Holy Transfiguration Monastery, 2001), 96.

47 Christopher Merrill, talk delivered at The Frost Place, Franconia, New Hampshire, in 2005.

48 This lecture was first delivered at a Frost Place advanced writers' workshop in Franconia, New Hampshire. —*Ed.*

49 Sheehan, *Psalms*, LXX numbering. References to this translation of Ps 118 (reprinted in full in Part Two) are hereafter given in the text. —*Ed.*

50 Jane Kenyon, "Having It Out with Melancholy," *Constance* (St. Paul, MN: Graywolf Press, 1993). Used by permission.

51 Akathist Hymn "Glory to God for All Things"; Ikos 1, Ikos 2, Ode 6, Ikos 6 are quoted. Available online from many sources. A handwritten copy found in Hieromartyr Gregory Petrov's papers after his death in the Soviet Gulags in 1940 was assumed to have been authored by him and remained in the Russian underground for many years. When it was later published in Russia, it emerged that the poem was written by Metropolitan Tryphon (Prince Boris Petrovich Turkestanov) not long before his death in 1934. I thank Mark Montague for bringing the question of authorship to my attention. —*Ed.*

52 See the author's account of this event in Chapter 5. —*Ed.*

53 Sydney Lea, *Pursuit of a Wound* (Urbana and Chicago, IL: University of Illinois Press, 2000), 69–70.

54 Met. Hilarion Alfeyev, *The Spiritual World of Isaac the Syrian (Cistercian Studies)* (Collegeville, MN: Cistercian Publications, 2000), 219, quoting St. Isaac from *Isaac of Nineveh, "The Second Part,"* Chapters IV–XLI, Sebastian Brock, trans.; Corpus Scriptorum Christianorum Orientalium 555, Scriptores syri 225 (Louvain, 1995).

55 Archimandrite Sophrony, *St. Silouan the Athonite*, trans. Rosemary Edmonds (Crestwood, NY: St. Vladimir's Seminary Press, 1991), Chapter XI, 208 ff., entitled "Keep thy mind in hell, and despair not."

56 See Archimandrite Sophrony, *Wisdom from Mount Athos* (Crestwood, NY: St. Vladimir's Seminary Press, 2001).

57 This introduction is adapted from four sources: the "Translator's Preface" and "Introduction" to Sheehan, *Psalms*, xv–xviii and xxxii–xxxvii; handwritten "Notes Toward a Psalmic Poetics," prepared for a lecture given at The Frost Place in Franconia, New Hampshire, on August 12, 2005; a few points from Chapter 8 herein, "The Action of a Merciful Heart"; and material from the author's Psalms journal, pp. 13–27 (second numbering sequence), also dated August 2005. —*Ed.*

58 Mother Maria, *The Psalms: An Exploratory Translation* (North Yorkshire, UK: Greek Orthodox Monastery of the Assumption, 1973).

59 This first section is adapted from Sheehan, "Translator's Preface," *Psalms*, xv–xviii.

60 The author has written at length on this question in his Introduction to *The Psalms of David*. Much of the following material is drawn from that essay, pp. xxxii–xxxvii.

61 John Breck, *The Shape of Biblical Language: Chiasmus in the Scriptures and Beyond* (Crestwood, NY: St. Vladimir's Seminary Press, 1994), 29.

62 For theological clarification concerning human reason and antinomy, I refer the reader to the following comments kindly provided to me by Fr. Matthew Baker: Fr. Georges Florovsky has written that "the divine Logos is no antinomy which undermines the 'logical'; rather, here is the full measure of Logos. . . . Antinomy is removed in 'contemplation': *theoria—henosis* [union]. In any case, the Divine Being is neither a-logical nor paralogical, and hence theological knowledge (the gnosis of John the Theologian) cannot be a-logical ('irrational') or paralogical." G. Florovsky to S. Sakharov, May 15, 1958, in Arkhimandrit Sofronii [Sakharov], *Perepiska s Protoiereem Georgiem Florovskim* (Essex/Moscow: Svyato-Ioanno-Predtechenskii Monastyr'/ Svyato-Troitskaya Sergieva Lavra, 2008). Fr. Baker notes that Fr. Florovsky's comment accurately reflects the teaching of the Greek Fathers, and is supported in the last century also by the theology of Fr. Dumitru Staniloe. Creaturely reason is but an image of the Logos, but is transformed in the process of deification, along with the whole person. Thus, while knowledge of God may be supra-rational, it is not irrational, and may (according to a wider definition of reason) be rightly called "rational." —*Ed.*

63 See also Glossary entries for *Chiasm* and *Antinomy*. —*Ed.*

64 Ronald E. Heine, *Gregory of Nyssa's Treatise on the Inscriptions of the Psalms* (New York, NY: Oxford University Press, 1995), 91. Hereafter cited in text as Heine.

65 See Chapter 8, "The Action of a Merciful Heart."

66 Jerome Groopman, "A Model Patient: How Simulators Are Changing the Way a Doctor Is Trained," *The New Yorker*, May 2, 2005.

67 See Glossary, and Breck, *Shape*, to understand the importance of a poem's center.

68 A further argument the author has made for the identification of line 93 as the midpoint is that *lamed*—the letter of the Hebrew alphabet that begins all lines of the Hebrew stanza—is considered cognate with both *limod* (study [of Torah]) and *lav* (heart), thus suggesting that the twelfth rather than the eleventh stanza is the poem's heart. —*Ed.*

69 This incarnative significance, the author has written (in notes for a lecture delivered in 2005 at The Frost Place), is intensified by the grammatical modes of the Hebrew

and the Greek verbs: the iterative mode in Hebrew and the aorist mode in Greek. For the ongoingness in the Hebrew verb becomes the actualization in the Greek. Thus, the incarnative intensification of the statutes opens into the Orthodox experience of the Resurrection: and life becomes forever ongoing. And the next three words of the LXX *Lamed* stanza beautifully match the single Hebrew word: that is, *sos eimi ego* translates *lek'ni*, "I am thine"—a matching wherein the Hebraic semantic oneness becomes the LXX trinity, thereby underlining the line's entire incarnative meaning.

Here, then, is the key to the stanza: the way of psalmic personhood is the way of an incarnative relation between the divine "thou" and the human "I." As the "I" gives itself entirely to "thee"—*incarnatively* gives itself—two things happen at once. First, the eternally enduring *logos* of line 89 (Heb. *Dabar*)—that is, the divine voice to which all of the Creation is a response—becomes the finite human voice responding. Second, the human mind and heart become the fully able instruments of divine study. And the object of this divine study is the "enduring-ness" of the statutes. Thus, as the human heart moves always deeper into intimate contact with the divine *logos*, the human heart beomes 'en-statute-ed'; that is, the instrument of human knowing becomes transfigured by—and *into*—the divine Intelligence.

And therefore the stanza's focus in the first three lines (89–91) is on what *remains*, what *persists*, what *endures* in this asymmetrical encounter. In Line 89, God's word endures (Gk. *diamenei*; Heb. *hamad*) in heaven; in line 90, God's truth endures (Gk. *diamenei*; Heb. *nagov*) on the earth; and in line 91, each earthly day endures (Gk. *diamenei*; Heb. *nagov*). —Ed.

70 The numbering of Psalms is according to the Septuagint (LXX) Greek (see Glossary and Appendix A). The translation is from Sheehan, *Psalms*, and based on Alfred Rahlfs, ed., *Septuaginta* (Stuttgart, Germany: Deutsche Bibelgesellschafte, 1979). For further commentary on the translation see the Translator's Preface to Sheehan, *Psalms*. —Ed.

71 This translates the Greek word *mese* and denotes the point where, during the Orthodox service of Matins for the departed, Psalm 118 is divided in half, as opposed to the usual division into three *stases*.—Ed.

72 In support of this thesis from a liturgical perspective, the kathismata schedule appoints Kathismata 16 and 17 (which is the whole of Psalm 118) for every Saturday of the year, including Lazarus Saturday (see Mother Mary and Bishop Kallistos, *Lenten Triodion* [South Canaan, PA: St. Tikhon's Seminary Press, 2002], p. 476). As the author notes elsewhere, however, these two kathismata come out of order in the weekly reading of Psalms, so there is something distinctive about having Psalm 118 on Saturday morning. That is, Friday morning finishes off the cycle with Kathismata 19 and 20, then Friday evening has Kathisma 18, and Saturday morning 16 and 17 (cf. n. 78 below). What is unusual about Lazarus Saturday (and Holy Saturday) is that Kathisma 17 is followed by the troparia (or hymns sung after the Psalter reading) of the Resurrection. On Memorial (or Soul) Saturdays, Kathisma 17 would be followed instead by the funeral Evlogitiaria. Both sets of Evlogitaria (hymns sung after the reading of the Psalter) are connected liturgically to Psalm 118, borrowing their refrain ("Blessed art thou, O Lord, teach me thy statutes") from 118:12. More liturgical support for the author's assertion concerning the resurrectional meaning of the Great Psalm comes from the appointment of Psalm 118 to be sung at Sunday Matins throughout the year whenever the Polyeleos (a festive portion of Matins or Vigil observed on higher-ranking Feast days) is not sung. That is, Psalm 118 would

not be sung at these points or at Sunday Matins at all if it were not understood by the Church to be resurrectional in meaning.

Lazarus Saturday, when Jesus raises Lazarus from lying dead four days in the tomb, is the beginning of the highest holy days in the Orthodox Church. It is followed by Palm Sunday, Jesus' triumphal entry into Jerusalem, and then the five deeply penitential days of Holy Week that culminate in His crucifixion on Holy Friday. Holy Saturday Matins is served Friday night, with Jesus' tomb in the center of the church. In many practices, the people gather around the tomb during the service in antiphonal chanting of the Lamentations (see Glossary) and Psalm 118.

Holy Saturday itself is understood as having what Fr. Patrick Reardon calls "two *spatial* aspects."

> The first is earthly, in the sense that the immolated body of Jesus lies in the tomb. We may think of this aspect as *visible*, in the sense that anyone watching within the tomb would have seen him there. There is also an invisible aspect to Holy Saturday, inasmuch as Jesus' soul has left that body (a "cadaver" now, in Mark's language) and gone elsewhere . . . ("Jesus cried out again with a loud voice," wrote Matthew, "and yielded up his spirit" [28:50]) . . . Foreshadowed by the experience of Jonah, Jesus hands himself over to death for the sake of us, his shipmates. And prophesying this deed, he declares, "For as Jonah was three days and three nights in the belly of the sea monster, so will the Son of Man be three days and three nights in the heart of the earth" (Matt 12:40).

Fr. Patrick asks, "What *happens* to Jesus' soul?" and answers as follows:

> Nothing really *happens* to Jesus, for the simple reason that he is no longer a *passive* being. Death has no hold on him. In fact, the creeds and ancient sources use the active voice when dealing with this subject; we are told that Jesus "descended first into the lower parts of the earth" (Eph 4:9) and "he went and preached unto the spirits in prison" (1 Peter 3:19). Although his body lies helpless in the hands of those who bury him, *no one* controls his soul. He is . . . "free among the dead." [Moreover,] . . . he penetrated the region of darkness with the abundance of his unconquered light, shattering the bars of Sheol, and liberating those ancients who in faith awaited his arrival . . . He arrives . . . in utter majesty . . . When, on Sunday [Holy Pascha], he would rise from the dead, Christ had already invaded the house of the strong man armed, had despoiled him, and had left his realm in ruins. (From *Jesus and the Atonement*, forthcoming [2015] from Ancient Faith Press. Quoted by permission. —*Ed.*)

73 Sheehan, Introduction to *Psalms,* "The Mind of David and the Mind of Christ."
74 All citations of Psalms herein are from Sheehan, *Psalms.* Numbering is according to the Septuagint. See Appendix A.—*Ed.*
75 An ancient Jewish text in which each element of creation, from the celestial to the animal, sings God's praises in biblical or rabbinic verses, many of them psalmic. I do not know which edition the author used. —*Ed.*
76 *Tehillim,* I, 73.
77 Heine, 91.

78 In this practice, beginning Saturday night with the first Kathisma (Pss 1–8), we pray Kathismata 2 and 3 (Pss 9–23) on Sunday; 4, 5, 6 (Pss 24–45) on Monday; 7, 8, 9 (Pss 46–69) on Tuesday; 10, 11, 12 (Pss 70–90) on Wednesday; 13, 14, 15 (Pss 91–108) on Thursday; 19, 20, 18 (Pss 134–150 and 119–133) on Friday; and 16, 17 (Pss 109–118) on Saturday morning.

79 St. Ignatius Brianchaninov, *The Arena: An Offering to Contemporary Monasticism*, trans. Archimandrite Lazarus (Jordanville, NY: Holy Trinity Monastery, 1983), 129.

80 Elder Ephraim of Katounakia, *Obedience Is Life* (Mt. Athos, Greece: Vatopaidi Monastery, 2003), 103.

81 *Way of a Pilgrim*, 93. I made a few tiny changes.

82 Heine, *Treatise*, page unknown. —*Ed.*

83 St. Isaac, *Homilies*, 26:129; brackets in original.

84 Ibid., 26:130; second brackets mine.

85 Ibid., 26:131, fn 14.

86 For the text of the Liturgy of St. John Chrysostom, see *Service Books of the Orthodox Church: The Divine Liturgies*.

87 St. Dionysius, *On the Divine Names*, in *Pseudo-Dionysius: The Complete Works*, 697B.

88 Robert Alter and Frank Kermode, eds., *The Literary Guide to the Bible* (Cambridge, MA: Belknap Press of Harvard University Press, 1990), 631.

89 Cf. n. 72 above.

90 Fabre d'Olivet, *The Hebraic Tongue Restored*, 1815, trans. Nayán Louise Redfield (New York, NY: G. P. Putnam's Sons, 1921). Page number unknown. —*Ed.*

91 Pierre Kovalevsky, *Saint Sergius and Russian Spirituality* (Crestwood, NY: St. Vladimir's Seminary Press, 1976), 79.

92 Ibid., 81.

93 Ladislaus Boros, *Hidden God* (New York, NY: Seabury Press, 1973).

94 2 Kings 12:16, Alter's translation, *Literary Guide*. This and the subsequent quotations in this paragraph are from pp. 260–62.

95 Quoted by Heine, 72.

96 *Patrologia Graeca*, J. P. Migne (Imprimerie Catholique, 1857–66), 44:949.

97 John N. Day, "The Pillars of Imprecation: How to Pray for Your Enemies by Praying Against Them," *Touchstone: A Journal of Mere Christianity* (November 2006), 34.

98 Book I: Pss 1–40; II: 41–71; III: 72–88; IV: 89–105; and V: 106–150.

99 A deep bog in John Bunyan's *Pilgrim's Progress*; by allegory, a state of extreme depression. In Bunyan's story, "This miry Slough is such a place as cannot be mended."

100 Read at his brother's funeral. The author himself inserted the letter at this point in the manuscript. —*Ed.*

101 The twins' older sister. —*Ed.*

102 Dn. Mark Barna, a friend of the family, is co-author of *A Christian Ending* (Manton, CA: Divine Ascent Press, 2011) with his wife, Elizabeth. He was assisted in the process of preparing the body by Fr. John Parker of Holy Ascension Orthodox Church in Charleston, South Carolina. Their church has adopted Dn. Mark's guidelines for helping families make their own arrangements for the end-of-life transition and routinely conducts funerals without the aid of a professional funeral director. —Ed.

GLOSSARY

Compiled by Fr. Moses Hibbard, Mark Montague, and Xenia Sheehan.
Indicates that a word is glossed in a separate entry.

Abba Philemon—One of the greatest desert dwellers of all according to the *Philokalia*. No historical date is available as to when exactly he lived, but he was said to be a great man of prayer, experiencing constant tears of *repentance and practicing extreme *asceticism.

Agape—The Greek word itself connotes love in varying aspects. In Christian parlance, it expresses a philanthropic quality by which Christians are called to love the world just as God does. This is seen in such examples as John 3:16, "For God so loved ['agapied'] the world . . . ," and the Early Christian ritual of the Love (*Agape*) Feast.

Akathist—A 24-stanza hymn sung in the *Orthodox Church, generally composed to honor or petition different saints. The Akathist Hymn to the Mother of God (seventh-century Byzantium) is the prototype for all hymns that have been fashioned after this style. Akathists continue to be composed as new saints are *canonized, or as a way of praying for help with a particular issue.

Amvon—An elevated platform in the center of an *Orthodox church. Traditionally, it was located in the center of the church, whereas today it most commonly refers to a promontory extending from the raised area preceding the altar area of an Orthodox church known as the solea.

Anaphora—The word is of Greek origin, literally meaning "to bear upward." In a liturgical context it refers to that moment during the Divine *Liturgy when the gifts of bread and wine are offered up to become the Body and Blood of the Lord Jesus Christ.

Angels—The angels are one part of a threefold created order: angels, humankind, and the rest of material creation. St. John of Damascus (eighth-century Syrian priest monk and polymath) tells us that, "Compared with us, the angel is said to be incorporeal and immaterial, although in comparison with God . . . everything proves to be gross and material" (*Exact Exposition*, II, 3; 37:205). There are nine ranks of angels, of which the ones that concern us most are those who serve as God's messengers to humankind (Gr. *angelos*) and watch over peoples, nations, and each person to assist in the working out of God's Providence (see Makarios, *Synaxarion*, II, 63–66). The *Orthodox Church understands the goal of this Providence to be the raising of humankind to be even higher than the angels. For we are told, "Therefore you shall be perfect, just as your Father in heaven is perfect" (Matt 5:48). See also *Demons*.

Antinomy/Antinomic—The term *antinomy* has been used in Orthodox theological discourse to describe "the affirmation of two contrasting or opposed truths, which cannot be reconciled on the level of the discursive reason although a reconciliation is possible on the higher level of contemplative experience . . . In order to reach out towards that which is inconceivable, the Christian tradition speaks in 'antinomic' fashion . . ." (Timothy Ware [Met. Kallistos of Diokleia], "The Debate about Palamism," *Eastern Churches Review* IX: 1–2, 46). "If we exclude the antinomic dimension," Met. Kallistos continues, "the danger is that we shall never ascend to the level of spiritual understanding" (51). See also Sheehan, *Psalms of David*, Introduction, esp. n. 10, and n. 62 herein.

Antiphonal Singing/Antiphony—The word *antiphony*, in church singing, means one voice singing in response to, or counter to, another. The goal is to integrate two realities into one, thereby emphasizing unity, especially with regard to true worship of the Triune Godhead. The author often uses *antiphony* in the context of the psalmist's (or our) dialogue with God as we move toward a deeper relationship with Him.

Apolytikion—A Greek term referring to the dismissal hymns, sometimes called **troparia*, placed at the end of Vespers or at either end of the *Matins service.

Aramaean—The Aramaean people are thought to have originated from an area near modern-day Syria. Although the original race of people died out in the eighth century, many modern-day Syrians consider their heritage to be Aramaean. The dialect that was spoken by this group has greatly informed modern-day Aramaic.

Ascesis—A Greek term originally referring to athletic training, an analogy that St. Paul was wont to use (Phil 3:12–16; 2 Tim 4:7). The practice of asceticism within the Orthodox Christian tradition is not merely a physical exercise, although it has this as one component, but rather a setting aside of secondary pursuits and concerns to focus on "the one thing needful" (Lk 10:42) in order to achieve full actualization of the person in the life of God in the Church. See also *Monk/ Monasticism; Deification; Great Lent; Hesychia; Theoria; Theosis*.

Athonite—see *Mt. Athos*.

Blessedness/Beatitude—The blessedness spoken of in the Psalms refers to our reception into God's life, and of His life into us, in every turn we make toward Him throughout our own lives in true* repentance. That is, as we learn to turn away from the poverty of our sinful condition we are raised to our Godly purpose, blessedness. The paradoxical reality of self-abasement leading toward divine uplifting is testified to by Jesus Christ Himself: "Whoever exalts himself will be humbled, and whoever humbles himself will be exalted" (Matt 23:12, ESV]). See also *Deification*.

Blessing—In the *Orthodox Church, it is customary for the faithful to ask for a blessing from their priest. This is done by placing the right hand in the left, palm up, whereupon the priest, forming the blessing with his right hand, crosses it over the faithful's coupled hands. The recipient of the blessing then kisses the priest's hand as an act of veneration, as the priest's hand is understood to be the image of the very hand of Jesus Christ, who offers His Body and Blood in the Eucharist, which the priest is ordained to perform. It is also a sign of respect for the authority of the Church, which has ordained the priest to represent Christ in the context of the Liturgy.

Bright Week—The week following the celebration of *Pascha (Easter), in which the faithful are understood to be living *within the Resurrection*. Distinctive aspects of Bright Week in the *Orthodox Church include: daily Divine *Liturgy, continuous opening of the Holy Doors between the altar and the nave, pure white vestments on the celebrants and church furniture, flowers in the church, feasting focused on the meat and dairy products abstained from during *Great Lent, and no fasting or *prostrations.

Cadence/Cadential Shape—Rhythmic flow of a sequence of words or sounds; poetic form governed by cadence rather than a fixed metrical pattern. In Psalm 118, the author identifies two kinds of cadence that give shape to the poem: (1) fixed (alphabetic sequence of stanzas; by extension, God's unchanging presence in the poem and His statutes); (2) flowing, which partakes of the incarnate and is driven by many different factors, such as the particular nature at any given point of the encounter between the angelic and the human, the nature and interaction of voices, the nine words (see Part Two, Chapters II and III), as well as metric and sonic qualities inherent in Hebrew and the language of translation. Cadential shape is also, if not primarily, given by the interaction or "fit" between the two types of cadence.

Canon—A hymn chanted during the *Matins service that celebrates the particular saint or feast being commemorated that day. The Canon usually consists of eight or nine odes, the first eight being based on the eight canticles of the Old Testament, and the ninth ode on the New Testament canticle also known as the *Magnificat.

Canonization—The *Orthodox Church keeps a list of saints, known as a canon, simply meaning "rule." Throughout the liturgical year, saints are commemorated each day in the Church's services. One who is recognized as a saint after his or her death is confirmed by the faithful, who have seen and experienced that this particular person led a holy life, pleasing to God, and is now in a position to intercede for those faithful still living on the earth. It is critical to note that in the Eastern Orthodox *tradition, canonization does not *make* a person a saint, but rather *confirms* that person's holiness as an already established fact.

Cappadocian Fathers—This term refers to the three great *Church Fathers: St. Gregory of Nyssa, St. Gregory Nazianzus, and St. Basil the Great, who lived in Cappadocia in Asia Minor in the fourth century. They were instrumental in articulating the Church's understanding of personhood and other *ontological concepts in the context of early conciliar discussions regarding the two most central teachings of the Church: the three Persons and one essence of the Holy *Trinity, and the one Person and two natures of Christ.

Chiasm/Chiasmus/Chiastic—A rhetorical form based on concentric parallelism, by which the first line of a poem in some way parallels the last, the second the penultimate, and so on, creating, in addition to the normal linear progression, both a centripetal and centrifugal flow of meaning. That is, "meaning is developed from the beginning and end of the passage toward the middle. Accordingly, the ultimate meaning of a chiastically structured passage is expressed not at the *end*, in what we understand to be the 'conclusion.' The real meaning or essential message of the text is to be found rather at its *center*" (Breck, *Scripture in Tradition*, 93). See also Breck, *The Shape of Biblical Language*.

Christ Pantocrator—The term could be rendered as "Christ Almighty, Ruler of All" or "Christ, holder of all things" in the sense of sustaining all of creation. It is customary in *Orthodox churches to have an icon entitled "Christ Pantocrator" in the central dome of the nave, showing Jesus Christ above all with his right hand held up in blessing and an open Gospel text in his left.

Church Fathers—A title given to the collective body of saints in the *Orthodox Church that has helped to bequeath and pass on the Orthodox Christian tradition through the ages. Note that this title is not reserved for a select group that ceased to exist after an arbitrary date in the third or fourth century, but still serves to describe those who facilitate the life and witness of the Church in our own day.

Church Slavonic—A liturgical language developed by St. Cyril of Thessalonica in the ninth century to aid Byzantine missionary activities among the Slavic peoples.

The language is still the normative liturgical language of nearly all Slavic churches today, and can be heard in many churches in America.

Compunction—Deep* repentance that combines consciousness of one's sinfulness with the tenderness and joy of knowing God's forgiveness. See *Philokalia* IV, 314.

Consubstantial—The word literally means to have shared substance. That is to say, the essential aspects of one person or idea are shared with another. This word is the Latin equivalent of the Greek *homoousion* chosen at the Council of Nicaea in 325 to describe the relations of the Three Persons of the *Trinity.

Deacon—In the clerical ranks of the *Orthodox Church, the deacon stands just below the presbyter, or priest. The ministry of the deacon has taken on many and varied forms since its inception in the book of the Acts of the Apostles in the New Testament. In large part, the deacon of today functions in a liturgical context, assisting the priest or bishop during the Divine *Liturgy. It is still commonplace, however, to see the deacon offering up varied ministries in the Church such as teaching or taking Holy Communion to the sick.

Deification—Also known as *theosis or divinization, deification is the normative underlying goal of all Orthodox Christian spirituality. It is the process of participating in the Life of God by sharing in His Divine Energies. See also *Blessedness; Theoria; Theosis*.

Demons—The Orthodox understanding of demons is that, in the first moments of the creation of the invisible world, Lucifer, highest and brightest of the *angels, thought to rival God's power and immediately fell into the depths of hell, bringing down with him a multitude of angels of every rank. These once-free angelic spirits became what we know as demons. They were confined to the earthly sphere of existence with a limited power to disturb and try the souls of humankind. The *Orthodox Church teaches that Christ, in accepting death for our sake, ended forever, for all who follow Him, this demonic power that would lead us to share in the eternal death of the fallen angels. For the Orthodox, this following of Christ is a lifelong *incarnative practice leading through *repentance to *theosis and a glorification beyond even that of the angels. For further information, see Rose, *Soul After Death*. See also *Holy Saturday; Angels*.

Diapsalma—See *Selah*.

Dionysius the Areopagite—Originally mentioned in the Acts of the Apostles as a companion of the Apostle Paul, he is the purported author of some of the most well-known mystical works in the body of Christian literature—mystical in the sense of focusing on the union of man with God. These include *The Celestial Hierarchy, The Ecclesiastical Hierarchy, On the Divine Names*, and *The Mystical Theology*. Scholars today attribute these works to an unknown author of the sixth century; however, the *Orthodox Church has historically upheld in its Church calendar and hagiographic writings that the works are those of the noble and well-educated Bishop of Athens St. Dionysius the Areopagite, martyred for his faith under the emperor Domitian in the year 96. Influential in both the East and the West, his works, aside from their purported authorship by a disciple of the apostles, have been especially valued for their explanation of *kataphatic* and *apophatic* theology: while *kataphatic* theology makes positive statements about God, our understanding of their content must be purified through their negation, so that we may pass beyond the limitations of both toward God. His feastday is celebrated in the Orthodox Church on October 3.

Divinized—See *Deification*.

Eastern Orthodox Church—See *Orthodox Church*.

Elder—In the Orthodox tradition it is common to seek out the counsel of a spiritual father. This is an intensely real relationship in which the spiritual father plants seeds of truth in the soul of his spiritual child, consistently watering them with his hope and prayers that the seeds may bear fruit in that person's life. An elder is one who has become, by the grace of God, a spiritual father to many and is given the gifts of the Holy Spirit to lead many toward the Kingdom of God in Christ Jesus.

Eucharist—see *Holy Gifts*.

Fast, Fasting—see *Great Lent*.

Fathers, Orthodox—See *Church Fathers*.

Great Lent/Lenten/Lent—Also known as the Great Fast, in the Eastern *Orthodox Church Great Lent is a forty-day period preceding *Holy Week, which culminates in the celebration of Holy *Pascha (Easter). It begins with a communal rite of forgiveness on Forgiveness Sunday. Characteristics of the Lenten season are abstinence from certain foods: meat, fish, eggs, dairy products, and on most days wine and oil; on a few festal days fish is allowed during the Great Fast. Eucharistic liturgies are celebrated only on Saturdays and Sundays during the Fast, with the exception of Wednesday and Friday *Liturgies of the Presanctified Gifts. The Lenten Fast does not exist solely for the purpose of eating less food, however, but so that the fully engaged Christian may strengthen his or her *repentance, prayer life, and almsgiving to the poor. The goal of the Fast is to reach, in purity of heart, the much-anticipated Pascha of the Lord so as to participate in His Resurrection and be, with Him, quickened into Life. See also *Ascesis*.

Heart—Defined by the translators of the *Philokalia* as "not simply the physical organ but the spiritual centre of man's being, man as made in the image of God, his deepest and truest self, or the inner shrine, to be entered only through sacrifice and death, in which the mystery of the union between the divine and the human is consummated" (IV:431).

Hesychia/Hesychast—A Greek word meaning "stillness." Hesychasts are ascetic monks who live in full or partial solitude and practice inner prayer, especially the *Jesus Prayer, in order to achieve inner stillness. In a sense, anyone with an uncompromising commitment to and practice of prayer may be said to be practicing hesychia. Such prayer cleans the vessel of the *heart so that it may be filled by God. Its goal is *deification, union with God through participation in His uncreated energies. Rooted in ancient Orthodox *tradition, the practice of hesychia received conciliar affirmation in the fourteenth century, after considerable controversy (known as the Palamite controversy), and continues today, especially in great monastic centers such as *Mt. Athos.

Holy Gifts—The elements of bread and wine that are offered at the *Anaphora of the Divine *Liturgy to become the Body and Blood of Jesus Christ and given to the faithful as the Eucharist.

Holy Saturday—The Saturday that ends *Holy Week, preparatory to *Pascha (Western Easter). It is on this day that Christ, after His death and burial, descended into Hades to release from the bondage of sin and death all those who had died prior to this time. A Resurrectional joy is already present in the *Liturgy of this day, to which the change to white vestments and many of the Scripture readings give witness. Cf. n. 72.

264 ■ *The Grace of Incorruption*

Holy Spirit—The Third Person of the Holy *Trinity, who, as the Nicene-
Constantinopolitan Creed states, "proceeds from the Father and with the Father
and the Son is worshipped and glorified, who spoke by the prophets." The Holy
Spirit is of the same Uncreated Essence as the Father and the Son, yet was shared
energetically with the Church on the first Pentecost (see Acts of the Apostles 1).

Holy Trinity—See *Trinity*.

Holy Week—The liturgical sequence beginning after Palm Sunday that marks the Lord
Jesus' final progress into Jerusalem and culminates in His crucifixion and death
on Holy Friday, His descent into Hades to free its captives on *Holy Saturday,
and His Resurrection on Holy *Pascha. It is observed in the *Orthodox Church
by intensified fasting and two services daily (including the Eucharist) until Holy
Friday, when there are three services (but no Eucharist). See also n. 72.

Homoousios—A Greek word literally meaning "of the same essence"; the word used
by Latin Fathers to translate it is *consubstantial (i.e., of the same substance). The
term was adopted at the Council of Nicaea in 325 to describe the relationship
of Jesus Christ and the Father (i.e., they are of the same divine nature). Later
the term was applied to the Holy Spirit as well; all three are one in essence. By
extension, the term is applied in this text to ideas and words to indicate that
essential features are shared while distinction is maintained.

Hours—Liturgical offices read throughout the day at the first, third, sixth, and ninth
hours (6 and 9 AM, noon, and 3 PM, though in practice they are often adjoined
to whatever services are being served in the Church). Generally they consist
in psalm reading, hymns, and other prayers. The tradition itself goes back to
the ancient practice of marking time in such a manner and to Jewish Temple
worship.

Humility—The greatest of all the Christian virtues, because without humility it is impossible to attain any other virtue. The greatest example of humility in the Christian
tradition is Christ Himself, whose supreme act of self-emptying love on the Cross
fuels the ability for anyone who follows Him to attain to a humble spirit. Humility
is the antidote for the initial sin of humanity in the Garden of Eden: pride.

Hymn of the Entrance—In English also often referred to as the Cherubic Hymn. Beginning with the words, "Let us who mystically represent the Cherubim . . . ," the
hymn is sung at the Divine *Liturgy during the Great Entrance, when the *Holy
Gifts are transported from the Table of Oblation to the Altar Table where they
will be consecrated to become the Body and Blood of Jesus Christ.

Hypostasis—A Greek term denoting a complete, unique realization of a nature, and often
translated into English as "person." Throughout the writings of the Orthodox
*Church Fathers, hypostasis is used to distinguish between the three Persons
(hypostases) of the Holy *Trinity: Father, Son, and Holy Spirit, distinct in
personhood, yet united in Divine nature. Likewise the term is used to affirm that
Christ is one Person with two natures. All human beings are distinct hypostases.
See also *Ontological*.

Iconostasis—Lit. *icon stand*, the iconostasis is a screen-like apparatus that houses icons in a
particular order, distinguishing the sanctuary (altar area) of an Orthodox temple
from the nave and surrounding area in the church. Not in any sense a barrier, the
iconostasis with its iconic "windows to Heaven" is understood rather as focusing
and guiding the worshippers' attention and prayers *toward* the altar where the
*angelic presences gather for the consecration of the *Holy Gifts.

Ikos—A hymn that follows the *kontakion within the structure of a *canon.

Image and Likeness—In Genesis 1:26 God speaks, saying, "Let us make man in our image, after our likeness." This has traditionally been understood as a distinction in *patristic theology; each man has within himself the *image* of God given at the initial creation, and through the process of *deification is able to attain to the *likeness* of God.

Incarnate/Incarnation/Incarnative—A word of Latin origin literally meaning *enfleshment.* The Incarnation proper is the coming of the Son of God into the world and taking on human flesh through the conception and birthgiving of the Virgin Mary (*Theotokos). Incarnation is discussed in various contexts herein, reflecting the idea that the Christian is called to *incarnate*—that is to realize in one's body and in one's earthly life—the qualities of the divine life, which have their origin in God, the Holy *Trinity. Something is said to be *incarnative* when it tends toward this end.

Jesus Prayer—The full prayer is "Lord Jesus Christ, Son of God, have mercy upon me, a sinner," but shorter forms are also used. In the *Orthodox Church, this prayer, centering in on the name of Jesus, is widely practiced as a way of following St. Paul's counsel to "pray without ceasing" (1 Thess 5:17). Its use may date to the Egyptian desert of the third or fourth century, but it is also alluded to in the Scriptures themselves (see Matt 9:27). Certain methods are employed at times to facilitate its practice, such as posture, breathing technique, or the use of a prayer rope (woolen or beaded; *chotki* in Russian, *komboskini* in Greek), by which the prayer is repeated knot by knot. See also *Hesychia.*

Kathisma (*pl.* kathismata)— A division of the Psalter used by the Eastern Orthodox Church and Eastern Rite Catholics. In monastic practice, three of the twenty divisions are chanted daily (but only two on Sundays) in a particular order, as described in note 78 herein. See Mother Mary and Bp. Kallistos, *The Lenten Triodion,* pp. 533–34, for the Lenten order.

Kellia—Monastic cell or a small community of *monks.

Kenosis/Kenotic—Derived from the Greek verb *kenoo,* which carries the meaning of draining something empty. In the Christian context, an act of *kenosis* is an act of extreme humility, epitomized in the self-emptying love of Jesus Christ seen in His Incarnation and His death on the Cross (see Phil 2:6–7).

Kissing a priest's hand—See *Blessing.*

Kontakion—A hymn sung at certain points during the Divine *Liturgy in honor of the saint or feast of the day, following the *Troparia. It is also placed after the sixth ode of the *canon at *Matins.

Lamentations—An Orthodox service set within the Matins for Holy Saturday, also known as the Burial Lamentations or Lamentations at the Tomb because it takes place around the tomb of Christ in the center of the Church. The service follows Gospel readings describing Jesus' capture, trial, and crucifixion. The Lamentation verses are sung antiphonally with the clergy chanting verses of Psalm 118. See Mother Mary and Bp. Kallistos, *The Lenten Triodion.*

Lent—See *Great Lent.*

Liturgy/Liturgical—Greek *leitourgia,* which in a Christian context refers to an act of worship to God involving both clergy and laity. All of the worship in the Eastern *Orthodox Church is done liturgically, as it always involves the mind of the *Church Fathers and the inherited *traditions of worship received from God Himself (i.e., Eucharistic Communion). Even private prayer in the homes of the faithful involves the liturgical influences of the larger Church community. The Divine Liturgy proper, resurrectional and paschal in spirit, is the Eucharistic service composed by Saints John Chrysostom and Basil the Great that is celebrated on Sundays and special Feast days (and daily in most monasteries) by the faithful gathered together.

Liturgy of the Presanctified Gifts—During the weekdays of *Great Lent it is not permitted to celebrate the Divine *Liturgy, in order to preserve the penitential character of the Fast. As a result the Presanctified Liturgy is celebrated as part of daily Vespers, usually on Wednesdays and Fridays. The Gifts themselves (the Eucharist) are consecrated at the previous Sunday Liturgy, hence the term Presanctified. See also *Anaphora; Holy Gifts*.

LXX—The Roman numerals signifying *seventy*. This is a common abbreviation for the *Septuagint text of the Old Testament, a translation carried out by seventy-two scholars (six from each of the Twelve Tribes of Israel).

Magnificat—The song or canticle spoken by Mary, taken from Luke 1:46–55, when she visits her cousin Elizabeth, who is pregnant with John the Baptist.

Masoretic Hebrew—Refers to the extant Hebrew text (abbreviated MT) of the Old Testament Scriptures, dating from around the tenth century AD. It differs in significant ways from the Hebrew original, of which much was lost in the destruction of Jerusalem in 70 AD. Most English-language Bibles today are based on the Masoretic text (MT). The *Orthodox Church, however, prefers and has always used the *Septuagint as a more accurate witness to the original Hebrew and as the text quoted throughout the New Testament.

Matins—The morning office of the daily liturgical cycle. In Greek practice, Matins (Orthros) is celebrated in the morning preceding the Divine *Liturgy. In Slavic churches, it is often customary to follow Vespers with the Matins service in the evening. The Matins service has many distinctive characteristics, one of which is the reading of the *canon in honor of the saint or feast of the day.

Matushka—A Russian term of endearment and respect for the wife of a clergyman, meaning "little mother." The term is counterpart to the common practice of calling Orthodox Priests "Father" or, in Slavic cultures, "Batyushka" ("little father").

Mind of Christ—Derives from St. Paul, 1 Corinthians 2:16: "We have the mind of Christ." The author has written that "we possess in ourselves the mind of Christ *solely because* God has given us this mind in order that we may know—in St. Paul's own words—'the things freely given us by God' (1 Cor 2:12). Itself a gift, the mind of Christ in us is thus the mode wherein we know God's gifts" (Sheehan, "The Mind of David and the Mind of Christ," *Psalms*, xxv).

Monarchianism—A heresy that developed early in the Church's history as an overzealous attempt to preserve monotheism in light of the Church's teaching on the divinity of the Father and the Son. The emphasis on divine unity by monarchian theologians resulted in a claim that Jesus was not of the same measure of divinity as God the Father, a teaching rejected by the Church.

Monk/Monasticism/Monastery—In Greek, *monos* means alone, corresponding to the Latin *solus*. The monastic life is characterized by various forms ranging from a community of persons (living within a coenobitic monastery) to the solitary eremitic life. The goal of monastic life is separation from the world in order to attain union with God. The goal in such separation is not to cut oneself off from the world utterly, but to be better able to love and pray for the world, having gained a spiritual state unaffected by the distractions and demands of worldly life through rigorous self-denial, volitional obedience, and the practice of inner prayer. Since the fourth century, monasticism and its spiritual witness have provided a crucial foundation and balance-point within the *Orthodox Church. See also *Ascesis; Hesychia; Jesus Prayer; Mt. Athos*.

Mother of God—See *Theotokos*.

Mt. Athos/Athonite—A peninsula and mountain geographically located in the northeasternmost part of Greece, jutting out into the Aegean Sea. It is an autonomous polity of the Hellenic Republic. According to Orthodox tradition, the Virgin Mary was traveling with St. John the Evangelist through the Aegean and, forced to land on the peninsula, was so moved by its beauty that she blessed it and asked that her Son give it to her to be her garden. His voice was heard to answer: "Let this place be your inheritance and your garden, a paradise and a haven of salvation for those seeking to be saved." Also called the Holy Mountain, it has existed as a *monastic stronghold since the mid-tenth century when St. Athanasius founded the first monastic community known as the Great Lavra, which still exists today. The peninsula today is home to twenty monasteries as well as numerous *sketes and hermitages.

MT—Masoretic text. See *Masoretic Hebrew*.

Name-Saint—It is common practice in most Orthodox churches for the faithful to take the name of a saint at Baptism. At times, the name of the saint is the person's given name or a like name, but it need not be. The Name-Saint is considered a special protector for that person and the day of that saint's commemoration in the Church a special day, called a Name Day. By this saint's name, an Orthodox Christian receives the Holy Mysteries (i.e., Confession and Eucharist, etc.) and is typically identified in all activity related to the Church. Thus the author and the Orthodox members of his family are at times herein referred to by their saint's name: Donatos, Xenia, Benedict, Maria (for St. Mary of Egypt). See *St. Donatos*.

Nous/Noetic—Defined by the translators of the *Philokalia* as "the highest faculty in man, through which—provided it is purified—he knows God or the inner essences or principles of created things by means of direct apprehension or spiritual perception" (I, 362). This faculty is distinguished from the reason or mind (*dianoia*), which works by sequences of logical connections. See also *Heart*.

Ontological—Derived from Greek *ontos*, "being." Ontology is concerned with the existence and manner of existence of beings, be they created beings—anything that exists in the cosmos—or uncreated—the Father, Son, and Holy Spirit. Thus terms like *essence, nature, person, hypostasis*, and *energy* are used to discuss the way that beings exist, what they have in common and what distinguishes them, and how they interact or are related to each other. To be affected on an ontological level is to be changed in a manner that is so fundamental as to change one's very being. See also *Hypostasis*.

Orthodox Church—The second largest Christian Church in the world, also called the Eastern Orthodox Church because of a division between the Eastern (centered in Constantinople) and Western (centered in Rome) halves of the Roman Empire that culminated in 1054 with mutual excommunication. The schism was based on growing differences of doctrine, politics, and practice (such as the Roman papal claim to primacy), leading finally to a change in the Nicene-Constantinopolitan Creed by Rome that was rejected by the East. Today the Orthodox Church has approximately 300 million members, distributed among more than a dozen autonomous local Churches (Russian, Greek, Romanian, etc.) throughout the world. These local churches are in communion with each other and are united in faith and worship as inheritors of the ancient Christian tradition as expressed, for example, by the seven Ecumenical Councils (Nicea I in 325; Constantinople I, 381; Ephesus, 431; Chalcedon, 451; Constantinople II, 553; Constantinople III, 680; and Nicea II, 787). The Orthodox Church found its way to North America with the arrival of Russian missionaries (including *St. Herman) in Kodiak, Alaska, in 1794; and over the next centuries, through Greek, Slavic, Middle Eastern, and other Eastern Orthodox peoples' immigration to the East Coast of North America. Estimates of North American Orthodox today, both ethnic and converts, range from 1.2 to 3 million.

Panikhida—A Slavic title for the Orthodox memorial service for the dead. The root of the word is the Greek *pannychis*, which literally means "all night," thereby signifying the earlier practice of an all-night vigil on the occasion of someone's death. The panikhida is not the funeral service proper, but a shortened version of it. It consists mainly of the reading of Psalms, singing of hymns, and other customary prayers. It is served also on particular later commemorations of the departed, such as the fortieth day after a person's death, and on the anniversary each year; also on designated Memorial Saturdays and, in *monastic practice, every Saturday.

Pascha—The Feast of the Resurrection of Jesus Christ, commonly known as Easter in Western Christendom (though sometimes not celebrated at the same time in the East and West because of differing practices in calculating the date). In the *Orthodox Church, every Sunday is celebrated as a little Pascha, but Pascha proper is celebrated annually as the culmination of *Great Lent and *Holy Week. It is the central and highest Feast of the Orthodox festal cycle. Generally celebrated from midnight until nearly dawn, the Holy Doors are thrown open, everything in the church is dressed in white, a great procession moves three times around the church, and proclamations of "Christ is Risen!" resound. The liturgical celebration is followed by a joyous feast. See also *Bright Week*.

Patristic—Those writings and teachings that were written by or refer to the Fathers of the Church. See *Church Fathers*.

Philokalia—A five-volume anthology of patristic writings on the spiritual life compiled by St. Nikodimos of the Holy Mountain and St. Macarius of Corinth in the latter half of the eighteenth century. The title means "Love of the beautiful," conveying the goal of the work, which is to guide us in a life of purification from sin, attaining of the virtues, and ultimately deification. The *Philokalia* has played a crucial role in reinvigorating the spiritual tradition of the Orthodox Church throughout the world. It was translated into English in the 1980s. See the Bibliography.

Prayers for parting of the soul from the body—A service that is ideally read at the very moment when a person's soul leaves the body. If possible, the priest will hear the confession of the dying person's sins prior to reading the office.

Presanctified Liturgy—See *Liturgy of the Presanctified Gifts*.

Procession—In the liturgical context of the *Orthodox Church, processions are a common occurrence marking the most significant events in the life of the Church. The term is also used in Orthodox theology to describe the mode by which the Holy Spirit derives His being from God the Father. Christ is "begotten by the Father"; the Holy Spirit "proceeds from the Father." By analogy, the term is used herein to describe the Father's movement toward the psalmist and the prayer of the psalmist toward Him.

Prosphora—A round loaf (or loaves) of bread prepared for use in the Liturgy, five of which (or in Greek practice, one large loaf) are specifically reserved for offering up in the Eucharist. Prior to baking, the loaf or loaves are stamped with a seal with several distinctive marks, the primary one being a cross marked with "IC XC NI KA," which in Greek means "Jesus Christ Conquers."

Prostration—In the *Orthodox Church, it is customary to do full-body prostrations (bowing all the way to the ground with knees and head touching the ground) at certain times during both liturgical and personal prayers, especially during the season of *Great Lent. Prostrations are a physical way to enact *repentance. Many Orthodox do a series of prostrations daily except on Sundays or during the Paschal season.

Repentance—Known as *metanoia* in Greek, it simply means a change of mind or purpose, a "turning around." John the Baptist, called the Forerunner, first sounded the call to "Repent, for the Kingdom of heaven is at hand!" (Matt 3:2). One of Christ's first proclamations was to "Repent and believe in the gospel" (Mk 1:15). It is therefore with such primacy that the *Orthodox Church regards repentance. While the act of repentance may have a simple inward movement behind it, it calls for the reorientation of one's whole life to God.

St. Arsenios the Great—Virtuous and noble Deacon of the Church of Rome in the time of Theodosius the Great (379–395) and tutor to the emperor's young sons. Surrounded by luxury, he prayed tearfully to God to guide him to salvation and was answered, "Arsenios, flee from men, and thou shalt be saved." He fled to Alexandria and then to Scete to become a monk, once more receiving the instruction to flee as his fame increased. He reposed in peace around 449, at the age of ninety-five, having attained spiritual heights reached by few.

St. Donatos—A fourth–century bishop whose philanthropy and Christ-like meekness gained him favor among the poor and destitute. Beyond his natural good works, the bishop was granted supernatural gifts from God whereby he healed the sick, slew a dragon that was poisoning the local water by making the sign of the cross over it with his riding whip, and even brought a dead man back to life, as the author relates.

St. Ephraim the Syrian—A fourth–century Syrian hymnographer and poet, who is well-known for his theological hymns found in works such as *Hymns on Paradise, Hymns on Faith,* and *Hymns of Nisibis.* Ephraim was an ordained deacon in the Church of Syria and also spent the latter part of his life ministering to those afflicted by a plague.

St. Febronia—A Virgin martyr who was brutally tortured and killed under the reign of the Roman Emperor Diocletian. Roman soldiers, arriving at the *monastery where she resided, sought to promise her worldly wealth if she would renounce Christ. At her rejection of the soldiers' offer, and her affirmation of her commitment to her true Heavenly Bridegroom Jesus Christ, she was beaten and tortured and finally beheaded. Her steadfast dedication to Jesus Christ in the face of the greatest suffering gained her a heavenly reward, attested to by the many miracles attributed to her.

St. Gregory of Nyssa—One of the great *Cappadocian Fathers, St. Gregory was the younger brother of St. Basil the Great and bishop of Nyssa. A profound theologian and prolific author, well-versed in the theology of Origen and Neoplatonic philosophy, some of his most famous works include *On the Making of Man*, *The Great Catechism*, *The Life of Moses*, and *Contra Eunomium*. He played a leading role in championing the Orthodox theology of the first two Ecumenical Councils after the death of St. Basil in 379.

St. Herman of Alaska—A member of the first missionary group sent to Alaska from Russia, he became one of the most beloved Saints to ever set foot on American soil. Although Apa Herman, as the native Alaskans called him, was never ordained into clerical orders, he was able to offer Christ-like love and humility as an example to those people he was sent to evangelize. Many miracles of healing and protection have been attributed to him both before and after his repose and it is still commonplace for Orthodox Christians to make pilgrimage to the place where his relics reside. There exists a monastic community on Spruce Island, St. Herman's former abode, to this day, and a new monastery is under construction at "Monk's Lagoon."

St. Ignatius Brianchaninov—A Russian bishop of the nineteenth century who is well-known for his work entitled *The Arena*. St. Ignatius was a talented youth who sought *monasticism early on, but was not allowed because the Tsar wanted to utilize his strengths in military service. Through several bouts with ill health, he was eventually granted his desire to enter monastic life, in which he advanced to Archimandrite and finally Bishop.

St. Isaac the Syrian—Also known as Isaac of Nineveh, he was born in Kurdistan in the first half of the seventh century and resided as a *monastic near modern-day Qatar. He was elected to the episcopacy in Nineveh, but sought to be released from this responsibility in order to pursue *ascetic discipline. Having retired to the wilderness, he labored in fasting, prayer, and writing spiritual works, being so zealous in his labors that he lost his sight. He reposed in a monastery at the end of his life and is commemorated on January 28. His *Homilies* have been called "the indispensable guide, along with the *Ladder* [of St. John Climacus], for every Orthodox soul to journey safely towards God" (Makarios, *Synaxarion*, III, 337).

St. John Climacus—Born in the latter part of the sixth century, he entered the Monastery of St. Katherine on the Sinai Peninsula at the age of sixteen. Throughout his *monastic life he advanced as a true example of *asceticism and became the Abbot of the Monastery. The name "Climacus" literally means "of the ladder" and refers to his *Ladder of Divine Ascent*, a work describing thirty stages of spiritual development leading to *theosis. This work has been a cornerstone of monastic literature since the time it was written and is widely read by Orthodox today, both lay and monastic. The fourth Sunday of Great Lent is dedicated to St. John.

St. Sergius of Radonezh—Born in Russia sometime between 1314 and 1322, he was raised with the name of Bartholomew. From a young age he sought a solitary life and later took monastic vows, then being given the name Sergius. He is a leading figure in Russian Orthodox *monasticism, and the monastery he originally founded bears his name to this day: Trinity–St. Sergius Lavra. He is commemorated in the Orthodox Church on two days—September 25, the day of his repose in 1392, and July 5, the finding of his incorrupt relics in 1422.

St. Silouan—A nearly contemporary saint especially beloved for his teachings on humility and simplicity. A native Russian, he lived from 1866 to 1938, spending many years as a *monastic at the Russian monastery of St. Panteleimon on *Mt. Athos. He was *canonized in 1987. His biography and writings are most readily available in the publication *Silouan the Athonite*, written and compiled by Archimandrite (now Saint) Sophrony (Sakharov, † 11 July 1993) of St. John the Baptist Monastery in Essex, England.

Salvific—An adjective used to describe things pertaining to salvation; that is, those things which enact *theosis in the life of an Orthodox Christian, transforming the entire being so that it may partake of the divine life of the Holy *Trinity.

Satan—See *Demons*.

Selah/Diapsalma—An enigmatic word that occurs throughout the Psalter, which, according to *St. Gregory of Nyssa, marks a specific moment in the psalm in which God speaks to the psalmist and thus to one truly praying the psalm.

Semitic—Denotes a people group or language group in the Middle East; especially those of Hebrew or Arab descent.

Septuagint/LXX—The Greek translation of the Hebrew Old Testament Scriptures. The title refers to the traditional understanding that seventy-two Hebrew scholars (six from each of the Twelve Tribes) were called to Alexandria by the Pharaoh Ptolemy (*ca.* 300 BC) to translate the Hebrew Scriptures into Greek, as knowledge of Hebrew was seen to be declining in the Empire. The Septuagint represents a closer historical link to the original writings of the Old Testament than any other translation that exists today. For this reason, and because of its use in the Hellenistic world during the spread of Christianity, it is the preferred text of the Old Testament in the *Orthodox Church. For Septuagint numbering, see Appendix A. See also *Masoretic Hebrew*.

Sin/Transgression—Sin (Greek *hamartia*) literally means to miss the mark. Contrary to conceptions of sin that view sin as incurring God's just judgment or anger and wrath, the Orthodox *tradition views sin as a disease with which all humanity is afflicted; a disease stemming from Adam and Eve's free but immature will, and abetted or abated by each individual's choices. Rather than inheriting the *guilt* of Adam's sin in the Garden of Eden (a Western Augustinian viewpoint based on a slight but crucial mistranslation into Latin of Rom 5:12), humankind is afflicted with the *effects* of that sin, especially death, under the shadow of which we are inclined, over and over, to "miss the mark" of union with God. "Transgression" implies a deliberate trespass that results from the condition of sin, though often the two are used synonymously.

Skete—A small monastic community that exists in practice somewhere between the full community life of coenobitic monasticism and solitary, eremitic monasticism. A skete is often composed of a few small cells for the monastics to dwell in, organized around a central church for communal worship, especially the reception of the Eucharist. The name is derived from the first communities formed in this fashion in the Egyptian region of Scetis. See also *Monasticism*.

Slavonic—See *Church Slavonic*.

Son of God—A title properly given to Jesus Christ, the Uncreated Son of God, begotten of the Father before all time began. The title denotes Christ's role within the Holy Trinity as well as His fully divine nature, which He joined with human nature in His single *hypostasis (person) in the *Incarnation. Cf. n. 31 herein.

Spirit—See *Angels; Demons*.

Spiritual Father—The tradition of spiritual fatherhood is ancient, being expressed in the Bible as far back as Elijah and Elisha (see 2 Kgs 2:9–14), and continues in the *Orthodox Church today. The role of a spiritual father ranges from that of a priest who is the consistent confessor for a person, to one who is a spiritual guide in all aspects of life, down to the most practical elements. The role of a spiritual father also differs depending on whether one lives within a *monastic community or in the world, though many Orthodox who live in the world seek out spiritual fathers from within the monasteries.

Subdeacon/Subdiaconate—One of the minor clerical orders in the *Orthodox Church. It follows that of Reader, and precedes that of *Deacon. Modern-day subdeacons function primarily as attendants in the Sanctuary (altar area) of the Church, especially in the presence of the Bishop.

Theoria—True divine theoria does not refer to theory in the sense that the modern scientific community would use it, but to the direct spiritual apprehension of God or His creations. Far from being a matter subjected to human reason, divine theoria is supra-rational and bestowed by the grace of God. Contemplation of God occurs when a person has been cleansed from sin and the passions and can therefore begin to behold the Beauty of God by divine grace. Theoria is the second of three stages of the spiritual life described in the *Philokalia* following catharsis (purification) and preceding *theosis (*deification).

Theosis—Theosis "literally means to become gods by Grace. The biblical words that are synonymous and descriptive of theosis are: adoption, redemption, inheritance, glorification, holiness and perfection. Theosis is the acquisition of the Holy Spirit, whereby through Grace one becomes participant in the *Kingdom of God*. Theosis is an act of the uncreated and infinite love of God. It begins here in time and space, but it is not static or complete, and is an open-ended progression uninterrupted through all eternity" (Archimandrite George, *Theosis*, 86). See also *Deification*.

Theotokos—A Greek term meaning *Birthgiver of God* used in the *Orthodox Church as a title of veneration for the Virgin Mary, the mother of Jesus Christ. The title was officially endorsed at the First Council of Ephesus in 431 and later ratified at Chalcedon in 451, in confirmation of the Orthodox understanding that the son to whom Mary gave birth was in very truth the *Son of God, both wholly human and wholly divine. An often-used synonymous title is Mother of God. Greek Orthodox often use Panagia, meaning the All-Holy One.

Tradition—Stemming from the Latin root *traditio* (Greek *paradosis*), the word itself generally implies transmission, especially with regard to teaching and practice. In the *Orthodox Church tradition can be understood in two aspects: Holy Tradition, which bears witness to the unchangeable doctrines of the Christian faith, such as the Virgin Birth, Jesus Christ being both God and man, etc.; and tradition that relates more to custom, that is, those details of Church life practiced especially with regard to various ethnicities and localities, and practices that come down to us through commonly accepted local historical witness. However, in the Orthodox view, these two aspects of Tradition are in no way separable but are part of a single all-encompassing reality of the life of the Church, continually inspired by the Holy Spirit in every age and in every place.

Transgression—See *Sin*.

Trinity/Holy Trinity—The Holy Trinity is the communion of God the Father, God the Son, and God the Holy Spirit. While the three persons are distinct in personhood (*hypostasis), they all share the same uncreated divine essence, incommunicable to human beings or to anything in the created world, and the same uncreated divine energies, which permeate and sustain creation. While the doctrine of the Holy Trinity is common to all traditional Christian confessions, the emphasis in the *Orthodox Church is distinctive, beginning with reference to the three distinct Persons, as opposed to the One Essence.

Troparion—Plural: *troparia; tropar* in the Russian tradition. A short hymn of one stanza, or one of a series of stanzas, sung in the *Orthodox Church.

Unction—Generally, unction refers to the anointing with oil. While the Unction service is a specific rite extant in the *Orthodox Church today, used at prescribed times including but not limited to the approach of death, unction in the general sense of anointing is also prevalent, as many of the faithful experience anointing with oil in various contexts.

BIBLIOGRAPHY

Bibliographic abbreviations used in text:

BDB   Brown-Driver-Briggs Hebrew-English Lexicon
LSJ   Liddell-Scott-Jones Greek-English Lexicon

Alfeyev, Met. Hilarion. *The Spiritual World of Isaac the Syrian (Cistercian Studies)*. Collegeville, MN: Cistercian Publications, 2009.

Alter, Robert, and Frank Kermode, eds. *The Literary Guide to the Bible*. Cambridge, MA: Belknap Press of Harvard University Press, 1990.

Bailie, Gil. *Violence Unveiled: Humanity at the Crossroads*. Chestnut Ridge, NY: Crossroad Publishing, 1996.

Barna, J. Mark, and Elizabeth J. *A Christian Ending*. Manton, CA: Divine Ascent Press, 2011.

Boros, Ladislaus. *Hidden God*. Seabury Press. New York, NY: Harper and Row, 1973.

Breck, John. *The Shape of Biblical Language: Chiasmus in the Scriptures and Beyond*. Crestwood, NY: St. Vladimir's Seminary Press, 1994.

———. *Scripture in Tradition: The Bible and Its Interpretation in the Orthodox Church*. Crestwood, NY: St. Vladimir's Seminary Press, 2001.

Brenton, Lancelot C. L. *The Interlineary Hebrew and English Psalter*. Grand Rapids, MI: Zondervan, 1979.

———, *The Septuagint Version, Greek and English*. Grand Rapids, MI: Zondervan, 1970.

Brown, Francis. *The New Brown–Driver–Briggs–Gesenius Hebrew and English Lexicon*. Peabody, MA: Hendrickson, 1979. Cited in text as BDB.

Chryssavgis, John. *Beyond the Shattered Image*. Minneapolis, MN: Light and Life, 1999.

———, and Bruce V. Foltz, eds. *Toward an Ecology of Transfiguration: Orthodox Christian Perspectives on Environment, Nature, and Creation*. New York, NY: Fordham University Press, 2013.

Day, John N. "The Pillars of Imprecation: How to Pray for Your Enemies by Praying Against Them." *Touchstone: A Journal of Mere Christianity*. November 2006.

[Pseudo-]Dionysius, Saint. *The Mystical Theology* and *On the Divine Names*. In *Pseudo-Dionysius: The Complete Works (Classics of Western Spirituality)*. Translated by Paul Rorem. Mahwah, NJ: Paulist Press, 1987.

Dostoevsky, Fyodor. *The Brothers Karamazov*. Translated and annotated by Richard Pevear and Laryssa Volokhonsky. San Francisco, CA: North Point Press, 1990. Reprinted New York, NY: Vintage, 1991. [The author strongly recommended this translation, as done by Orthodox believers who understood and faithfully represented the Orthodox culture about which Dostoevsky writes. —*Ed.*]

———. *Demons*. Translated and annotated by Richard Pevear and Laryssa Volokhonsky. New York, NY: Knopf, 1994.

Ephraim, Elder. *Counsels from the Holy Mountain*. Florence, AZ: St. Anthony's Greek Orthodox Monastery, 2010.

Ephraim of Katounakia, Elder. *Obedience Is Life*. Mt. Athos, Greece: Vatopaidi Monastery, 2003.

Ephrem the Syrian, Saint. *Hymns on Paradise*. Crestwood, NY: St. Vladimir's Seminary Press, 1997.

Frost, Robert. *Collected Poems*. New York, NY: Library of America, 1995.

George, Archimandrite. *Theosis: The True Purpose of Human Life*. Mt. Athos, Greece: Holy Monastery of St. Gregorios, 2006. Also available online at http://orthodoxinfo.com/general/theosis-english.pdf.

Girard, René. *The Girard Reader*. Edited by James G. Williams. Chestnut Ridge, NY: Crossroad/Herder, 1996.

"Glory to God for All Things." Akathist Hymn authored by Metropolitan Tryphon (Prince Boris Petrovich Turkestanov); originally attributed to Protopresbyter Gregory Petrov. Available online from many sources.

Gray, Archpriest George, ed. *Portraits of American Saints*. San Francisco, CA: Diocese of the West, Orthodox Church in America, 1994.

Groopman, Jerome. "A Model Patient: How Simulators Are Changing the Way a Doctor Is Trained." *The New Yorker*. May 2, 2005.

Hapgood, Isabel Florence. *Service Book of the Holy Orthodox-Catholic Apostolic Church*. New York: Association Press, 1922. [It is available in various later editions.]

Hatch, Edwin, and Henry A. Redpath. *A Concordance to the Septuagint*. 2nd edition. Grand Rapids, MI: Baker Books, 1998.

Heine, Ronald E. *Gregory of Nyssa's Treatise on the Inscriptions of the Psalms*. New York, NY: Oxford University Press, 1995.

Ignatius (Brianchaninov), Saint. *The Arena: An Offering to Contemporary Monasticism*. Translated by Archimandrite Lazarus. Jordanville, NY: Holy Trinity Monastery, 1983.

Isaac the Syrian, Saint. *The Ascetical Homilies of St. Isaac the Syrian*. Brookline, MA: Holy Transfiguration Monastery, 1984.

Jarrell, Randall. *Poetry and the Age*. New York, NY: Knopf, 1953.

John Climacus, Saint. *The Ladder of Divine Ascent*. Boston, MA: Holy Transfiguration Monastery, 2001.

John of Damascus, Saint. *An Exact Exposition of the Orthodox Faith*. Vol. 37 in *The Fathers of the Church*. New York, NY: Fathers of the Church, Inc., 1958.

Kenyon, Jane. "Having It Out with Melancholy." *Constance*. St. Paul, MN: Graywolf Press, 1993.

Kovalevsky, Pierre. *Saint Sergius and Russian Spirituality*. Crestwood, NY: St. Vladimir's Seminary Press, 1976.

Lampe, G. W. H. *A Patristic Greek Lexicon*. Oxford: Clarendon Press, 1969.

Lea, Sydney. *Ghost Pain*. Louisville, KY: Sarabande Books, 2008.

———. *Pursuit of a Wound*. Urbana and Chicago, IL: University of Illinois Press, 2000.

Liddell, Henry George, Robert Scott, Sir Henry Stuart Jones, et al. *A Greek-English Lexicon*. Oxford: Clarendon Press, 1968. Cited in text as LSJ.

Little Russian Philokalia. Vol. III. A Treasury of Saint Herman's Spirituality. New Valaam Monastery, Ouzinkie, AK: St. Herman Press, 1989.

Lossky, Vladimir. *The Mystical Theology of the Eastern Church*. Crestwood, NY: St. Vladimir's Seminary Press, 1976.

Lust, Johan, Erik Eynikel, and Katrin Hauspie. *Greek English Lexicon of the Septuagint*. Part II. Stuttgart, Germany: Deutsche Bibelgesellschaft, 1996.

Makarios, Hieromonk, of Simonos Petra. *The Synaxarion: The Lives of the Saints of the Orthodox Church*. Seven Volumes. Translated from the French by Mother Maria (Rule) and Mother Joanna (Burton). Ormylia (Chalkidike), Greece: Holy Convent of the Annunciation of Our Lady, 2008.

Maria, Mother. *The Psalms: An Exploratory Translation*. North Yorkshire, UK: Greek Orthodox Monastery of the Assumption, 1973.

Mary, Mother. *The Festal Menaion*. South Canaan, PA: St. Tikhon's Press, 1990.

———, and Bp. Kallistos. *The Lenten Triodion*. South Canaan, PA: St. Tikhon's Press, 1998.

McVey, Kathleen, and John Meyendorff. *Ephrem the Syrian: Hymns (Classics of Western Spirituality)*. Mahwah, NJ: Paulist Press, 1989.

Mullins, Hilary. "The Transfiguration of Don Sheehan." *Numerocinq* online magazine, 2013. Available online at http://numerocinqmagazine.com/2013/08/06/the-transfiguration-of-don-sheehan-essay-hilary-mullins/.

Nellas, Panayiotis. *Deification in Christ: Orthodox Perspectives on the Nature of the Human Person.* Translated by Norman Russell. Crestwood, NY: St. Vladimir's Seminary Press, 1987.

O'Brien, Elmer, S.J. *Varieties of Mystic Experience.* New York, NY: New American Library, 1965.

d'Olivet, Fabre. *The Hebraic Tongue Restored.* 1815. Translated by Nayán Louise Redfield. New York, NY: G. P. Putnam's Sons, 1921.

Patrologia Graeca. Volume 44. J. P. Migne, Imprimerie Catholique, 1857–66.

Philokalia. Comp. St. Nikodimos of the Holy Mountain and St. Makarios of Corinth. Translated and edited by G. E. H. Palmer, Philip Sherrard, Kallistos Ware. Volumes I, II, IV. London, Boston: Faber and Faber, 1981.

Possekel, Ute. *Evidence of Greek Philosophical Concepts in the Writings of Ephrem the Syrian.* Walpole, MA: Peeters, 1999.

Rahlfs, Alfred, ed. *Septuaginta.* Stuttgart, Germany: Deutsche Bibelgesellschafte, 1979.

Reardon, Patrick. *Jesus and the Atonement.* Forthcoming in 2015 from Ancient Faith Press.

Rose, Fr. Seraphim. *The Soul After Death.* Platina, CA: The Saint Herman of Alaska Monastery Press, 1980.

Salinger, J. D. *Franny and Zooey.* New York, NY: Little, Brown, 1991.

Samaras, Nicholas. *Hands of the Saddlemaker.* New Haven, CT: Yale University Press, 1992.

Service Books of the Orthodox Church: The Divine Liturgies. Third Edition. South Canaan, PA: St. Tikhon's Press, 2013.

Sheehan, Donald. Introductions to the poets in *The Breath of Parted Lips: Voices from the Robert Frost Place.* Volume 1. Fort Lee, NJ: CavanKerry Press, 2001.

———, trans. and intro., with Olga Andrejev. *Iconostasis* by Pavel Florensky. Crestwood, NY: St. Vladimir's Seminary Press, 1996.

———. Journals kept by the author are in the possession of his family.

———, ed. *Mountain Intervals: Poems from The Frost Place 1977–1986.* Lunenberg, VT: Meriden–Stinehour, 1987.

———, trans. *The Psalms of David. Translated from the Septuagint Greek.* Edited by Xenia Sheehan and Hierodeacon Herman Majkrzak. Eugene, OR: Wipf and Stock, 2013.

Sophrony, Archimandrite (now Saint). *St. Silouan the Athonite.* Translated by Rosemary Edmonds. Crestwood, NY: St. Vladimir's Seminary Press, 1991.

———. *Wisdom from Mount Athos.* Crestwood, NY: St. Vladimir's Seminary Press, 2001.

Taylor, Bernard A. *The Analytical Lexicon to the Septuagint.* Grand Rapids, MI: Zondervan, 1994.

Vasileios, Archimandrite. *Beauty and Hesychia in Athonite Life.* Published in Greek, 1994, translated into English, 1996. Montreal: Alexander Press, 1996.

Ware, Timothy (Met. Kallistos). "The Debate about Palamism." *Eastern Churches Review* IX:1–2.

The Way of a Pilgrim and The Pilgrim Continues His Way. Translated by R. M. French. San Francisco, CA: HarperCollins, 1965.

Zizioulas, John D. "The Contribution of Cappadocia to Christian Thought." In *Sinasos in Cappadocia*, edited by Frosso Pimenides and Stelios Roades. National Trust for Greece: Agra Publications, 1986.

ACKNOWLEDGMENTS AND CREDITS

A version of Donald Sheehan's essay "'A New Man Has Arisen in Me!': Memory Eternal in Dostoevsky's *Brothers Karamazov*" has for many years been posted on the Dartmouth College website under the title "Dostoevsky and Memory Eternal: An Eastern Orthodox Approach to *The Brothers Karamazov*," concluding with the essay printed separately herein under the title "Coming Home." The latter was also distributed at his funeral and has been privately translated into both Russian and Greek.

The author's account of Fr. Vladimir Sovyrda's passing, included in the chapter on "The Syrian Penitential Witness," is used by kind permission of the Sovyrda family.

Psalm 118 and all other psalms quoted in this volume in their final form authorized by the translator, as well as portions of the "Introduction to Psalmic Poetics" in Part Two, were first published in *The Psalms of David, Translated from the Septuagint Greek by Donald Sheehan*, edited by Xenia Sheehan and Hierodeacon Herman Majkrzak (Eugene, OR: Wipf and Stock, 2013). Copyright © 2013 Carol (Xenia) Sheehan. This material is used by permission of Wipf and Stock Publishers, www.wipfandstock.com.

A version of the Psalm 118 translation (and other psalms quoted herein) first appeared in Thomas Nelson, *The Orthodox Study Bible: Ancient Christianity Speaks to Today's World* (Old Testament © St. Athanasius Academy of Orthodox Theology, 2008; NT text © Thomas Nelson, 1982). All material herein that resulted from Donald Sheehan's work in assisting the Academy in writing *The Orthodox Study Bible* is used by permission of the Academy, which has released any claim on its copyright to Carol (Xenia) Sheehan, her heirs and assigns.

Selections from St. Isaac the Syrian's *Ascetical Homilies*: Copyright © 1984 Holy Transfiguration Monastery, Brookline, MA, used by permission. All rights reserved.

A version of "'The Spirit of God Moved Upon the Face of the Waters': Orthodox Holiness and the Natural World" was previously published in John Chryssavgis and Bruce V. Foltz, eds., *Toward an Ecology of Transfiguration: Orthodox Christian Perspectives on Environment, Nature, and Creation* (New York, NY: Fordham University Press, 2013).

Nicholas Samaras' poem "Easter in the Cancer Ward" (*Hands of the Saddlemaker*, Yale University Press, 1992) is quoted in full herein by permission of the author.

A version of "The Way of Beauty and Stillness: Shakespeare's *Winter's Tale*" was previously published in James Jordan and James Whitbourn, *The Musician's Trust* (Chicago, IL: GIA Publications, 2013), under the title "Shakespeare's *The Winter's Tale*: The Way of Beauty and Stillness."

Robert Frost, "An Old Man's Winter Night" from the book *The Poetry of Robert Frost*, edited by Edward Connery Lathem. Copyright © 1916, 1969 by Henry Holt and Company, copyright © 1944 by Robert Frost. Reprinted by permission of Henry Holt and Company, LLC. All rights reserved.

Jane Kenyon, excerpts from "Having It Out with Melancholy" from *Collected Poems*. Copyright © 2005 by The Estate of Jane Kenyon. Reprinted with the permission of The Permissions Company, Inc. on behalf of Graywolf Press, Minneapolis, Minnesota, www.graywolfpress.org.

Sydney Lea's poems "Wonder: Red Beans and Ricely" (*Ghost Pain*, Sarabande, 2008) and "Phases" (*Pursuit of a Wound*, University of Illinois Press, 2000) are quoted herein by permission of the author.

Selections from Patrick Reardon's forthcoming book from Ancient Faith Press, *Jesus and the Atonement*, are quoted by permission.

ILLUSTRATION CREDITS

p. 13 Icon of St. Ephraim the Syrian. Copyright © Stefan Nedetu artabizantina.uv.ro. Used by permission.

p. 40 Icon of St. Isaac the Syrian. Copyright © Holy Transfiguration Monastery, Brookline, MA. Used by permission. All rights reserved.

p. 56 Icon of St. Herman Feeding the Ermine. Lasha Kintsurashvili of Georgia www.iconpainter.ge. Used by permission.

p. 59 Icon of St. Herman of Alaska, by Father Luke Dingman www.lukedingman.com. Used by permission.

p. 71 Monk's Rock at the mouth of Monk's Lagoon, Spruce Island, Alaska, where St. Herman often went for a retreat. Many icons show him standing on this rock, the rock itself transfigured by his presence. Photo: Fr. Joseph Huneycutt. Used by permission.

p. 71 Monk's Lagoon, Spruce Island, Alaska. Photo: Patrick Barnes. Used by permission.

p. 72 The path from the beach. Photo: Patrick Barnes. Used by permission.

p. 72 The kellia (monastic cell) built by Fr. Gerasim (Schmaltz; †1969), who spent thirty-five years here as a hermit, faithfully tending to the site where St. Herman lived, his relics, etc. Photo and caption: Patrick Barnes. Used by permission.

p. 72 The icon corner where Fr. Gerasim prayed. Photo: Patrick Barnes. Used by permission.

p. 172 Eleventh-century mosaic of Mary, the Theotokos, Oranta, in the apse of the Cathedral of St. Sophia in Kiev, Ukraine. Photo copyright © Natalia Bratslavsky/Shutterstock. Used by permission.

p. 196 Holy Trinity–St. Sergius Lavra, Sergiev Posad, Russia. Photo: Shutterstock.

p. 196 Pilgrims visiting St. Sergius' relics at Holy Trinity–St. Sergius Lavra, Sergiev Posad, Russia. Photo copyright © Arthur Lookyanov moscowdriver.com. Used by permission.

p. 201 Prosphora loaf from Holy Trinity–St. Sergius Lavra, Sergiev Posad, Russia, showing St. Sergius praying before the Theotokos; received by Donald Sheehan from Evgeny Tislenko via a pilgrim in 1989. Photo 2014: Maria Sheehan/Miriam Warren.

p. 235 Artist's proof of a portrait of Don Sheehan by Gary Grier. Painted a few months before Don's repose in Charleston, SC. Photo 2010: Maria Sheehan/Miriam Warren. Used by permission.

INDEX

This index, written by T.L. Ryan, follows recommendations in the 16th edition of the *Chicago Manual of Style* (2010); however, out of respect, titles for clergy and saints have been retained. The Foreword, Editor's Introduction, Epilogue, and Glossary are not indexed.

INDEX OF SCRIPTURAL REFERENCES

All indexed Scriptural references are listed as they are found within the text
and follow the *Septuagint* (LXX) numbering system.

OLD TESTAMENT

ABOUT THE AUTHOR

Donald Sheehan received a PhD in English literature, with an Italian minor, from the University of Wisconsin, Madison. He began his long and active teaching career at the University of Chicago in 1967 and concluded it at Dartmouth College, from which he retired in 2004. From 1978 to 2005 he served as Executive Director of The Frost Place in Franconia, New Hampshire, where he created internationally acclaimed poetry writing programs and inspired many contemporary poets.

He authored numerous lectures and essays, of which a selection is included in this volume. He also edited the poetry volume *Mountain Intervals: Poems from The Frost Place* (1987); co-translated, with Olga Andrejev, Fr. Pavel Florensky's *Iconostasis* (1996); and introduced the poets in *The Breath of Parted Lips: Voices from The Robert Frost Place*, Volume 1, edited by Donald Hall. Having taught himself both Hebrew and Greek, he translated the Septuagint Greek Psalter as *The Psalms of David*, published posthumously by Wipf and Stock in 2013. He seldom sought publication, however, valuing more highly the rich fruit of enabling others to develop and multiply their talents.

He was received into the Orthodox Church in 1984, serving for many years as a Subdeacon in northern New England parishes of the Orthodox Church in America. After his conversion, he turned much of his attention to praying, teaching, and writing about Psalms, praying through the entire Psalter each week. He reposed in the Lord May 26, 2010, and is buried at Panagia Prousiotissa Greek Orthodox Monastery in Troy, North Carolina.